The Presidency of
JAMES
MONROE

AMERICAN PRESIDENCY SERIES

Clifford S. Griffin and Donald R. McCoy, Founding Editors
Homer E. Socolofsky, General Editor

George Washington, Forrest McDonald
John Adams, Ralph Adams Brown
Thomas Jefferson, Forrest McDonald
James Madison, Robert Allen Rutland
James Monroe, Noble E. Cunningham, Jr.
John Quincy Adams, Mary W. M. Hargreaves
Andrew Jackson, Donald B. Cole
Martin Van Buren, Major L. Wilson
William Henry Harrison & John Tyler, Norma Lois Peterson
James K. Polk, Paul H. Bergeron
Zachary Taylor & Millard Fillmore, Elbert B. Smith
Franklin Pierce, Larry Gara
James Buchanan, Elbert B. Smith
Abraham Lincoln, Phillip Shaw Paludan
Andrew Johnson, Albert Castel
Rutherford B. Hayes, Ari Hoogenboom
James A. Garfield & Chester A. Arthur, Justus D. Doenecke
Grover Cleveland, Richard E. Welch, Jr.
Benjamin Harrison, Homer B. Socolofsky & Allan B. Spetter
William McKinley, Lewis L. Gould
Theodore Roosevelt, Lewis L. Gould
William Howard Taft, Paolo E. Coletta
Woodrow Wilson, Kendrick A. Clements
Warren G. Harding, Eugene P. Trani & David L. Wilson
Calvin Coolidge, Robert H. Ferrell
Herbert C. Hoover, Martin L. Fausold
Franklin Delano Roosevelt, George T. McJimsey
Harry S. Truman, Donald R. McCoy
Dwight D. Eisenhower, Chester J. Pach, Jr., & Elmo Richardson
John F. Kennedy, James N. Giglio
Lyndon B. Johnson, Vaughn Davis Bornet
Richard Nixon, Melvin Small
Gerald R. Ford, John Robert Greene
James Earl Carter, Jr., Burton I. Kaufman
George Bush, John Robert Greene

James Monroe, LL.D., president of the United States. *Engraving, 19 ½ x 13 inches, by Charles Goodman and Robert Piggott after a painting by Charles Bird King. (Published by William H. Morgan, Philadelphia, 1817; courtesy of the Library of Congress)*

The Presidency of

JAMES
MONROE

Noble E. Cunningham, Jr.

UNIVERSITY PRESS OF KANSAS

Published by the University Press of Kansas (Lawrence, Kansas 66049),
which was organized by the Kansas Board of Regents
and is operated and funded by Emporia State University, Fort Hays State
University, Kansas State University, Pittsburg State
University, the University of Kansas, and Wichita State University

Library of Congress Cataloging-in-Publication Data

Cunningham, Noble E., 1926–
The presidency of James Monroe / Noble E. Cunningham, Jr.
p. cm.
(American presidency series)
Includes bibliographical references and index.
1. United States—Politics and government—1817–1825.
2. Monroe, James, 1758–1831. I. Title.
II. Series.
E371.C86 1995 973.5′4—dc20 95-34157
ISBN 0-7006-0728-5

British Library Cataloguing in Publication Data is available.

Printed in the United States of America

10 9 8 7 6 5 4

The paper used in this publication meets the minimum requirements
of the American National Standard for Permanence of Paper
for Printed Library Materials Z39.48–1984.

For
Mary Alice and Randy

CONTENTS

he read in the press, the more he began to question the document. He was elected as an antifederalist to the Virginia Ratifying Convention.[5]

Although Monroe generally approved of the structure of government devised in Philadelphia, he found certain provisions of the Constitution unacceptable and favored amendments before ratification. Unlike some antifederalists, such as Patrick Henry, Monroe favored strengthening the federal government, but he wanted a constitution that was more in harmony with republican ideals. He preferred that the Senate be apportioned according to population and directly elected by the people. He also believed that endowing the Senate with a share of executive authority violated the principle of separation of powers. Monroe approved of the veto and did not fear the executive power granted by the Constitution, but he thought the president should be popularly elected. He opposed the levying of direct taxes by the federal government but supported central control over the militia in order to obviate the need for a standing army. Like numerous others on both sides of the ratification debate, he deplored the absence of a bill of rights, yet unlike many who shared his concerns, Monroe was not willing to approve the Constitution and seek changes later. He thus opposed his friend Madison in the Virginia convention and voted in the minority against ratification.[6] Because antifederalism was strong in Virginia, Monroe's stand did not seriously impede his political career. Yet when he faced Madison in the first congressional elections, he lost his bid for a seat in the new House of Representatives.

In August 1789, the Monroes moved from Fredericksburg to a house and farm in Charlottesville, a few miles from Monticello.[7] Three months later, Jefferson returned to the United States from his service as minister to France, but he remained only briefly at Monticello, departing in March 1790 for New York to become secretary of state in President Washington's cabinet. Before the end of the year, the Virginia legislature elected Monroe to the United States Senate, and he joined Jefferson and Madison in the temporary capital, now in Philadelphia. As he took his seat in the Senate in December 1790, the differences within the legislature and the administration were becoming more clearly defined than at any time since Washington assumed office nineteen months earlier, and the new thirty-two-year-old senator promptly became an active and partisan member.

One week after Monroe was sworn into office, Secretary of the Treasury Alexander Hamilton sent to Congress his plan to create a national bank—a proposal that aroused the strong opposition of Madison in the House of Representatives and of Secretary of State Jefferson in the cabinet. In the Senate the bank bill did not generate the sharp division that it provoked in the House, but Monroe was in the minority that voted against the measure.[8] Like Jefferson and Madison, he was concerned about the direction the new government was taking and disturbed not only by Hamilton's fiscal policies but also by perceived antirepublican trends.

Monroe collaborated closely with Madison and Jefferson. Writing to Jefferson in June 1791, he confided: "Upon political subjects we perfectly agree, and particularly in the reprobation of all measures that may be calculated to elevate the government above the people. . . . The bulk of the people are for democracy, and if they are well informed the ruin of such enterprizes will infallibly follow."[9] In the early leadership of a republican party forming around Madison in Congress and coalescing behind Jefferson in the cabinet in opposition to Hamilton, Monroe would play a similar role in the Senate as an organizer of a republican bloc.[10]

Politics was a consuming interest for Monroe. More than either Madison or Jefferson, he was a pragmatic politician highly sensitive to contemporary currents. Monroe's letters to Jefferson and Madison dealt largely with the world of practical action, not with abstract speculation. Monroe's major biographer has found that in all the letters exchanged between Monroe and Jefferson over four decades, none dealt exclusively or at any great length with philosophical or scientific pursuits, in contrast to the correspondence between Madison and Jefferson, in which philosophical discussions frequently merged with practical politics.[11]

After Madison and Jefferson worked out arrangements with Philip Freneau in 1791 to establish the *National Gazette* in Philadelphia, Monroe became an early contributor. In the fifth issue (November 14, 1791) of the nationally circulated paper, Freneau published the first of a series of three essays by Monroe. Signed "Aratus" and directed against the sympathetic response to Edmund Burke's condemnation of the French Revolution, Monroe argued that the revolution in France was grounded in the same principles as the American Revolution. "As the friend of humanity, I rejoice in the French revolution; but as a citizen of America, the gratification is greatly heightened," Aratus told his readers, because the two revolutions were intimately linked and dependent on each other.[12] Identifying opponents of the French Revolution as enemies to republican institutions, Monroe plunged into a political debate that was at the core of party conflict during the 1790s. He quickly became an effective polemicist for the emerging Republican party.

Adept at practical politics, Monroe also engaged in organizing activities and was a key figure in the effort to defeat the reelection of John

Adams as vice-president in 1792. Joining in an alliance with New York Republicans in support of the candidacy of New York Governor George Clinton, Virginia Republican leaders were active in marshaling opposition to Adams. Clinton's fifty electoral votes were an embarrassment to Adams, although not enough to deny him reelection. The campaign, nevertheless, was striking evidence of the growing Republican strength.[13]

In May 1794 President Washington named Monroe as the United States minister to France, replacing Gouverneur Morris, whose lack of sympathy for the French Revolution led the French government to request his recall. Priding himself in maintaining a neutral stance, Washington saw the appointment of a prorepublican minister as the logical course to improve relations with France. After being turned down by Robert R. Livingston and James Madison, Washington offered the post to Monroe, whose admiration of the French Revolution was well known. The Virginia senator had the support of Republicans in Congress and of Secretary of State Edmund Randolph, who had succeeded Jefferson at the State Department at the beginning of 1794. Although aware of the political perils of accepting an assignment tendered by a president who did not share his partisan sentiments about France, Monroe considered it his duty to accept. But in doing so, he took an enormous risk, and it nearly wrecked his political career. After two years in Paris, Monroe would be recalled for being too conspicuously pro-French.[14]

When Monroe, his wife, and their young daughter sailed from Baltimore, Maryland, in mid-June 1794, John Jay was already in England for negotiations that would inevitably affect the relations of the United States with France. Yet Monroe was not shown Jay's instructions, and Secretary of State Randolph did not make it clear to him that Jay was authorized to discuss commercial matters. Monroe thus left the United States with the impression that Jay's mission was limited to settling disputes arising from the peace treaty of 1783. That misconception helps to explain many of his representations to the French government. At the same time, the American minister's words and actions reflected an ardent support for the French cause not in accord with the policy of the government that he represented. In a speech to the French National Convention in August 1794, Monroe spoke of the similarities between the American and French republics. "They both cherish the same principles and rest on the same basis, the equal and unalienable rights of man," he declared as he pictured France embarking on "the same noble career" as the United States. He praised the heroic valor of French troops, which commanded "the admiration and applause of the astonished world."[15] Such rhetoric was hailed by Republicans in the United States, but as Madison warned Monroe, it was "very grating to the ears of many."[16] After Timothy Pickering, an ardent Federalist, replaced Randolph as secretary of state, Washington agreed in July 1796 to Monroe's recall. Since the presidential election was approaching, Pickering waited six weeks before informing Monroe, to ensure that the ousted minister would not reach the country before the election.[17]

When the Monroes returned to the United States in June 1797, John Adams was president, and Jefferson—who had placed second in the electoral vote—was vice-president. By that time, Adams had made it clear that the Republican vice-president would not be in the confidence of the Federalist administration, and Jefferson had quickly resumed leadership of the Republican party after three years' absence from the national scene. Upon his arrival in Philadelphia, Monroe was met at the dock by Jefferson, Albert Gallatin (Madison's successor as the Republican leader in the House of Representatives after the Virginian's retirement), and Aaron Burr, the New York Republican leader, who was in the city to consult with Jefferson. The three men conferred with Monroe for two hours and so signaled their support for the recalled diplomat. A few days later, Republicans held a public dinner in honor of Monroe at Oeller's Hotel in Philadelphia, which was attended by Vice-president Jefferson and more than fifty members of Congress.[18]

Monroe found the political climate in the United States greatly altered in the three years he had been away. The Federalists were now entrenched in power in the national government, and he was disillusioned with the new regime. Returning to Virginia, he immediately devoted himself to defending his record as minister to France by preparing for publication an extensive volume of official papers introduced by a lengthy commentary.[19] Though he refrained from harsh criticism of Washington, Monroe severely indicted the foreign policy of his administration. Reflecting the partisanship of the 1790s, the work won praise from Republicans and condemnation from the Federalists. Jefferson, whom Monroe had consulted in composing his defense, was enthusiastic and told the author he had heard "unqualified eulogies" on the book by all who were "not hostile to it from principle."[20] On the other hand, Federalist stalwart Oliver Wolcott called it "a wicked misrepresentation of facts," and Secretary of State Pickering reported that the publication was spoken of in some circles as Monroe's "death warrant."[21] Federalist predictions of Monroe's political demise, however, were ill-founded. Monroe never lost the support of Republican leaders, including Jefferson and Madison, and he resumed his place in the party leadership. He also retained his popular support within the Republican sector of the electorate.

The Monroes now took up residence in Albemarle County on land adjoining Jefferson's at Monticello. With Madison nearby at Montpelier in Orange County, the Virginia triad of Republican leadership that had formed while Jefferson was secretary of state was restored. Although Jefferson was away about half of each year as vice-president, there was ample opportunity for consultation, as shown by the surviving records of meetings among the three men. Jefferson and Madison had hoped that Monroe would set his sights again on Congress, but that Federalist-dominated body was not an attractive prospect to Monroe, who decided instead to seek election to the Virginia assembly. He held back from that course, however, when he learned in 1799 that he was under consideration as the Republican candidate for governor—an office filled through election by the Republican-controlled legislature. Madison, a member of the House of Delegates, nominated Monroe and joined in defending Monroe's mission to France against Federalist criticism. Voting followed strict party lines, and Monroe was elected governor of Virginia on December 6, 1799. He was reelected in 1800 and 1801, completing the three one-year terms permitted by the Virginia Constitution.[22]

As governor of Virginia during the presidential campaign of 1800, Monroe was well positioned to advance Jefferson's election. Among other duties, he was empowered by the Republican-controlled legislature to appoint the officials in each county who supervised the election. In Virginia the Republican slate of presidential electors won in all twenty-one electoral districts and cast their votes for Thomas Jefferson and Aaron Burr. Because all Republican electors elsewhere repeated this performance, the election unexpectedly resulted in a tie between Jefferson and Burr.

The Constitution, as originally adopted, had not provided for a distinction between president and vice-president in the electoral balloting. The election was thus to be decided by the Federalist-dominated House of Representatives, though neither party controlled a majority of state delegations. The Federalists were in a position to prevent an election if the Republicans would not agree to accept Burr. In that constitutional crisis, the presence of a committed Republican leader and Jefferson's close friend as governor of Virginia—the largest state in the Union—was a factor that Federalist leaders had to weigh in any attempt to block Jefferson's election by the House of Representatives. Balloting began on February 11, 1801, in Washington, D.C., the new capital to which the government had moved in the summer of 1800. The first ballot produced a deadlock in which neither Jefferson nor Burr had a majority of states. When repeated balloting over several days brought no change in the voting, many Republicans feared the election might not be decided before John Adams's term of office ended on March 4. Some even feared a Federalist usurpation.[23]

As alarm over Federalist intentions mounted in Virginia, Monroe assured Jefferson that there was a determination throughout the state not to submit to any coup. Although he opposed a move to keep the Virginia assembly in session until the election was decided, Monroe promised Jefferson that he would convene the legislature without delay "should any plan of usurpation be attempted at the federal town."[24] Such action never became necessary. The Federalists in Congress eventually yielded before the adamantine Republican support of Jefferson, and on the thirty-sixth ballot, on February 17, 1801, Jefferson was elected the third president of the United States.

In his message to the Virginia legislature in 1801, Governor Monroe declared that he considered "the late election to the Executive of the United States, as having essentially contributed to secure to us the enjoyment of the blessings for which we contended in our revolution." He lauded Jefferson's election and the change in government in Washington as "an example which proves how competent the people are to self government! How wise and faithful in the exercise of the most important acts of sovereignty!"[25]

In Virginia the subordination of the executive to the legislature made the governor's office of limited value as a training ground for the presidency of the United States, but Monroe assumed a larger leadership role than most previous governors of Virginia had. Although his predecessors sent occasional messages to the legislature, Monroe introduced the practice of sending an annual message to the legislature modeled on the president's annual address to Congress. Here he gave an account of his administration, discussed state needs, provided information, and made recommendations. One of the proposals in his 1801 message concerned the establishment of an effective state-supported system of education. Echoing Jefferson's and Madison's earlier attempts to promote public education in Virginia, Monroe declared: "In a government founded on the sovereignty of the people the education of youth is an object of first importance. In such a government knowledge should be diffused throughout the whole society, and for that purpose the means of acquiring it made not only practicable but easy to every citizen."[26] This plea, like most of the other reforms that Governor Monroe advocated, fell on deaf legislative ears, but his efforts did not go unnoticed. Thomas Ritchie, editor of the Richmond *Enquirer*, praised Monroe for turning "the negative functions of a governor into the instruments of a most respectable influence."[27]

During the years following his governorship, Monroe broadened his political experience with diplomatic service on behalf of the Jefferson administration. The first of several missions resulted in the treaty for the purchase of Louisiana and brought Monroe widespread fame. Jefferson's decision in 1803 to send Monroe to Paris to join Robert R. Livingston in negotiating with France on the explosive Louisiana issue had been based not only on their close relationship but also on Monroe's popularity in the West. "You possess the unlimited confidence of the administration and of the western people and generally of the republicans everywhere," the president wrote to Monroe in urging him to accept the mission. Although Napoleon had already decided to sell Louisiana to the United States before Monroe reached Paris, Monroe and Livingston jointly negotiated the treaty that doubled the size of the United States. Before returning to the United States to receive acclaim, Monroe was appointed minister to England and was also sent on a special mission to Spain. In neither assignment did his efforts meet with much success.[28]

By the time he returned home in December 1807, Monroe's record as a diplomat was again under question. In his mission to Madrid in 1805, he had assisted Charles Pinckney, the United States minister there, in negotiations with Spain, but their endeavors were fruitless. In England he was joined by special envoy William Pinkney in parleys that led to the signing of a treaty in 1806, but the American negotiators failed to get the British to yield on the critical issue of impressment. As a consequence, President Jefferson declined to submit the Monroe-Pinkney treaty to the Senate for approval, and the episode left Monroe estranged from Secretary of State James Madison, who was being widely talked of as Jefferson's successor.[29]

Before leaving England, Monroe received letters from Virginia Congressman John Randolph of Roanoke urging him to be a candidate for president. Once a strong ally of Jefferson's, Randolph saw Monroe as an alternative to Madison, whom he bitterly opposed. Although given no encouragement by Monroe, Randolph persisted in trying to build support for him in Virginia. Monroe had been hurt by the administration's rejection of the British treaty and was in no mood to endorse the secretary of state; consequently, when he returned to the United States, he took no steps to halt Randolph's drive. At the same time, he never committed himself to Randolph and did not join in his assault on the administration.[30]

Monroe's support in Virginia was not limited to the followers of

Randolph. After a large majority of the state legislature voted to extend to him a complimentary address upon his return from England, one member declared that "many here believe Col. Monroe can be elected President, if his friends will take a firm ground."[31] But Madison's friends in Virginia were also active, and the competition resulted in two caucuses nominating opposing electoral slates—one pledged to Madison, the other to Monroe. Advocates of each candidate formed rival state campaign organizations.[32]

Outside Virginia, the movement for Monroe did not have wide support. A majority of the Republican members of both houses of Congress met in a caucus in January 1808 and nominated Madison for president. Supporters of Monroe and of George Clinton of New York, however, had declined to attend the meeting, and they refused to give up their candidates. Neither Monroe nor Clinton withdrew from the contest. Jefferson wrote to Monroe that he saw "with infinite grief a contest arising between yourself and another, who have been very dear to each other, and equally so to me." Pledging his own neutrality in the contest, Jefferson expressed concern about the political consequences of the split in Republican ranks.[33] Monroe responded that he had been, and would continue to be, an inactive spectator of the events. "Should the nation be disposed to call any citizen to that station it would be his duty to accept it. On that ground I rest. I have done nothing to draw the attention of any one to me in reference to it, nor shall I in future. No one better knows than I do the merit of Mr. Madison, and I can declare that should he be elected he will have my best wishes for the success of his administration."[34]

Monroe maintained that position until the closing weeks of the campaign, when he unexpectedly projected himself into the contest by making public his correspondence with President Jefferson relating to the election and his recent diplomatic service. Believing that his withdrawal from the campaign would have served as a repudiation of his record, Monroe published the papers—after receiving Jefferson's permission to do so—more for personal vindication than as a serious bid for the presidential office. The exchange of letters showed Jefferson expressing continued confidence in Monroe and neutrality in the contest with Madison. The disclosure did not alter the expected outcome of the election. In Virginia the Madison ticket for electors won 14,665 votes to 3,408 for Monroe, and Monroe won no electoral votes in any state. Later he insisted: "I allowed the nomination to be made and persevered in, as a trial of my character, and in support of my independence, of the administration, and of all others, and not in the expectation, or desire of being elected."[35]

Having declined to support the candidacy of Madison, who was clearly Jefferson's choice as his successor, the political prospects for Monroe at the beginning of 1809 were not bright. Madison organized his new administration without including or even consulting him. Nevertheless, Monroe pledged to back the new administration, and Jefferson worked quietly to reconcile his two old friends. In November 1809 President Madison asked Jefferson to sound out Monroe about accepting the governorship of Louisiana, but Monroe was more offended by the offer of an inferior post than appeased by Madison's gesture of confidence, which further tested Jefferson's skills at mediation. Monroe's political future also depended on regaining the favor of Virginia Republicans who had voted for Madison in the presidential election.

The political restoration of Monroe began with his election to the Virginia assembly in 1810. That was rapidly followed by his election in January 1811 to fill the vacancy in the governorship created when John Tyler resigned to accept a federal judgeship. The speed with which Madison offered the judgeship to Tyler when the post became open suggests that the president hoped to assist in Monroe's political comeback and the rebuilding of Republican harmony in his home state.[36]

Difficulties within his cabinet also influenced Madison's interest in Monroe's return to political life. A powerful faction in the Senate had blocked the president's first choice of Albert Gallatin as secretary of state and had forced the appointment of Robert Smith to that key post. As secretary of the navy under Jefferson, Smith had not shown the incompetence with which he has sometimes been charged, but he was a disaster as secretary of state. By 1811 Madison was determined to replace him. Although Monroe's earlier diplomatic career had generated controversy, no other Republican could bring so much experience in diplomacy to the post. In March 1811 President Madison asked Monroe to be secretary of state. In an exchange of vaguely worded letters, the two men satisfied themselves that they could overcome past differences and work together, and Monroe accepted.[37] The decision had momentous implications, because service as secretary of state had thus far been an important stepping stone to the presidency. Jefferson had served nearly four years as Washington's first secretary of state. Madison had held that post throughout Jefferson's two terms as president. Monroe was now in position to follow Madison's path to the presidency.

When Monroe took up his cabinet duties in the spring of 1811, he was aware of the critical state of affairs with Great Britain. Although many observers interpreted his appointment as an indication that the president was about to adopt a more favorable policy toward Britain, Monroe and Madison shared a common view of the fundamental interests of the United States. Any hope that his appointment might trigger a conciliatory gesture from the British government also proved illusory. By late summer the president and the secretary of state decided that if Britain did not respond to American demands by the end of the year, preparations for war should begin.[38]

When Congress assembled in October, Monroe became the president's most effective liaison with the new Congress—particularly the House of Representatives—and its new leadership, which favored standing up to England. After months elapsed with no change in British policy, Madison sent a war message to Congress on June 1, 1812, and by June 17 a declaration of war had passed both houses. Once the war began, Monroe was anxious to leave the State Department and take a military assignment. Although Madison considered giving him an army command, he saw the need for his services within the administration as more pressing. When early military reverses necessitated a change in the War Department, the president made Monroe acting secretary of war, but factional opposition in the Senate thwarted his permanent appointment. After ten weeks, Monroe returned to the State Department, and Madison named John Armstrong as secretary of war. Monroe now expected Madison to appoint him as lieutenant general to lead the invasion of Canada, but Armstrong persuaded the president to commission Monroe a brigadier general. Monroe refused the lesser rank. By then there were signs that negotiations for peace might soon begin, so Monroe remained at the State Department.[39]

In view of what he regarded as Armstrong's mismanagement of the war effort, Monroe did not confine himself to diplomacy. He made various suggestions about military affairs, including recommendations for the better defense of the capital, which Armstrong rejected. As hostility within the cabinet increased, Monroe urged the president to remove the secretary of war, but Madison deferred action. The president, however, did begin to review military plans more closely, and he depended more on Monroe for advice.[40]

Still, Madison's hesitation and Armstrong's conviction that the British would not attack Washington left the capital vulnerable to the disaster that overwhelmed the city in August 1814. Armstrong had so discounted the need for military preparations that there was no military intelligence. The secretary of state himself led a troop of cavalry out from Washington on August 18 to gather information about the large British squadron that had appeared in the Potomac River. Locating the British landing force some fifty miles from the city and correctly anticipating their movements, Monroe on August 21 brought back to Washington the only reliable intelligence about the British invasion. In the frantic American effort to halt the British advance at Bladensburg on August 24, Monroe was actively engaged in deploying the Maryland militia. After shooting began, the president, who had also come to the battlefield, suggested that the civilians withdraw and leave the fighting to the military.[41]

After the rout of the American forces at Bladensburg, Monroe was the last cabinet member to leave Washington as the British entered the city that evening. The exhausted secretary of state had slept no more than a few hours at a time and had worn the same clothes all week. Yet he returned with Madison to the devastated capital on August 27, two days after the British withdrew, whereupon the president asked him to assume command of the defense of the capital in the absence of the secretary of war. A week later the discredited Armstrong resigned, and once again Monroe became acting secretary of war. Although Madison was initially uncertain about making the appointment permanent, he sent Monroe's nomination to the Senate on September 26, and it was promptly confirmed. After Governor Daniel P. Tompkins of New York declined appointment as secretary of state, Monroe was also named acting secretary of state.[42]

The desperate straits in which the nation found itself in 1814, without adequate military forces or financial resources to support them, convinced both Madison and Monroe of the need to abandon the long-standing Republican hostility to a national bank and the traditional reliance on militia rather than permanent military forces for national defense. The finalization of the Treaty of Ghent in December 1814 and General Andrew Jackson's victory over the British at New Orleans in January 1815 brought peace to the nation before new measures were implemented. But before leaving office, President Madison would sign the bill to charter the second Bank of the United States, and one of Monroe's last actions as secretary of war was to draft a call for a military peace establishment composed of a regular army of twenty thousand men—twice its prewar strength.[43]

In March 1815 Monroe gave up his post at the War Department and resumed his duties as secretary of state. With the war over and Madison's second term entering its final two years, Monroe's attention and that of political leaders in Congress increasingly focused on the approaching presidential election of 1816.

2

★★★★★

THE ELECTION OF A PRESIDENT

As a presidential candidate, James Monroe brought to the contest of 1816 extensive political service at home and wide diplomatic experience abroad. He also had the advantage of close association with Thomas Jefferson and James Madison, but he risked comparison to those fellow Virginians, whose intellectual breadth and interests few contemporaries could match. Moreover, being from Virginia was itself a disadvantage, because presidents from his state had held the executive office for all but four years since George Washington was inaugurated in 1789.

New Yorkers, never rewarded with more than the second office for their allegiance to the Republican party, were bitter but remained divided over an alternative to Monroe. To some, William H. Crawford, who had joined Madison's cabinet as secretary of war, seemed promising. A popular and impressive figure, the forty-four-year-old Georgian had a strong following in Congress. Crawford also was a more conservative Republican than Monroe, whose advocacy of an expanded military and naval establishment indicated a willingness to depart from once-cherished Republican principles. There was some support for New York Governor Daniel P. Tompkins, popular and ambitious but little known outside New York and not highly regarded by many Republicans within his own state. Jonathan Fisk, appointed by Madison as United States attorney for the district of New York, thought Tompkins was completely unqualified. "May the day never arrive in the history of this republic, when any character however great and popular, shall be placed in the executive chair, who has never had any experience in the general government," he wrote to New York Congressman John W. Taylor. "It may do, to take green hands, for members of congress: but it would be madness to take such for the executive." Fisk was convinced that the great mass of Republicans in New York expected Monroe to be nominated and would support him. "He is certainly the most prominent public character," Fisk believed. "Public opinion centers upon him as unhesitatingly, generally, and steadily, as it did upon Mr. Jefferson, or Mr. Madison. He is the man most experienced in the government, most tried and approved in high political Stations, whom the republic can now Select as chief magistrate and altogether such a man, as in my Judgement promises the fairest, to promote and sustain in that office, the affections of the party and the welfare of the nation."[1]

A week earlier, former New York governor Morgan Lewis had written to Taylor expressing his resentment over the prospect of another Virginian as president. Even so, Lewis was willing to support Madison for a third term to keep out Monroe, since he believed that "there is no comparison, between the two men. Madison is quick, temperate and clear. Monroe slow, passionate and dull. Madison's word may always be relied on. I have known him from a Boy. I am sorry to say I cannot bear the same testimony to Monroe."[2]

These contrary views of Monroe that Taylor received from fellow New Yorkers—who knew he would play a key role in any congressional nominating caucus—reflected divisions and rivalries among New York Republicans. As the competition intensified, the New York legislature on February 14, 1816, adopted resolutions warning that since Virginians had held the presidential office for twenty-four out of twenty-eight years, another president chosen from the same state would jeopardize the continued ascendancy of the Republican party in New York. The legislature urged Republican members of Congress to work for the congressional nomination of Tompkins but pledged to support the candidate selected by the caucus. This endorsement of the New York governor was so muted that it may have been designed to promote Tompkins for vice-president.[3] George Hay, Monroe's son-in-law and manager of his campaign in Virginia, suspected that Tompkins was attempting to align with Crawford, hoping to become his vice-president and succeed him as president at the end of eight years.[4]

When the New York resolutions reached Washington, the New York delegation agreed to back Tompkins for president in the caucus, though the members were unanimous in believing that he could not be nominated. In that event, the New Yorkers would be nearly equally divided between Monroe and Crawford. Taylor, who favored Monroe and opposed congressional caucusing in principle, was convinced, as late as March 4, 1816, that a nominating caucus would not be held in Washington.[5] Not all of Monroe's New York supporters shared Taylor's opposition to nomination by caucus. Defending the practice as dependent on the selection of candidates with broad public support, Jonathan Fisk insisted, "Let a caucus once nominate him who is not the favorite of the people, and then it will be seen that a caucus nomination does not make the President of these United States."[6]

Every candidate was aware of the advantage conferred by a caucus nomination, even though its authority might be challenged. Yet Crawford, with less national visibility than Monroe, needed the congressional nod more than his rival. Some Monroe backers preferred no meeting of the caucus to one that they were unsure of controlling, since they could rely on Monroe's nomination by several state legislatures. While Crawford loyalists claimed that he had the support of a majority of Republicans in Congress, Hay thought it evident that he did not. "If he had, it would be proclaimed by a Caucus in 24 hours," he wrote privately. "Believe me he never had that majority; and the delay of the Caucus is a demonstration of the fact." The same inference should not be made in regard to Monroe's strength, Hay cautioned, predicting that the New Yorkers "will get right again."[7]

Hay's confidence in Monroe's ultimate success was substantiated. Although the circumstances surrounding the initial call for the caucus of 1816 remain elusive, contemporaries suspected—and events confirmed—that Crawford's forces were responsible for the unsigned, printed notices that all Republican members of Congress received on Sunday, March 10, calling a caucus on Tuesday evening, March 12, in the House chamber. According to the reports in the press, the meeting was attended by 58 senators and representatives out of an estimated 125 Republican members of Congress present in the city. All but about ten of those in attendance favored Crawford. With less than a majority of the Republican members of Congress present, the meeting confined itself to issuing a summons for a full caucus on Saturday, March 16. Monroe's friends had no choice but to attend, and on the preceding night, about forty Monroe supporters gathered in the Senate chamber to plot their strategy.[8]

At seven o'clock in the evening on March 16, the caucus met in the House chamber "for the purpose of taking into consideration the propriety of recommending to the people of the United States suitable persons to be supported at the approaching election for the offices of president and vice-president of the United States." Present were 118 members of the House and Senate and one territorial delegate. Press reports estimated that twenty-four Republican members of both houses did not attend the caucus, nine of them being absent from the city. After Samuel Smith of Maryland was called to the chair, Henry Clay opened the meeting by moving that it was inexpedient to make any caucus recommendation. This was defeated, but New York's John W. Taylor then introduced a similar resolution declaring that the practice of caucus nominations ought not to be continued. That motion also failed, and the caucus proceeded to vote. The outcome was close, but a clear victory for Monroe, who received 65 votes to 54 for Crawford. For vice-president the choice was between the two candidates most frequently considered for the nomination, Governor Tompkins of New York and Governor Simon Snyder of Pennsylvania. Tompkins won decisively, 85 to 30.[9]

The support that Monroe had in many states contributed to his success in the caucus. Endorsements by Republican state conventions in Rhode Island and Massachusetts and by the legislature of Pennsylvania were evidence of Monroe's popularity with state leaders, whom congressmen could not afford to ignore. Besides, Crawford himself was hesitant to oppose Monroe's candidacy, unwilling to risk failure and alienation from the next administration and expecting his deference to put him next in line as Monroe's successor.[10] Whatever the determinative circumstances, Monroe would owe his nomination to Congress, and that nomination was paramount to election in 1816. That reality would not be lost on either Congress or the president, and it would influence the parameters of presidential power.

Opposition to Monroe did not cease with the caucus nomination. One anonymous critic published a fourteen-page *Exposition of Motives for Opposing the Nomination of Mr. Monroe for the Office of President of the United States*, in which he renewed the attack on Virginia's domination of the presidency and challenged Monroe's qualifications for the high office. "His best friends allow him to be but of moderate capacity, and slow of comprehension," he wrote. While acknowledging Monroe's urbanity, he accused Monroe of allowing himself to be unduly influenced by those around him. Monroe was prone to keep talent at a distance and surround himself with mediocrity, this opponent charged, and "to commit the most important affairs of state to incompetent hands."[11] Other discontented Republicans urged DeWitt Clinton, who had challenged Madison's reelection in 1812, to enter the contest against Monroe, but Clinton offered no encouragement to such proposals.[12]

No Federalist actively challenged Monroe for the presidential office. No nominating caucus or any other meeting, public or private, named a Federalist candidate. It was tacitly understood that Senator Rufus King of New York was the Federalist standard-bearer, but he made no attempt to campaign or in any way advance his election prospects. In the fall of 1816, King wrote privately that the presidential election had been settled at Washington the previous winter: "So certain is the result, in the opinion of friends of the measure, that no pains are taken to excite the community on the subject. . . . In no preceding Election has there been such a calm respecting it."[13] King's later partisan assessment of the election was that Monroe "had the zealous support of nobody, and he was exempt from the hostility of Everybody."[14] King overstated the absence of opposition to Monroe, but he was on firm ground in concluding that Monroe's election was never in doubt once he received the Republican caucus nomination in March 1816.

When the electoral vote was cast in December 1816, Monroe won all but three states and captured 183 votes. Rufus King carried only Massachusetts, Connecticut, and Delaware for a total of thirty-four electoral votes. Receiving the same number of votes as Monroe, Governor Daniel D. Tompkins of New York was elected vice-president. When the Senate met on February 12, 1817, to count the electoral vote, a brief controversy erupted over Indiana's ballot, cast before it had been admitted as a state in December 1816. In the end, the three electoral votes of the nineteenth and newest state were duly read and recorded. In any event, their exclusion would not have altered the outcome.[15]

Long before the electoral vote was cast or counted, Monroe was making plans for his administration and receiving advice and recommendations about the composition of his cabinet. General Andrew Jackson wrote to Monroe in early November 1816, urging the appointment of William Drayton, a South Carolina Federalist, as secretary of war. With apologies for unsolicited advice, Jackson then asserted:

> Every thing depends on the selection of your ministry. In every selection, party and party feelings should be avoided. Now is the time to exterminate that *Monster* called Party spirit. By selecting characters most conspicuous for their probity, Virtue, capacity, and firmness, without any regard to party, you will go far to eradicate those feelings which on former occasions threw so many obstacles in the way of government; and, perhaps, have the *pleasure,* and *honor,* of uniting a people heretofore politically divided. The Chief Magistrate of a great and powerful nation should never indulge in party feelings. . . . Consult *no party* in your choice—pursue the dictates of that unerring judgment which has so long, and so often benefitted our country.[16]

In reply, Monroe offered an extended commentary on political parties in the United States and on the policy regarding partisanship that

19

he planned to follow while president. In doing so, he made it clear that he viewed the situation as more complex than that suggested by Jackson's proposal simply to ignore all party feelings and attachments. Monroe affirmed that he believed decidedly in the principle that the president "ought not to be the head of a party, but of the nation itself." But he went on to review the history of the rise of political parties in the United States and to point out fundamental differences between the Federalists and the Republicans. "That some of the leaders of the federal party entertained principles unfriendly to our system of government I have been thoroughly convinced; and that they meant to work a change in it, by taking advantage of favorable circumstances, I am equally convinced." The opposition of the Republicans, "carried on with great firmness, checked the career of this party, and kept it within moderate limits."[17]

The clash between the parties had not ceased, Monroe maintained, pointing to the Federalist opposition to the War of 1812 and to the Hartford Convention—opposition that had reduced the Federalist party to its present weakened state. Furthermore, the recent presidential election "has been made by the republican party . . . and of a person known to be devoted to that cause." Although the dangerous purposes of the Federalist party were largely confined to certain eastern leaders and never adopted, "still, southern and eastern federalists have been connected together as a party, have acted together heretofore, and altho' their conduct has been different, of late especially, yet the distinction between republicans and federalists, even in the Southern and Middle and Western States, has not been fully done away." And he asked: "To give effect to free government, and secure it from future danger, ought not its decided friends, who stood firm in the day of trial, to be principally relied on? Would not the association of any of their opponents in the Administration itself wound their feeling, or, at least, of very many of them, to the injury of the republican cause?"[18]

The president-elect answered his own question. "My impression is that the Administration should rest strongly on the republican party, indulging towards the other a spirit of moderation, and evincing a desire to discriminate between its members, and to bring the whole into the republican fold as quick as possible." The dream of converting Federalists to Republicans was the same vision Jefferson had held when he declared upon taking office in 1801: "We are all republicans—we are all federalists." Monroe rejected the view that the Federalist party was needed to maintain unity and order within Republican ranks, nor did he subscribe to the opinion that free governments could not exist without parties. To move to a nonparty system, the first step was to keep the

Republican party together "by not disgusting them by too hasty an act of liberality to the other party." The second object was to prevent the reorganization and revival of the Federalist party. "To accomplish both objects, and thereby exterminate all party divisions in our country, and give new strength and stability to our government, is a great undertaking, not easily executed," he wrote. "I am nevertheless decidedly of opinion that it may be done."[19]

In his lengthy letter to Jackson, Monroe stated that he was in no way committed to the appointment of any particular persons to his cabinet and indicated that he expected to give special attention to geographical representation. The plan he considered ideal was to take the heads of the four departments from the four sections of the union: the East, the Middle states, the South, and the West. He recognized that this would sometimes be unworkable and so should not be a hard-and-fast rule. "But it would produce a good effect to attend to it when practicable. Each part of the Union would be gratified by it, and the knowledge of local details and means, which would be thereby brought into the Cabinet, would be useful."[20]

Geographic considerations thus weighed heavily in Monroe's mind as he chose his cabinet. Because the office of secretary of state had been the bridge to the presidency and resentment against Virginia's domination of the high office was increasing, Monroe's first decision was to appoint no one from the South or the West to head the State Department. Deciding to select a candidate from the East, he turned to John Quincy Adams—"who by his age, long experience in our foreign affairs, and adoption into the republican party, seems to have superior pretentions to any there," he confided to Jefferson.[21] Adams had been minister to Great Britain since 1815, and he had a lengthy record of diplomatic service dating back to assignments in the Netherlands and in Prussia in the 1790s. During Madison's presidency he had served as minister to Russia (1809–1814) and had chaired the United States peace commission at Ghent, which ended the War of 1812. No competitor could match his diplomatic experience. Moreover, in abandoning the Federalist party and throwing his support behind the Jeffersonian embargo of 1807, Adams had been an early Federalist convert to Republican ranks.

By the third week in December 1816 rumors were circulating in Washington that Adams was the leading candidate for secretary of state. Congressman Hugh Nelson of Virginia sensed that there was "a strong disposition to find a Secretary of State to the Eastward. I should not be much surprised if J. Q. Adams should be the man."[22] Nelson also reported that Henry Clay, the Speaker of the House, had refused the Department of War. What Clay desperately wanted was to be secretary of state. Earlier in the year, he had turned down Madison's offer of the War Department, when Madison moved William H. Crawford to the Treasury. Having refused the post from Madison, the ambitious and proud Kentuckian was insulted to be offered the same lesser cabinet position by Monroe. The alienation of the popular congressman from the new president before his administration had even begun did not bode well for the working relationship between the executive and Congress, particularly at a time of weakening party allegiance. Clay would show his displeasure by declining to attend Monroe's inauguration.[23] William H. Crawford also coveted the office of secretary of state, but Monroe asked the Georgian to stay on at the Treasury. Monroe had long before decided to include his rival for the nomination in his administration—though not at the State Department. In fact, there is evidence that President Madison had consulted with Monroe before appointing Crawford as secretary of the Treasury in October 1816.[24]

With a secretary of state from the East and a Treasury chief from the South, the president-elect wanted a westerner at the helm of the War Department. After being turned down by Clay, Monroe considered naming Andrew Jackson to the post. While contemplating the wisdom of taking Jackson away from his command of the army in the South, he was informed by a close friend of Jackson's, Congressman George W. Campbell of Tennessee, that the general was not interested in the appointment.[25] Monroe then offered the position to Governor Isaac Shelby of Kentucky, who declined because of age.[26] Meanwhile, Monroe decided to retain as secretary of the navy Benjamin Crowninshield of Massachusetts, who had headed the Navy Department under Madison since 1814.

Monroe confided to Jefferson his proposed nominations a week before his inauguration and observed: "I can hardly hope, that our Southern gentlemen, who have good pretentions, will enter fully into this view of the subject, but having formed my opinion on great consideration, I shall probably adhere to it."[27] Monroe would not learn of Shelby's refusal until after taking office, and it would be October 1817 before John C. Calhoun accepted the War Department post, after it had also been rejected by South Carolina Congressman William Lowndes.[28] Calhoun assumed his duties as secretary of war in December 1817.

Meanwhile, John Quincy Adams, who was still in London when he received news of his appointment, did not arrive in Washington until late September 1817. In the interim, Richard Rush, attorney general under Madison, served as acting secretary of state as well as attorney general. As the counsel to the president, the attorney general sat in the cabinet, but there was no department of justice. After Adams's arrival, Rush was named minister to England, and in November 1817 Monroe appointed William Wirt of Virginia as attorney general.[29] In short, Monroe would be unable to assemble his new cabinet until after Congress met at the beginning of December 1817, some nine months after taking office as president. In the meantime, Monroe would begin to establish the identity of his administration with the electorate.

The United States over which Monroe was to assume leadership on March 4, 1817, was only two years removed from the debilitating war with Great Britain—a war that had divided the nation, burdened it with debt, and left nearly every government building in the nation's capital badly damaged or in ruins. Yet the army had repelled the British invasion at New Orleans, and Americans emerged from the conflict with a new sense of confidence and independence. The end of the War of 1812 marked the first time since the founding of the new republic that Americans were not preoccupied with foreign affairs. From the outbreak of the French Revolution—only a few months after the inauguration of President Washington—until the Congress of Vienna in 1815, the nearly continual wars in Europe and the ultimate engagement of the United States in the war with Great Britain in 1812 dominated the American political world. The peace in and with Europe meant that Americans could turn their attention to matters closer to home, especially to domestic economic concerns. As Henry Adams wrote in concluding his monumental history of the administrations of Thomas Jefferson and James Madison: "Every serious difficulty which seemed alarming to the people of the Union in 1800 had been removed or had sunk from notice in 1816. With the disappearance of every immediate peril, foreign or domestic, society could devote all its energies, intellectual and physical, to its favorite objects. . . . The continent lay before them, like an uncovered ore-bed."[30]

While the Congress of Vienna brought a balance of power and harmony among the major nations of Europe, it also suppressed the fires of revolution on the continent. At the same time, rebellions against Spanish rule in Latin America burned out of control. These movements for independence and republican government aroused the sympathy and support of North Americans, who saw themselves as the prototype. Although Monroe would enter office with Europe and North America at peace, the revolutions in Latin America, together with the presence of Spanish troops in Florida on the southern border of the United States, meant that foreign concerns would return to prominence on the national agenda.

The population of the United States in 1817 was approaching nine million—more than twice the 1789 total. The growing number of new states seeking admission to the Union reflected the accelerating westward movement of the population. The census of 1810 counted nearly 1,400,000 people living in the Mississippi Valley; by 1820 there were over 2,400,000 residents. Virginia still remained the largest state in the Union, but almost half the population of the United States lived in New England and the Middle Atlantic states. In the census of 1810, New York City had passed Philadelphia as the largest city in the United States, but both cities exceeded 100,000 in population by 1815.[31]

When Monroe took office, nineteen states composed the Union, and five more would be added before he left the presidency in 1825. With the increase in population and the number of states, the membership of the House of Representatives stood at 184 members at the beginning of Monroe's presidency, in contrast to 106 members when Jefferson became president in 1801. An even more striking indication of the growth of the country was the increase in the number of post offices, which totaled only 75 in 1789, soared to 1,025 by 1801, and reached 3,459 in 1817.[32]

By 1817 the American economy was recovering from the disruption of the War of 1812. The national debt was down $4 million from the previous peak of $127 million in 1816. It would continue to diminish during Monroe's two terms, totaling under $84 million when Monroe retired in 1825.[33] Two months before Monroe's installation as president, the second Bank of the United States, established in the last year of Madison's presidency, began operations in Philadelphia on January 1, 1817. The revival of the national bank, whose charter had not been renewed in 1812, inspired hope that stability would return to a banking system that had proved inadequate to the demands of the wartime and postwar republic.

The United States in 1817 was still predominantly an agricultural society. The period from 1810 to 1820 was the only decade in the history of the United States when urbanization did not increase.[34] Even so, the War of 1812 had given a strong stimulus to manufacturing. Between 1810 and 1815 the number of spindles in operation in cotton spinning increased from 87,000 to 130,000 and would reach 220,000 by 1820.[35] In 1815 Hezekiah Niles dedicated a volume of the *Niles' Weekly Register* "To the Manufacturers of the United States; whose labors are eminently calculated to build up a national character, and insure the real independence of our beloved country."[36] In raising the tariff in 1816, Congress gave increased encouragement to manufactures.

Agriculture remained not only the principal base of the economy but also the foundation for the institution of slavery. While slavery was gradually being abolished in states north of Maryland and Delaware and prohibited in western areas north of the Ohio River, it was becoming more deeply entrenched in the South. The rapid growth of cotton production in the Lower South was accelerating the transfer of slaves from the Upper South to the developing lower region, leading to a dependence on slavery over an expanding area.

With the increasing application of steam power to water transport, the United States in 1817 was on the verge of a revolution in transportation. During Monroe's presidency, steamboats would come into ever-increasing use on American waterways, in both the East and the West. Meanwhile, federal government support for building roads and canals had been restrained by Madison's veto of an internal improvements bill in one of his last acts as president, and the constitutional power of Congress regarding internal improvements remained an issue throughout Monroe's presidency. On the state level, New York began building the Erie Canal during the first year of Monroe's administration, and it would be formally opened to traffic six months after Monroe left office.

Americans in 1817 were deeply involved in politics at all levels of government. Over three hundred newspapers were published in the United States in 1817, and they were filled with extensive political news and commentary. Frances Wright, who arrived from England to travel around the nation during the second year of Monroe's presidency, wrote that "it would be impossible for a country to be more completely deluged with newspapers than is this. . . . It is here not the amusement but the duty of every man to know what his public functionaries are doing."[37] Members of Congress saw to it that newspapers circulated in their districts. Texts of all acts of Congress were published in the papers, which were also vigorous organs in political campaigns.

The United States in the early nineteenth century continued to look to Europe for models and leadership in the arts, architecture, and literature. The novels of Sir Walter Scott were immensely popular, and by 1823, Americans had bought 500,000 copies of Scott's works. Before Monroe took office, Washington Irving had written Diedrich Knickerbocker's *History of New York* (1809) and was on his way to becoming a man of letters. His greatest success still lay ahead, and in his lifetime—though not in Monroe's—Irving would be surpassed by a flowering of American literary talent.[38]

As he had for decades, Gilbert Stuart dominated American portrait painting, particularly of public figures, and during his first year as president Monroe would sit for the famed artist in Boston. Younger American painters, such as John Vanderlyn and Thomas Sully, were challenging Stuart's hegemony, but his portraits remained the most favored images in popular prints.[39] John Trumbull, who had begun his tableau of the adoption of the Declaration of Independence before the Constitution was drafted, continued his historical painting and would be commissioned to create paintings for the Rotunda of the United States Capitol while Monroe was president.

In architecture Benjamin Henry Latrobe had already left his mark on the nation's capital, now in the process of rebuilding after the destruction of the War of 1812. Meanwhile, Thomas Jefferson attracted a steady stream of visitors to Monticello and was putting into action his plans for the founding and building of the University of Virginia. One of Monroe's first public appearances as president was his attendance on May 5, 1817, at the first regular meeting in Charlottesville of the Board of Visitors of the recently authorized Central College, which Jefferson was grooming to become the University of Virginia.[40] The astute Jefferson had invited former president Madison as well as Monroe to be members of the board, and the meeting drew the publicity that Jefferson desired. At this moment in history, however, public interest centered less on the two former presidents than on the recently inaugurated executive. James Monroe now commanded the nation's attention.

3

★ ★ ★ ★ ★

FIRST MONTHS IN OFFICE

"Under the auspices of a delightful day, yesterday took place the interesting ceremony attendant on the entrance of the President elect of the United States, on the duties of his arduous station. The ceremony and the spectacle were simple, but grand, animating and impressive." Thus did the Washington *National Intelligencer* describe the inauguration on March 4, 1817, of James Monroe, fifty-eight-year-old Virginia veteran of the revolutionary war, recent secretary of state, and now the fifth president of the United States.[1]

On March 1, Monroe had written to John Marshall requesting the chief justice to administer the presidential oath of office prescribed by the Constitution at twelve o'clock on the fourth in the chamber of the House of Representatives. Marshall replied with a gracious consent the same day. Two days later the *National Intelligencer* published the order of proceedings for the inaugural, indicating seating arrangements within the chamber and specifying—among other details—that "ladies will be accommodated with seats in the Chamber to the utmost extent" consistent with the other arrangements.[2]

On the morning of inauguration day, the *National Intelligencer* published a last-minute notice announcing that the committee of arrangement had altered the location of the inaugural ceremony and that the president-elect would take the oath of office in a portico to be erected for that purpose in front of the Congress hall. The editor explained that the change was made because of fears about the strength of the temporary building in which Congress was meeting, but he added that it was "in a degree also imputable to a difference between the two Houses, or their officers, in the mode of appropriation of the Representatives Chamber to the purposes of this ceremony." What the editor did not report was that members of the Senate had wanted to move their red velvet chairs to the House floor, where they were to sit during the ceremony, but Henry Clay, the Speaker of the House, was already miffed at Monroe and had refused to permit it. The outdoor ceremony was the result of the impasse between the two houses.[3]

A mild day on March 4 drew a large crowd to the inaugural ceremonies, and the drama of the occasion quickly overcame the petty controversy over seating. At half past eleven in the morning, the president-elect, accompanied by the vice-president-elect, left the private residence at 2017 I Street where the Monroes had lived while he served in Madison's administration. "Attended by a large cavalcade of citizens on horseback, marshalled by the gentlemen appointed to that duty," noted the reporter for the *National Intelligencer,* the party reached the Congress hall a little before noon, where they were met by President Madison and the justices of the Supreme Court. After military honors presented by the Marine Corps, the Georgetown Riflemen, a company of artillery, and two companies of infantry from Alexandria, they entered the Senate chamber, where the vice-presidential oath of office was administered to Daniel Tompkins.[4]

The assemblage then moved to the elevated portico erected for the occasion, and "in the presence of an immense concourse of officers of the government, foreign officers, strangers, (ladies as well as gentlemen) and citizens," Monroe delivered his inaugural address. The oath of office was then administered by Chief Justice Marshall, followed by gun salutes from cannon on the grounds and at military installations in Washington. "It is impossible to compute with anything like accuracy the number of carriages, horses, and persons present," the *National Intelligencer* exclaimed, though the reporter estimated the crowd at five thousand to eight thousand and observed that "such a concourse was never before seen in Washington."[5] Sally Otis, wife of Federalist Senator Harrison Gray Otis of Massachusetts, condescendingly described the crowd at the inaugural ceremonies as "not equal I should think to those assembled on our last Artillery Election and by no means so well conditioned." Still, she was struck by the view down "the broad Pennsylvania Avenue three miles in length crowded as far as the eye could extend with carriages of every description, the sidewalks with foot passengers men women and children fiddles fifes and drums altogether presented a scene picturesque and animating."[6]

After the ceremony, President and Mrs. Monroe returned to their house on I Street and received friends, members of Congress, governmental officials, foreign dignitaries, and the general public. Mrs. Otis thought that there were more people outside the president's quarters than at the inaugural. "It was nearly an hour before we could get to the door and then pushing our way through all the Scavengers and wash women of the City who were laying violent hands on the waiters of cake and refreshments," she wrote to her father.[7] The evening concluded with a ball at Davis's Hotel, attended by President and Mrs. Monroe, James and Dolley Madison, the heads of departments, foreign ministers, and "an immense throng of strangers and citizens."[8]

The events of the day were all the more memorable because Washington in 1817 was a city still bearing the scars of war left by the British burning of the capital in 1814. Restoration of the President's House had proceeded rapidly, but it was not yet ready for occupancy. Monroe and his wife would not take up residence there until September 1817, and even then the East Room remained unfinished. Meanwhile, they would continue to live in their house on I Street, four blocks from the White House. Congress was meeting in a brick hall on the site of the present Supreme Court building. The structure had been hurriedly built in six months in 1815 by private interests anxious to keep the legislature in Washington, while the burned-out Capitol was rebuilt. From the portico erected for the inauguration, Monroe looked out on a Capitol shadowed by scaffolding, on unfinished construction, and on other evidence of the seat of government rising again from the ruins of 1814. Nearly three years would elapse after his inaugural before the Capitol was ready for Congress to return, and work on it would continue throughout his presidency.[9]

Monroe's inaugural address was not particularly memorable. It lacked well-turned phrases and contained few, if any, image-filled passages likely to be recalled by listeners or quoted by future readers. Monroe reviewed the impressive progress of the United States since the Revolution, the remarkable success of the Constitution, the expansion of the Union, and the healthy state of the national economy. The first president to take office since the end of the War of 1812, he commended his countrymen for meeting that test and pictured the nation that had emerged from the struggle as vigorous and flourishing. Dangers from abroad still existed, he cautioned, urging attention to military forces, coastal fortifications, and the state militia.

Among issues of wide popular interest, Monroe stressed the importance of additional roads and canals, but he left unclear his view of national authority to build them by referring to the necessity of "proceeding always with a constitutional sanction." He also spoke in general terms about the need to provide manufactures with "the systematic and fostering care of the Government," but he did not suggest specific measures. He noted the healthy state of the Treasury and projected the discharge of the national debt at an early period. In closing his address, the new president remarked on "the increasing harmony which pervades our Union. Discord does not belong to our system." The American people "constitute one great family with a common interest." In language typical of his literary style he concluded: "To promote this harmony, in accord with the principles of our Republican Government, and in a manner to give them the most complete effect, and to advance in all other respects the best interests of our Union, will be the object of my constant and zealous attentions."[10]

The editor of the *National Intelligencer* summed up Monroe's address: "The principles developed in his Inaugural Speech, are such as, adhered to, will triumphantly bear him through. They are those of the honest Republican, and at the same time of the practical statesman. They afford us the highest presage of an upright and unsophisticated administration of public affairs, on the solid principles of the constitution, regulated by reason, and tempered by the wisdom of experience."[11] Less generous in assessing the content of the address was the editor of the *National Register,* a weekly newsmagazine published in Washington. "As to the *style* of the speech," he conceded, "it is, like the suit of clothes which president Monroe wore on the occasion, very good home-spun, and quite fine enough. It forms no objection with us, that there are no flowers of rhetoric scattered through it."[12] Within a week after the inaugural ceremony, the text of Monroe's speech had reached Boston. Henry Dearborn, who had served in Jefferson's cabinet, wrote the president on March 11: "I have this morning with peculiar pleasure read your address, or speech. I think it cannot fail of giving full satisfaction to all sound and truehearted Americans."[13]

After a special session of the Senate confirmed the presidential appointments and adjourned on March 6, 1817, Monroe had ample time to organize his administration and formulate the policies of his presidency before the new Fifteenth Congress convened on December 1. The lull was fortunate for the new president because John Quincy Adams was not expected at the State Department until autumn and Monroe had not yet received an acceptance of the War Department post. In these circumstances, Monroe decided to revive the precedent set by Washington at the beginning of his presidency—but followed by no subsequent executive—of making a tour through part of the country.

Like Washington's journeys, Monroe's travels would foster national unity. Monroe, however, was primarily interested in promoting the nation's military defenses, which he saw as implementing the plan enacted by Congress after the War of 1812 to construct a chain of fortifications along the coasts, bolster defenses on the northern border, and strengthen the navy by establishing naval depots and dockyards. His tour would not only help him administer the program but also build public support for the costly projects. He planned to travel northeastward along the coast and then westward, giving particular attention to coastal work, dockyards, forts, and other military installations. As acting secretary of war at the time of the British burning of Washington in 1814, Monroe well remembered the vulnerability of the United States to hostile invasion. Building military defenses would become one of his major undertakings as president.[14]

When Monroe informed Nicholas Biddle, a frequent correspondent, of his trip, the Philadelphian warmly endorsed his plans. Biddle, who had been Monroe's secretary when he was minister to England and would be appointed by him as one of the five directors of the Bank of the United States, told Monroe that ever since the time of Washington, the president had "unfortunately appeared to the nation too much like the Chief Clerk of Congress,—a cabinet man, stationary at his desk relying exclusively on Secretaries, and invisible except to those who seek him." Biddle thought it would "be highly gratifying to the community to see the Chief Magistrate examining for himself and taking care that the operations confided to him are not marred by the negligence or infidelity of agents."[15]

Monroe initially conceived of the tour as strictly confined to government business, and Biddle encouraged him to believe that the public would appreciate his motives for "abstaining from all exhibitions of mere ostentation or festivity."[16] But by the time Monroe made the first stop on a journey that would extend for nearly sixteen weeks, he was dissuaded from that notion. "When I undertook this tour, I expected to have executed it, as I might have done, in an inferior station, and even of a private citizen," he confided to Jefferson, "but I found at Baltimore that it would be impracticable for me to do so."[17]

Hezekiah Niles, who edited his *Weekly Register* in Baltimore, reported Monroe's arrival in the city on June 1: "Mr. Monroe travels as privately as he can, except he were to pass incognito—his dress and manners have more the appearance of those supposed to belong to a plain and substantial, but well informed, farmer, than such as, from our perverted *notions*, are attached by many to a personage so distinguished." Niles also made an observation that explained why the president could not expect to travel as a private citizen: "The pressure of the people that continually surrounded him though grateful to his feelings,

31

inconvenienced him not a little, and has a tendency materially to defeat the objects of his journey; yet we cannot find fault with the people for desiring to see and pay respects to their chief magistrate."[18]

In the first exchange of addresses that would become a ritual throughout Monroe's tour, the mayor of Baltimore delivered a welcoming speech, praising the increasing harmony within the United States and commending the president for not being satisfied with dated or secondhand information. The mayor was gratified "to see the chief magistrate of this great and powerful nation making an official tour through their country in the style of a private citizen, guarded only by the respect paid to the high station he occupies, and the affections of a virtuous people."[19]

In his response, Monroe made specific references to the locality, as he did at later stops along his route. The president commended the gallant conduct of the citizens of Baltimore during the War of 1812 and recalled the "glorious victory" on the Maryland shore. Before the formal exchange of greetings, Monroe had already visited Fort McHenry and the battlefield where the British invasion had been blocked, and he had paid his respects at the monuments to the battle and to George Washington in the city. In accordance with his efforts to reduce ceremonial attention, Monroe declined an invitation to a public dinner, and early the next morning he left Baltimore by steamboat for Philadelphia.[20]

Though joined by various military officers and local officials at stops along the way, Monroe was accompanied on his tour only by a private secretary and Brigadier General Joseph Gardner Swift, chief of the Army Corps of Engineers and superintendent of West Point. Reaching Philadelphia on the evening of June 5, the president was escorted into the city by three troops of cavalry and a large number of citizens. His hope of avoiding such public display was already shattered. The next day he exchanged greetings with the Pennsylvania Society of the Cincinnati, whom he addressed as "the surviving members of my associates in arms, who distinguished themselves in our revolutionary contest." At Philadelphia, Monroe inspected the navy yard, visited the penitentiary, the Pennsylvania Hospital, the Academy of Fine Arts, and Peale's Museum. He also viewed Thomas Sully's paintings.[21]

On his way from Philadelphia to New York, Monroe passed through Trenton. As bells rang and a salute was fired, Monroe was greeted by municipal authorities, volunteer companies, and a large crowd. The president was formally welcomed to "the scene of some of the services you have rendered your country." Monroe replied spontaneously, referring to Trenton as "the place where the hopes of the country were revived in the war of the revolution by a signal victory obtained by troops under the command of General Washington."[22] Though he did not mention it, his mind must have been flooded with memories of the engagement there in 1776, in which he was severely wounded on the day after Christmas.

In his early reports on Monroe's trip, editor Hezekiah Niles announced that he would "not follow the president step by step, and retail all the chit-chat stuff that appears in the papers about him—as irksome to the republican mind and manners of Mr. *Monroe* as to the people at large." In his opinion, "We by no means find fault with the marks of respect paid to the chief magistrate on a tour of duty, but think there is more of pomp and parade given to it by the people than the fitness of things requires."[23] Nevertheless, considering his *Weekly Register* to be a recorder of official proceedings, Niles continued to report the tour and to publish the text of numerous addresses to the president along with Monroe's replies. During the remainder of the summer, most issues of his newsmagazine contained items taken from the heavy coverage in the newspapers in the towns and cities through which the president passed. Editor Thomas Ritchie of the Richmond *Enquirer* was also critical of the president's tour, denouncing "all the idle pageantry, all the ridiculous and noxious pomp which it has called forth," but he did see it as contributing to the calming of party spirit.[24]

Monroe reached the home of Vice-president Tompkins on Staten Island on the evening of June 9 and stayed there while visiting the military installations in the vicinity. He entered New York City on June 11, landing at the Battery, where he was greeted with a military salute. After reviewing the troops, the president and the general officers led a column of soldiers to the city hall for the official welcoming ceremony. The mayor's speech was one of the longest on the tour, and Monroe tried to match it in length. In New York, he also exchanged addresses with the Society of the Cincinnati, visited the arsenal and other sites, and paid particular attention to manufacturing establishments. Along with the three living former presidents of the United States, he was admitted as a member of the Society for the Encouragement of Domestic Manufactures.[25]

At major stops on his tour, the exchange of formal addresses was an expected convention, leading the editor of the *Essex Register* to observe:

> We have been pleased with every thing we have heard in the visit of the president of the United States, besides the addresses. In this we are guided as much by his pleasure as our own. We do not expect that he comes to us to read and write, but to see us. We should deem it

very absurd on a private visit to give a gentleman a letter, and oblige him to read and answer it, before we conversed with him. Send to Washington as many addresses as you can, and let him read them there; but at your own house . . . only bid him welcome.[26]

Monroe had no set speech that he delivered at every sojourn, nor did he have a speech writer. At shorter stops, he made brief remarks extemporaneously. Longer speeches he composed himself, and the drafts of some of them are extant among his papers. His style was ponderous, lacking the brilliant conciseness of Jefferson or the profundity of Madison. But the thoughts were his own, and his speeches were published in the local papers everywhere he visited. They were also reprinted in distant newspapers throughout the nation and then collected and republished in book form for popular distribution.[27]

For Monroe, the demands of travel and especially of speech making were exhausting. "You can form no idea of the exertion I have been called on to make, and which it has been impossible to avoid," he wrote from West Point after two weeks of travel.[28] Following two months on the road, he complained that he had "been compelled to answer four or five addresses in a day as I have passed forward, not one of which I had seen, or heard, till read." Yet he took satisfaction in meeting the challenge and asked his son-in-law George Hay how this success could "correspond with the dullness, and slowthful operation of faculties imputed to me by Mr. Wirt. I have been particularly hurt by that allegation against me, from so respectable a quarter," he confided, "because I candidly think that if I have any marked feature of character it is that of promptitude in any and all situations in which I have been or may be placed."[29]

The characterization to which Monroe referred had appeared in *The Letters of the British Spy*, William Wirt's essays on Virginia manners and mores published in the Richmond *Virginia Argus* in September 1803 and afterward reprinted as a book. Wirt had written of Monroe: "Nature has given him a mind neither rapid nor rich; and therefore, he cannot shine on a subject which is entirely new to him." On the other hand, Wirt observed, "to compensate him for this he is endued with a spirit of generous and restless emulation, a judgment solid, strong and clear, and a habit of application, which no difficulties can shake, no labours can tire." Wirt's widely circulated portrait of Monroe was the more unflattering to him because Wirt had contrasted Monroe unfavorably with Jefferson. Yet it was not a wholly negative assessment. While Wirt had contended that Monroe's acquaintance with the fine arts was very limited and superficial, he had followed this by stating that "making allowances for his bias towards republicanism, he is a profound and even an eloquent statesman." And Wirt declared at the end of his sketch that "it would be a matter of no surprise to me, if, before his death, the world should see him at the head of the American administration."[30]

Wirt's description could be quoted in Monroe's favor to stress his judgment, application, and tireless labors. But Monroe was offended by the claim that he was slow of mind—though it did not deter him from naming Wirt to his cabinet as attorney general—and he was pleased that this exhausting journey disproved Wirt's evaluation. "The trial of my faculties, and of the prompt command of them, was the greater, from the consideration that my movement was so rapid," he wrote, "that I was seldom more than five or six hours in bed, in any one day of 24; that the committees of arrangement who met me at the entrance into every town, with numerous escorts who attended me through it, kept me always in a crowd; that the heat was great the dust excessive, and above all, that my health was delicate."[31]

Monroe engaged in these reflections at the end of the eastern segment of his tour, which though grueling, had been eased somewhat by the use of steamboats whenever possible. He had gone by steamboat from Baltimore to Philadelphia, and from New York he made a trip by steamboat to West Point, returning to Staten Island before leaving by steamboat for New Haven on June 20.[32] Monroe also used steamboats in visiting Rhode Island. Nothing so clearly illustrates the rapid and widespread employment of steamboats in the United States during this period as their repeated use by the president in his travels in 1817. A revolution in transportation was under way in the United States, and the president was an eager participant. John Quincy Adams marveled in 1817 that a passage between New York and Boston could be completed in forty hours. The steamboat *Connecticut* left New York for New Haven at seven in the morning on Mondays, Wednesdays, and Fridays and arrived at five or six o'clock in the afternoon. Passengers transferred to the steamboat *Fulton* for New London, docking there at five or six the next morning. At New London, a line of stages waited to take passengers immediately through Providence on to Boston, where they arrived before midnight the same day.[33] Monroe also used naval ships at times on his trip, including revenue cutters and the sloop of war *Enterprize* off the New England coast.[34]

The president paid the expenses of his travels out of his own pocket. To finance this trip, he drew on six thousand dollars advanced to him for the household furniture that was to be used in the President's House. Monroe later expressed appreciation that the cost of his tour was "much diminished by the hospitality and accommodation afforded me throughout the Union, and especially in the principal cities, where the expense was greatest." Often traveling by mail stages, he had been pleased when the post office, "unsought and unexpected," provided land transportation, but he was surprised when he received a bill for $1,912—an amount that he regarded as exorbitant.[35]

Monroe's visit to New England attracted nationwide attention, for the Virginia president was entering the domain of the Federalists, his political enemies since the beginning of his career in national politics. It was also in New England where opposition to the War of 1812 had been greatest and from which a threat of disunion had been heard. The visit was widely regarded as a demonstration of Monroe's commitment to the words of his inaugural address, in which he had asserted that the American people constituted one great family with a common interest. After touring much of New England, the president used his stop at the village of Kennebunk, Maine, to reiterate that his travels confirmed "how much we are one people, how strongly the ties, by which we are united, do in fact bind us together; how much we possess in reality a community, not only of interest, but of sympathy and affection." He was prompted to make this remark, he said, "because you are pleased to express a confident hope that a spirit of mutual conciliation may be one of the blessings which may result from my administration."[36]

In Connecticut the editor of the New Haven *Herald*, reporting Monroe's visit to that city, commented on the republican simplicity of Monroe's dress by noting that he wore "a plain blue coat, a buff under dress, and a hat and cockade of the revolutionary fashion." The editor also sensed an unreserved display of public patriotism.

> It was not the sound of artillery, the ringing of bells, nor the splendid processions alone, from which we are to judge the feelings and sentiments of the people on this occasion. It was the general spirit of hilarity which appeared to manifest itself in every countenance, that evinced the pride and satisfaction with which the Americans paid the *voluntary* tribute of respect to the ruler of their own choice—to the magistrate of their own creation. The demon of party for a time departed, and gave place for a general burst of NATIONAL FEELING.[37]

Visiting a number of towns and smaller cities in New England before reaching Boston, the president was warmly welcomed by local officials, as townspeople and militia companies turned out to greet him. The mayor of New London, Connecticut, praised the new era "when party spirit is assuaged, and a spirit of mutual charity and forbearance nationally prevails."[38] Monroe interpreted the large turnout of people in the New England states as prompted by their concern that their reputation had suffered because of their conduct during the War of 1812 and by a desire to demonstrate that they now were firmly attached to the Union and republican government.[39]

In Boston, Federalists vied with Republicans to welcome the president. Monroe spent five days in Boston, with visits to surrounding places.[40] "The President . . . rides hard, visits everything, and in so rapid a manner that it is utterly impossible he should burden his mind with any superfluous knowledge," Federalist Christopher Gore wrote to a friend. Gore reported that on a single day Monroe "inspected an arsenal at Watertown, a cotton manufactory a Waltham, examined Mr. Lyman's villa, stopped at my house, ate a strawberry, bowed and shook hands cordially, returned to Boston to meet the Town oration, the Governor's collation, and the Cincinnati address and their dinner, take tea at Governor Gray's, etc., etc., etc."[41]

For the celebration of the Fourth of July, Monroe visited the ship *Independence*, elegantly decorated with the flags of various nations, and climbed Bunker Hill. "It is impossible to approach Bunker Hill, where the war of the revolution commenced, with so much honor to the nation, without being deeply affected," he told the people of Charleston. "The blood spilt here roused the whole American people, and united them in a common cause in defence of their rights—That union will never be broken." Monroe was guest of honor at a dinner hosted by former president John Adams and later paid a visit to Adams at Quincy and made other private calls in Boston. He received an honorary degree of doctor of laws from Harvard University and found time to sit for Gilbert Stuart (fig. 1), who had painted portraits of all his predecessors in the presidential office.[42]

Monroe's visit to Boston was closely covered in newspapers throughout the country. Even Hezekiah Niles, who had said he would not dog the president's steps in his *Weekly Register*, confessed that he had devoted more time and space to an account of Monroe's trip to Boston than many might think it deserved. But Niles justified it by noting what newspaper editors were saying about the effect of Monroe's tour on reducing party animosities. The *Independent Chronicle and Boston Patriot* declared that "the visit of the *President* seems wholly to have allayed the storms of party. People now meet in the same room who would before scarcely pass the same street—and move in concert, where before the most jaring discord was the consequence of an accidental rencounter."[43] The *Boston Gazette* noticed that in every place through which the president had passed, the people had "most generously and without distinction of party" manifested their respect. It was the Boston *Columbian Centinel* that referred to the times as the "era of good feelings," observing that "during the present jubilee many persons have met at festive boards, in pleasant converse, whom party politics had long severed. We recur with pleasure to all the circumstances which attended the demonstrations of good feelings."[44]

Monroe confided to Jefferson that in Boston the reconciliation was not as universal as the newspapers depicted. "In all the towns through which I passed, there was an union between parties, except in the case of Boston. . . . Some of our old and honest friends at Boston were, however, unwilling to amalgamate with their former opponents, even on our own ground."[45] Later, on the floor of the House of Representatives, Henry Clay questioned the harmony and extinction of party spirit associated with popular demonstrations for Monroe on his tour, and he ridiculed the scenes where "the people of those parts through which the President passed, rise *en masse*, as the audience at the Theatre Français or Covent Garden, upon the entrance of the Sovereign, to greet, to honor, and to salute him."[46]

While Monroe was still on his travels, the criticisms from Thomas Ritchie in the Richmond *Enquirer* reached him and aroused concerns that he revealed privately to George Hay. Waiting at Sackets Harbor for the winds to shift on Lake Ontario before setting sail westward, Monroe worried that his recent reception in upstate New York would bring new attacks from Ritchie, writing:

> The whole population turned out, from the surrounding country, and met me at each village en masse. In crossing a bridge a mile from this town, there were 19 triumphal arches raised over it, one in honor of each State, whose name was inscribed on it, and on the first was a large Eagle alive, and another on the last. I could not control this movement, more than those which occurred to the Eastward, and indeed at Baltimore, Philadelphia, through the whole State of Jersey, and at New York. . . . The military had nothing to do in this business. It was exclusively the act of the citizens.[47]

Ritchie also condemned the president's private visits to Federalists on his trip, which prompted Monroe privately to defend his intentions. Monroe saw it as facilitating an eventual Federalist union with the Republican party, but he regarded the future conduct of Federalists as the surest test of their trustworthiness and was not prepared to rush into appointing them to office. The whole population should join in support of republican government, but that could be accomplished "only by a union of parties on republican principles." A premature appointment of a leading Federalist would excite the resentment of Republicans and cement the Federalists, "who would infer that it proceeded from fear of them as a party." Monroe was convinced that his tour was promoting national unity, but he was not ready to ignore previous party attachments. He noted that he had gone out of his way more than once on his tour to speak well of his Republican predecessors, Jefferson and Madison, during whose administrations opposition had centered in the areas he visited.[48]

Monroe's journey, which carried him as far westward as Detroit, was the first visit to the West by a president of the United States. It reflected Monroe's long-standing interest in the West as well as a growing national recognition of that section's vital role in the Union. Above all, it gave westerners a new sense of confidence as they built communities beyond the mountains. An address from the citizens of Lancaster, Ohio, praised the rising importance of the West and told the president that "its citizens feel an additional confidence that the intimate information which this journey has enabled you to collect, will be used for its benefit and protection."[49]

Western spokesmen who greeted the president were sometimes apologetic about the few amenities they could offer. As the mayor of Chillicothe, Ohio, declared, "the progress of the arts and sciences has not reached in our State the height which they possess in some of our Sister States, but our love of Country and devotedness to her welfare is not surpassed by any. The plain reception of our Chief Magistrate is consonant, we hope, with his republican principles." The town official expressed pride in western accomplishments, telling the president that "in this country, which when a wilderness attracted your early and persevering attention, you may now trace the footpath of industry and the highway of enterprise."[50] Not to be outdone by their eastern neighbors, the people of Detroit welcomed the president with an evening illumination of the city and gave a "splendid ball" in his honor.[51]

Monroe had expected to be back to Washington by the end of August, but it was September 17 before he returned, having covered some three thousand miles by land and water. In keeping with the receptions given the president throughout his trip, Monroe received a final salute upon his arrival in the District of Columbia. Met by the mayor of Georgetown and a delegation of citizens at the boundary of the district, he was accompanied into the city by a cavalcade of citizens on horseback and in carriages, a troop of cavalry from Alexandria, and a band. A surprise awaited the president when he reached Pennsylvania Avenue. A Marine Corps detachment was there to welcome him, and with the war damage mostly repaired, the White House was ready for him to take up residence.[52]

A few months later, looking back on his tour, Monroe expressed the hope that some unanticipated advantage might result from his journey. But he confessed that "the exertions which I was incessantly called on to make, had nearly overwhelmed me, on more than one occasion."[53]

4

THE NEW PRESIDENT AND
A NEW CONGRESS

Three days after President Monroe returned from the West, John Quincy Adams arrived in Washington to take up his duties as secretary of state. The fifty-year-old son of the former Federalist president brought to his post not only his diplomatic experience but also the habits of a compulsive diarist, and he left for posterity an extremely detailed record of the inner workings of the Monroe administration. Almost immediately upon Adams's arrival in the capital, Richard Rush escorted him to the White House, where the president was eager to confer with his new department head before leaving to join his wife in Virginia. As the former secretary of state under Madison, Monroe entered office fully versed on matters of foreign affairs. During his final year in office, however, Madison had largely refrained from initiating any new foreign policies, and Monroe was now anxious to deal with a backlog of issues. In their first conference Monroe and Adams discussed relations with Great Britain, Spain, and France, but they gave most attention to South America, where the spread of revolutions posed grave questions for the nation that had first raised the banner of rebellion against European rule in the American hemisphere.[1]

During the month that Monroe was in Virginia, Adams inundated the president with papers to review, and the secretary of state learned immediately to expect no perfunctory readings or cursory stamps of approval from the president. Monroe scrutinized all of the communications received and responded carefully to issues raised. In reviewing drafts of documents prepared by Adams, he frequently indicated words,

41

sentences, or paragraphs to be altered or deleted. For example, the president wrote to Adams from Albemarle on October 11, 1817, that "it will be advisable for you to omit the last paragraph in the project of a reply, which I lately received, and is now returned to you, and to substitute for it, something of the kind enclosed."[2] This was but one sentence in a letter of nearly three pages in his own hand offering an informed commentary on the questions under discussion.

Meanwhile, other department heads were also broaching matters to the president, who had hoped to attend to his private affairs but found little time to do so. Acknowledging papers sent to him by George Graham, acting secretary of war, Monroe explained in a letter from Albemarle that "the business pressing on me from the other departments, which has been considerable, has prevented my attention to some communications from you." But he promised early answers and also to return other papers "with notes on them as I find them, for my table is covered with such."[3] The day after he wrote this letter, a busy Monroe officiated at the laying of the cornerstone of the first pavilion at the University of Virginia.[4]

The president's close involvement in administrative duties continued after he returned to Washington on October 20. When Adams sent him the draft of sixteen pages of official instructions that Richard Rush was to carry with him as minister to Great Britain, Monroe returned it with a page of suggested alterations on three points. After discussing these with Monroe, Adams felt that his own views had prevailed on two of the three issues and that the third change was "inconsiderable."[5] On another of many similar occasions, Adams recorded: "On calling at the President's this morning with the draft that I had made of an answer to Mr. Correa, according to his directions yesterday, I found it did not exactly suit his ideas, and I was obliged to make an alteration of the draft." Again, Adams noted after a visit with the president: "He read over my draft of instructions to the Commissioners for South America, and directed alterations and additions, which I accordingly made at home this evening." Though Adams sometimes changed the president's mind and at other times yielded to him with reluctance, Monroe clearly possessed and exercised the final authority.[6]

Monroe included all members of his cabinet in deliberations over major foreign policy issues, which dominated the early cabinet meetings held after his return from his long tour and his trip to Virginia. The principal topics under consideration related to South America, and the president posed a series of specific questions that, beyond their content, illustrate the administrative style employed by Monroe as president:

Has the Executive power to acknowledge the independence of new States whose independence has not been acknowledged by the parent country, and between which parties a war actually exists on that account?

Will the sending, or receiving a minister to a new State under such circumstances be considered an acknowledgement of its independence?

Is such acknowledgement a justifiable cause of war to the parent country? Is it a just cause of complaint to any other power?

Is it expedient for the United States, at this time, to acknowledge the independence of Buenos Ayres, or of any other part of the Spanish dominions in America now in a state of revolt?

What ought to be the future conduct of the United States towards Spain, considering the evasions practiced by her government, in procrastinating negotiations, amounting to a refusal to make reparation for injuries?

Is it expedient to break up the establishments at Amelia Island and Galveston, it being evident that they were made for smuggling, if not for piratical purposes, and already perverted to very mischievous purposes to the United States?

Is it expedient to pursue the measure which was decided in May last, but suspended by circumstances, of sending a public ship along the Southern coast, particularly that of the Spanish Colonies, with three citizens of distinguished abilities and high character, to examine the state of those colonies, the progress of the revolution, and the probability of its success, and to make a report accordingly?[7]

Most of the concerns raised by these queries were not of recent origin, but they were matters that the new administration could not long postpone. Indeed, Monroe had turned to some of these problems before making his postinaugural tour, for the declaration of independence by Buenos Aires in 1816 demanded renewed attention to events in South America. Monroe had attempted to enlist Joel Poinsett to make the intelligence-gathering trip along the coast of South America referred to in the final question put to the cabinet.[8] But Poinsett had declined the mission, and Monroe delayed further action until after his tour.

The cabinet met for four-and-a-half hours on October 25, deliberated another four hours on October 28, and held a long session on October 30. It was agreed that the activities on Amelia Island—located at the mouth of the St. Mary's River between Georgia and East Florida—required an immediate response and that orders be issued for the army to break up the marauding parties on the island. Similar action was to be taken at Galveston. The cabinet also decided that the frigate *Congress* should be dispatched with a fact-finding commission to Buenos Aires.

Adams opposed the recognition of the government of Buenos Aires, and the president deferred a determination on this key point.[9] Though formal answers had not been framed for all of the questions raised by the president, they had been thoroughly discussed in the cabinet, and Monroe had established a procedure that he would follow throughout his presidency.

Congress was scheduled to convene on December 1, but Monroe had not yet prepared his message, so he took steps to better organize his days and his office. Soon after taking office, Monroe had decided to abandon the practice that Jefferson had initiated, and Madison had continued, of permitting foreign diplomats to call at the President's House at will and without appointments. Instead, he returned to the diplomatic etiquette followed by Washington and John Adams and modeled on practices in the capitals of Europe. Relations between the president and foreign diplomats would be reserved and formal, placing ministers to the United States on the same footing as American ministers in European courts. They would be granted appointments with the president when requested and received formally by him. Monroe told Adams in early November that he did not have a moment free, day or night, for any foreign visitors but that as soon as he had a secretary, he would fix a regular time for receiving them.[10]

After being turned down by William C. Rives—who declined rather than give up his seat in the Virginia assembly—Monroe named his brother Joseph Jones Monroe as his private secretary. With a secretary on duty, Monroe left instructions that heads of departments were to be admitted at all times but other visitors only at or after one o'clock. Cabinet meetings, called by the president as needed, were usually scheduled for noon or one o'clock and sometimes lasted most of the afternoon.[11]

Monroe appears to have drafted his first message to Congress without soliciting written reports or suggestions from his department heads, but he assembled the members of his cabinet on November 28, three days before Congress convened, to consider his draft. Present were Secretary of State Adams, Treasury Secretary William H. Crawford, Navy Secretary Benjamin Crowninshield, Attorney General William Wirt, and George Graham, acting secretary of war (John C. Calhoun not yet having arrived in Washington). Monroe first read his message to them without interruption; then he read it by paragraphs. "There was a variety of discussions upon certain passages, and some alterations were made," Adams recorded in his diary, without providing any clues as to the points of controversy. The debate was no doubt lengthy, for dinner was announced before they had completed the review by paragraphs.[12]

On December 2, 1817, President Monroe sent to Congress the longest annual message that had yet been addressed to that body. Like Jefferson and Madison before him, he did not deliver his speech in person but forwarded it to Congress to be read by a clerk. His private secretary carried copies to both houses of Congress. As initiated by Washington, the annual address of the president to Congress had become the main vehicle for the president to review the past year and the state of the Union, to anticipate developments, and to propose an agenda for legislative action. After the reading of the message at noon on December 2, the Senate ordered two thousand copies printed, and the House ordered five thousand copies. Because the address was also widely republished in the newspapers, it served as a report to the nation as well as to Congress.[13]

The president began his message by declaring that "at no period of our political existence had we so much cause to felicitate ourselves at the prosperous and happy condition of our country." He expressed satisfaction at burgeoning national unity and reported that preparations for defense in case of war were "advancing under a well-digested system with all the dispatch which so important a work will admit." Monroe thus affirmed at the outset of his presidency a strong commitment to the coastal and border defense of the United States, which his tour earlier in the year had also signaled.[14]

Turning to a survey of foreign affairs, the president devoted considerable attention to relations with Spain and the struggle of the Spanish colonies in Latin America for independence. Although negotiations with Spain over claims and the boundaries of the Louisiana Territory remained suspended, the president held out hope that they would be reopened. As to Latin America, he noted that "it was natural that our citizens should sympathize in the events which affected their neighbors," but he stressed that the policy of the United States was to maintain an "impartial neutrality" in the conflicts between Spain and the colonies. Discussing the situations at Amelia Island and Galveston, Monroe described the pirating, smuggling, harboring of fugitive slaves, and the illicit introduction of slaves from Africa and indicated that he had given orders to suppress those activities. He rejected the claims of the invaders occupying Amelia Island that they acted under the authority of South American colonies. Monroe also reported the plan to send a fact-finding mission to South America.[15]

The president sketched an auspicious view of the internal affairs of the country. Revenues from imposts and tonnage duties were up, the debt was being reduced, and the balance sheet of the federal government was such that Monroe recommended the repeal of the internal taxes imposed during the War of 1812. In reporting various treaties with Indian tribes, lands purchased from them, and the expansion westward of American settlements, Monroe added:

> In this progress, which the rights of nature demand and nothing can prevent, marking a growth rapid and gigantic, it is our duty to make new efforts for the preservation, improvement, and civilization of the native inhabitants. The hunter state can exist only in the vast uncultivated desert. It yields to the more dense and compact form and greater force of civilized population; and of right it ought to yield, for the earth was given to mankind to support the greatest number of which it is capable, and no tribe or people have a right to withhold from the wants of others more than is necessary for their own support and comfort.[16]

In recommending to Congress that in its Indian policy more provisions be made for "their improvement in the arts of civilized life," Monroe reflected the prevailing wisdom that Indians could survive only by adapting to the white man's culture.

Referring to the public lands that were becoming available as Indian titles were surrendered in treaty agreements, Monroe expressed a strong opinion that "the public lands are a public stock, which ought to be disposed of to the best advantage for the nation. The nation should therefore derive the profit proceeding from the continual rise in their value." He believed that if "great capitalists" had the opportunity of amassing vast tracts of land at low prices, "the profit will accrue to them and not to the public." While proposing no specific plan, he urged that in making provisions for the sale of public lands, Congress do so with a view to the public interest.[17]

As he extolled the vast territory of the United States, Monroe turned to the subject of internal improvements and stressed the many advantages afforded by good roads and canals and the need for their construction. On the controversial issue of the constitutional power of Congress to construct a system of roads and canals, however, the president announced the "settled conviction in my mind that Congress do not possess the right. It is not contained in any of the specified powers granted to Congress, nor can I consider it incidental to or a necessary means." He recommended to Congress the submission of a constitutional amendment that would confer the explicit power to build roads and canals. Monroe also suggested another amendment that would empower Congress to institute "seminaries of learning, for the all-important purpose of diffusing knowledge among our fellow-citizens throughout the United States."[18]

Of all the subjects touched on in his address, Monroe's announcement concerning taxes attracted the most interest. Even before the president's message arrived, word had circulated among members of Congress that the cabinet had agreed to recommend the repeal of all internal taxes, which included licenses to distillers and retailers, taxes on refined sugars, sales at auction, carriages, and stamped vellum, parchment, and paper.[19] After Monroe's address was delivered to the House, Congressman Hugh Nelson remarked, "If not popular in any other sense, it will be so from recommending a repeal of the internal taxes."[20] But former Federalist senator Jeremiah Mason of New Hampshire said the recommendation was "what I least expected and dislike most. . . . This is the only tax which tends to an equalization of burdens between the sea-board and interior states."[21]

Members of Congress had been anxious to hear Monroe's position on internal improvements since it was not known whether the new president would depart from his predecessor on the controversial question. The issue was particularly lively because Madison, on his last day in office, had vetoed a bill to appropriate money to construct roads and canals from the funds obtained from granting the charter to the second Bank of the United States.[22] Although President Madison had reversed his earlier opposition to the first Bank of the United States as unconstitutional and signed the act chartering the second national bank, he rejected congressional authority to build roads and canals on the same constitutional grounds employed by Monroe in his message. Congressman Nelson, who supported Monroe's stand, thought the president had "gratuitously tendered his opinion" on the power of Congress regarding internal improvements but had done so in "a gracious candid manner that can excite no unpleasant feelings." Yet Nelson believed that Monroe could expect opposition from some members and that the advocates of internal improvements in Congress would try to carry a new measure "with an overwhelming constitutional majority."[23]

Two weeks after publishing the text of Monroe's message to Congress in his *Weekly Register,* Hezekiah Niles observed that "every one of the quill-driving family of editors seems to feel it his *right* and *duty* to offer some remarks on the annual messages of the president," and he proceeded to offer his own review. In analyzing the "very plain and very interesting communication," Niles found the greatest fault with the president's reference to the nation's profitable and extensive commerce. While admitting that it was augmenting federal revenue, he insisted that commerce was not as profitable or extensive as it should be. "It is very certain that our commerce is *not* flourishing," he wrote, arguing that a considerable part of the nation's trade was in foreign hands, many American ships were idle, and shipbuilding had almost ceased in many ports. Still, he concluded that "the message, in the whole, shows a sound intelligence faithfully devoted to the best interests of the republic and will do much to rivet Mr. Monroe to the affection of his fellow citizens, and exalt his character, with that of his country, abroad."[24]

As he would continue to do in subsequent years, Monroe sent copies of his annual message to friends and political acquaintances throughout the country. His comments to one correspondent indicate that he viewed the statements about Spain and South America, including the measures taken regarding Amelia Island and Galveston, as the most important part of his message. It was his object to support the colonies as much as possible without a confrontation with the allied powers, who could be expected to side with Spain against the colonies. The administration would continue to take the pulse of the European nations, while remaining at liberty to act as the interests of the United States required.[25]

Many of the recipients of the president's message replied with words of praise. "The lucid exposition it gives of the state of the nation, in its external and internal aspects—the prosperous and happy condition of the country it develops, must strengthen in the people their love of country and increase their confidence in its government," wrote Governor John Brooks of Massachusetts.[26] John Jacob Astor, wealthy fur trader and real estate investor, claimed that "there is but one opinion among the publick which is that this your message is the best publick document which has ever appeared in this country."[27] Applauding the president's position on internal improvements, Virginia strict-constructionist Spencer Roane rejoiced that Monroe, at the beginning of his administration, had acted on "a principle that the founders of our Constitution have deemed all important to preserve our liberties."[28]

Former president Madison was more critical and questioned Monroe on "the latitude of the principle on which the right of a Civilized people is asserted over the lands of a savage one."[29] To this Monroe responded that "the history of our settlements, from the first discovery of this country, is a practical illustration of the doctrine contained in my message respecting Indian titles, and I think that it is supported by natural law." He added candidly that "the more we act on it, taking the Indians under our protection, compelling them to cultivate the earth, the better it will be for them."[30] At the same time, it is noteworthy that two months before sending his message to Congress, Monroe had rejected Andrew Jackson's assertion that any treaty with Indians over lands was an absurdity because treaties with other nations transferring territories to the United States had made no reservations in favor of the Indians.

Monroe maintained instead that "within our limits, where the Indian title is not extinguished, our title is good against European powers only, and it is by treaty with the latter that our limits are formed."[31]

While Congress was organizing its committees and getting under way, Monroe and his cabinet prepared for anticipated congressional calls for position papers and other legislative actions. The members of the administration, with Secretary of War Calhoun now at his post, were also evaluating one another. In early January 1818 Adams recorded in his diary that if he understood the characters of his colleagues, "Crawford's point d'honneur is to differ from me, and to find no weight in any reason assigned by me. Wirt and Crowninshield will always be of the President's opinion. Calhoun thinks for himself, independently of all the rest, with sound judgment, quick discrimination, and keen observation. He supports his opinions, too, with powerful eloquence." Reflecting on the frequent meetings of the cabinet where the president discussed all the major policies of his administration, Adams confided: "These Cabinet councils open upon me a new scene and new views of the political world. Here is a play of passions, opinions, and characters different in many respects from those in which I have been accustomed heretofore to move." As he watched the president, who after long cabinet debates frequently postponed his final determination, Adams concluded, "There is slowness, want of decision, and a spirit of procrastination in the President, which perhaps arises more from his situation than his personal character."[32]

Adams early recognized the political circumstances that complicated the president's decision making. The secretary of state noted that within a week after Monroe sent his first annual message to the Congress, Henry Clay "had already mounted his South American great horse." Clay's object, Adams believed, was "to control or overthrow the Executive by swaying the House of Representatives," and his first maneuver was to bring forward a motion to recognize the independence of Buenos Aires. Adams quickly associated Clay's actions with the jockeying of aspirants to succeed Monroe as president. He also realized that as secretary of state, he too was regarded as a potential rival for the presidency. Adams immediately interpreted Crawford's resistance to him in the cabinet as springing from the Treasury secretary's ambitions for the presidency, and he saw similar motivations in the conduct of Clay. The Kentuckian's jealousy of him was exacerbated because Adams had won the cabinet post Clay coveted. Adams accordingly viewed Clay as the head of a new opposition in Congress to the administration and suspected that "he makes no scruples of giving tone to all his party in run-ning me down." As the congressional session dragged on, Adams believed that Clay's recalcitrance was the president's greatest worry. "The subject which seems to absorb all the faculties of his mind," he recorded in his diary, "is the violent systematic opposition that Clay is raising against his Administration."[33]

The Fifteenth Congress to which Monroe addressed his first annual message had the largest number of new members since the First Congress in 1789. Of the total membership of the preceding Congress, over 63 percent did not return.[34] One new member, Congressman Louis McLane of Delaware, cast his eye around the chamber at the opening of the session and observed: "The house of representatives presents a group of all descriptions of people, in looking upon which you would be inclined to suppose they had been gathered together from all climes, as samples of their respective nations. There may be great talent hidden under their exterior, but the time has not arrived to develop it."[35] As a Federalist, McLane belonged to a dwindling partisan minority, but he was one of the majority of new members. The unprecedented turnover in Congress was largely attributed to the passage of a bill in 1816 to raise the pay of representatives and senators from six dollars a day to fifteen hundred dollars per year.[36] There had been no increase in congressional pay since the First Congress, despite a depreciation of the currency. The new salary was no more than that of the sergeant of arms or the doorkeeper of the House, or many clerks in government offices, but the measure excited a public outcry throughout the country. "From every quarter it was severely anathematized, and all were forced to acknowledge that the great majority of the People required its repeal," Congressman John Tyler admitted to his constituents in reporting the repeal of the act in 1817, just before Monroe took office.[37] Although Tyler was reelected, the quick rescission of the measure was not enough to save the seats of other legislators.

Despite the significant number of new members in the Fifteenth Congress, the leadership had largely escaped the voters' retribution. Henry Clay had not been turned out by his Kentucky constituents and had again been elected Speaker of the House of Representatives. William Lowndes of South Carolina, who had been chairman of the House Ways and Means Committee in the preceding Congress, returned and was renamed as head of that powerful committee. Also resuming their positions were the chairmen of the House committees on elections, manufactures, public lands, post office and post roads, and accounts. Moreover, only two of the nineteen chairmen of standing committees of the new House had not served in the preceding Congress.[38]

In connection with the large number of first-time members, the party composition of the new Congress shifted. In the House of Representatives there were 142 Republicans and 40 Federalists, representing a considerable loss of Federalist strength; in the previous Congress, the party division had been 116 Republicans and 67 Federalists. In reporting these figures in his *Weekly Register,* Hezekiah Niles interpreted them not only as giving the Republican side of the House an enormous gain but also as showing a great decline of the power and spirit of party. "The real or apparent moderation of party spirit," Niles instructed his readers, "has caused the present to be called 'the era of good-feelings.'"[39]

Some in the preceding Congress had already observed the loosening of party ties. Congressman Lewis Williams told his North Carolina constituents in 1816 that "among the most auspicious appearances of the times, is the obliteration of party spirit. No question at the present session of Congress has been discussed or determined on the ground of party."[40] On the day that Monroe was inaugurated, another North Carolina representative wrote to his constituents that in Congress "party spirit is so far extinct, that the time seems to have passed away, and I fondly hope will never again occur, when party measures, ruinous to the best interests of the country, can be carried by the mere force of a name; and the fate of the most important questions, decided or known by the file leader of a party."[41] As the first session of Congress under Monroe drew to a close, John Tyler concluded that "party distractions have entirely been forgotten."[42]

Tyler and others may have overstated the wane of the parties, for the presence of forty Federalists in the House of Representatives showed that the opposition to the Republicans had not been totally vanquished. Nor was President Monroe ready to ignore past party alignments in making appointments to office. Yet the absence of party as a critical factor in Congress had wide implications for Monroe's leadership as president. Unlike Jefferson, Monroe could not appeal to members of Congress in the name of party or party unity and had to govern without the benefit of a congressional following that accepted the necessity of party discipline to implement the president's program. "The Government has been carried on so long by mere party spirit, that I expect our rulers will be somewhat perplexed to carry it on by any other principle," Jeremiah Mason predicted.[43] And at the end of Monroe's first year as president, Justice Joseph Story observed that "the Executive has no longer a commanding influence. The House of Representatives has absorbed all the popular feeling and all the effective power of the country."[44] Clay, as Speaker of the House, played a major role in the rising stature of the lower house.

In his message to Congress at the opening session of the Fifteenth Congress, Monroe had outlined only a limited legislative program. His key recommendation on taxes was quickly implemented by the repeal of all internal taxes.[45] Congress also passed legislation to admit two new states, Mississippi and Illinois, into the Union, set its new pay at eight dollars a day, and increased veterans' benefits. But few other important measures made it through the legislative process. Members spent a great deal of time debating the constitutional implications of internal improvements but did not act on the president's proposal for an amendment explicitly granting congressional authority. Instead, the House of Representatives, while not asserting the power of Congress to *build* roads and canals, adopted a resolution stating that Congress had the power, under the Constitution, to *appropriate money* for the construction of roads and canals.[46]

Before the close of the session, the policy Monroe announced in his annual message of maintaining neutrality between Spain and its rebellious colonies was endorsed by the House of Representatives, but not without a fight. The explosive issue was brought to the floor when Clay proposed to appropriate funds for a minister from the United States to "the independent provinces of the River Plata, in South America." Tantamount to the recognition of independence, such a mission to Buenos Aires was a step that the president was not prepared to take, though he clearly sympathized with the South American patriots. In a week of animated debate, Clay spoke at length on three separate days, his longest speech lasting three hours. His motion was nevertheless defeated by a vote of 115 to 45. One congressman who opposed the measure explained to his constituents that he regarded it not only as likely to involve the United States in a war with Spain but also as "an unnecessary and improper interference with Executive authority."[47]

Reflecting on the debate, Monroe wrote privately that his policy had been "to favor the colonies, to the utmost extent, consistent with the peace, security, and happiness of our own country." That objective had been achieved by the fact-finding mission to Buenos Aires, "whereby they have all the advantages of recognition of their independence without its dangers to ourselves, and even to themselves, for, if such recognition led to war, I think it would do them more harm than good." The colonies had equal access with Spain to American ports, by which they got arms and "every munition of war." He pointed out that "this they might lose if we became a party to it."[48] The president had won one contest with the Speaker of the House, but it was not the last challenge to his leadership.

After four months of congressional proceedings, John Quincy Adams wrote to a friend that "the present session will stand remarkable in the annals of our Union, for showing how a Legislature can keep itself employed, when having nothing to do."[49] Some members of Congress were even less charitable. "Perhaps there was no session of Congress, since the adoption of the federal constitution, in which so little was apparently done in the same length of time," Congressman James Stewart reported to his North Carolina constituents.[50] In their defense, Stewart and other members pointed to the inexperience of the new legislators, the long debates on constitutional issues of an abstract nature, and an unusually large number of claims. One new member, anxious to get home, wrote that he had been told by seasoned representatives that "there never was one third part so much business before any former Congress, even at the commencement of a session, as we have now on our table and in the Committee rooms—more than 1500 petitions are said to have been presented this session."[51]

Looking back on the session after Congress adjourned, Monroe complained to Madison that, considering the flourishing state of the country, the Fifteenth Congress had been "unusually oppressive on every branch of the Executive department." There had been more calls for information than he could ever remember, and in a portion of the House of Representatives "a very querulous spirit has been manifested." Monroe observed that "the questions, involving the right in Congress to make roads and canals, and the policy of the Executive respecting South America, produced the greatest difficulty. They were those from which the opposition expected to make the greatest impression, but happily the result did not correspond with their views."[52]

Monroe had intended to make an extensive tour along the coast to Savannah, westward to St. Louis, and back home through Kentucky. But the late adjournment of Congress caused him to delay the trip until the following year.[53] Instead, he inspected the fortifications on the Chesapeake Bay and at Norfolk, and he took some time to recuperate, since his health had suffered during the difficult winter. The president could not leave behind the burdens of office, however, and he carried with him the worries of a crisis that he had quietly dealt with during 1817: the military operations against the Seminole Indians. It was soon to become the subject of loud public controversy, the echoes of which would outlast his presidency.

5

ANDREW JACKSON AND
THE FIRST SEMINOLE WAR

On the day that James Monroe was inaugurated, Andrew Jackson wrote a long letter to the new president from the headquarters of the southern division of the army at Nashville. "I have waited with anxious solicitude for the period to arrive, when I could congratulate my Country and myself on your being placed into the Presidential chair of this rising Republic," the general began. He followed with a list of national military needs, starting with the defenseless situation of New Orleans and Mobile and the insufficient attention to the protection of the frontier. After several pages of advice on matters of defense and Indian policies, Jackson came to the issue that was uppermost in his mind: the powers assumed by William H. Crawford as secretary of war under Madison, "which strike at the very root of all subordination, that ought and must exist in an Army." Specifically, he referred to the case of Major Stephen H. Long of the Corps of Topographical Engineers, who had been given a special assignment from the secretary of war without the orders going through Jackson, to whom the major had reported. Jackson expressed high alarm over "the right, assumed by the Secretary of War to direct the Topographical Engineers to perform special duties, the manner in which they shall report, and even directing them to report to an independent department, and all this without the knowledge of the Commanding General." He told the president that he could not forbear bringing the matter to his early notice, "that it may find a correction before its disorganizing features take root, and hereafter be quoted as precedents."[1]

Monroe did not reply to Jackson's letter before departing on his tour in the spring of 1817. Carrying the relevant papers with him, he intended to write to the general during one of his steamboat passages. Along the way he sent Jackson several brief notes assuring him of a reply.[2] However, it was October before Monroe finally responded, while he was at home in Virginia, by which time he saw his letter as notifying Jackson of "the decision which he must have inferred I had already and long made."[3] The basic issue was clear. On April 22, Jackson had forbidden compliance with any order from the War Department that did not come through the proper channel; consequently, Major General Eleazer W. Ripley at New Orleans, on Jackson's responsibility, had refused a direct order from the War Department.[4] Thus, the authority of the secretary of war, and of the president, had been directly challenged.

It seems likely that Monroe's delay in confronting Jackson was partly influenced by his difficulties in filling the office of secretary of war, temporarily occupied by George Graham, formerly the chief clerk of the War Department. Though the position was still open when he wrote to Jackson on October 5, five days later he offered the post to John C. Calhoun, who promptly accepted.[5] In any event, the president now dealt with the issue directly, though he sought to do so without humiliating the proud general. "I will put the affair at rest, and in a way conciliatory to him, as I presume," Monroe wrote to the acting secretary of war.[6]

In answering Jackson, Monroe took a firm position and supported it with conviction. "Your order of the 22d of April makes the issue, by prohibiting obedience to any order from the department of war by the officers of your division, or by any officer who had reported and been assigned to duty in it, which did not pass through you its commander," Monroe wrote to Jackson. "This order involves the naked principle, of the power of the Executive, over the officers of the army, in such cases, for the department of war cannot be separated from the President." The War Department was instituted to convey the president's orders to the army and to perform other services, he pointed out. The orders of that department were therefore the orders of the president, and the president was the commander in chief of the army. His authority was limited only by the Constitution and the laws of the United States. "Under these circumstances I cannot perceive on what ground an order from the Chief Magistrate, within the limitation stated, can be disobeyed." Never concise in developing his arguments, Monroe expounded for several pages on the supremacy of presidential authority over military forces. At the same time, he acknowledged the practical importance of orders going through the chain of command, except in cases of urgency.

When a situation departed from normal procedure, the commander of the district should be advised of it and sent a copy of the order. Because Jackson had previously threatened to retire, the president closed his letter by expressing his earnest desire that the general remain in service.[7]

Although Monroe hoped for an earlier resolution of the issue, he had not received Jackson's answer to his letter when he sent the general a copy of his message to Congress on December 2. Professing his desire to end "this unpleasant affair, in the most honorable manner for you, that it may be possible, consistent, with principles, which it is my duty to maintain," Monroe stated that as soon as Calhoun arrived in the capital, he would ask the secretary of war to prepare a set of regulations to deal with the matter. "A few rules will be sufficient for the purpose," the president wrote, "and in them, the principle may be laid down, that as a general rule, the order should go to the Commander of the division, and that in all cases, when deviated from, a copy should be sent at the same time to him. This will, I presume, terminate the affair, with perfect delicacy to you."[8] To this letter Jackson replied promptly, indicating that "the plan proposed fully meets my approbation, for I see in it that magnanimity of conduct only to be met with in great and good minds."[9]

When Calhoun took up his duties as secretary of war, one of his first tasks was to issue a general order specifying the policy that Monroe had outlined to Jackson. Sending a copy of the order to Jackson, Calhoun, in a covering letter, elaborated on the arguments supporting the policy, but it was Monroe who had worked out the principles and obtained Jackson's approval.[10] The day before Calhoun sent oficial notification to the general, the president informed Jackson of the order being forwarded by Calhoun and assured him that it was "in strict conformity with my letters to you." Monroe reaffirmed that "the justice of it is acknowledged in your letters to me, and indeed cannot be controverted." No reference or allusion to Jackson's case had been made, Monroe pointed out, and in fact it was not necessary for him to revoke his order of April 22. "With this measure the affair may terminate, as I hope, and presume, it will," Monroe wrote with obvious relief.[11] And it was none too soon.

Monroe also notified Jackson that the same mail would bring him "an order to repair to the command of the troops acting against the Seminoles, a tribe which has long violated our rights, and insulted our national character. The movement will bring you, on a theatre, where possibly you may have other service to perform, depending on the conduct of the banditti at Amelia Island and Galvestown. This is not a time for you to think of repose."[12] The decision to send Jackson to the Georgia frontier had been reached at a cabinet meeting on December 26, when the members had also confirmed the policy of pursuing the Seminoles across the border into Florida, if required, to put down their raids.[13] Ten days earlier, the following orders had been dispatched to General Edmund Pendleton Gaines at Fort Scott:

> On receipt of this letter, should the Seminole Indians still refuse to make reparation for their outrages and depredations on the citizens of the United States, it is the wish of the President that you consider yourself at liberty to march across the Florida line, and to attack them within its limits, should it be found necessary, unless they should shelter themselves under a Spanish post. In the last event, you will immediately notify this department.[14]

Jackson received copies of all orders to Gaines but no special, additional instructions regarding intrusions into Florida. Acknowledging these communications—received before his assignment to assume command of forces on the Florida border—Jackson wrote from Nashville to the president on January 6, 1818. He applauded all the actions taken except the restraint on Gaines from attacking Spanish posts. "Permit me to remark," he wrote, "that the arms of the United States must be carried to any point within the limits of East Florida, where an Enemy is permitted and protected or disgrace attends." He recommended that all of East Florida be "seized and held as an indemnity for the outrages of Spain upon the property of our citizens." This would save the United States from a war with Great Britain or some continental power combined with Spain. He then added that "this can be done without implicating the Government; let it be signifyed to me through any channel, (say Mr. J. Rhea) that the possession of the Floridas would be desirable to the United States, and in sixty days it will be accomplished."[15]

On January 11, 1818, General Jackson received his orders from the secretary of war to take command of the operations against the Seminoles. The next day, on his own authority, he began raising one thousand volunteers of mounted riflemen from western Tennessee to serve in the campaign. While requesting that the thousand Georgia militia drafted into service be kept in the field, he did not wish to depend solely on them for numerical superiority. With the Tennessee volunteers acting in conjunction with the regular troops, he promised to move promptly and, "with the smiles of heaven," successfully against any force the Seminoles could concentrate against them. "The Volunteers that have been invited to the field are of tried materials and such as can be relied on in the day of danger and trial," he told Calhoun.[16] With assurances from "old companions in arms" that they would join him on the Georgia frontier, Jackson set out for Fort Scott on January 22.

Meanwhile, in Washington the welcome news arrived that Amelia Island had been peacefully occupied.[17] But, while awaiting word about the conflict with the Seminoles, concerns in Congress mounted. On March 24 John Forsyth, chairman of the House committee that considered the foreign affairs raised in the president's message, inquired of Calhoun whether generals Gaines and Jackson had been authorized to invade Florida in fighting the Seminoles. Calhoun responded that the president would transmit the requested information to Congress.[18] The next day Monroe laid before both houses of Congress all the information in his possession respecting the war with the Seminoles. He stressed the utter inability of the Spanish government to check the attacks of the Seminoles against the United States and concluded that "when the authority of Spain ceases to exist there, the United States have a right to pursue their enemy on a principle of self-defense." He also reported that orders had been given to the general in command not to enter Florida unless in pursuit of the Seminoles, to respect Spanish authority wherever it was maintained, and to withdraw his forces as soon as order and security against further hostilities had been established.[19]

Congress adjourned before the news reached the capital that General Jackson had seized the Spanish fort at St. Marks in Florida on April 7.[20] Accusing the Spanish of providing aid and refuge to the Seminoles, Jackson ordered his troops to storm the fort. They took it without resistance. Inside, they discovered Alexander Arbuthnot, a Scotsman who gave his American captors no satisfactory explanation for his presence. The subsequent capture of Arbuthnot's schooner led to the discovery of papers regarded as incriminating and then to the arrest of Robert Ambrister, who was charged with being a fellow conspirator. A trial by court-martial resulted in the execution of the two men as inciters of the Indian war. Jackson was convinced that even if the men were not British agents, the British government knew of their activities.[21] In reporting his various actions to the secretary of war, Jackson enclosed documents that he said clearly evinced "the duplicity of the Spanish Commandant at St Marks in professing friendship towards the United States while he was actually aiding and supplying her savage enemies; Throwing open the gates of his garrison to their free access, Appropriating the King's stores to their use, issuing ammunition and munition of war to them, and knowingly purchasing of them property plundered from the Citizens of the United States." Jackson justified his deeds as in pursuance of his instructions and necessary to ensure the peace and security of the southern frontier of Georgia.[22]

After hearing reports that the Seminoles had free access into Pensacola and were assembling warriors and receiving arms and ammunition there, Jackson decided to move westward. When the governor refused to permit a peaceful occupation of Pensacola, Jackson attacked and forced the surrender of Fort Carlos de Barrancas and the recognition of American authority in Pensacola on May 28. "This step became absolutely necessary to put down the Indian war, and give 'peace and security' to our Southern frontier," Jackson wrote to President Monroe. "I have established peace and safety, and hope the government will never yield it, should my acts meet your approbation, it will be a source of great consolation to me, should it be disapproved, I will have this consolation, that I exercised my best exertions and judgment and that sound national policy will dictate holding possession as long as we are a republick."[23] To Calhoun, Jackson insisted that tranquility on the southern frontier could be maintained only by a cordon of military posts along the Gulf of Mexico. To think that a boundary line in a wilderness could be defended was "visionary in the extreme."[24]

Before Jackson's official communications reached the president and the secretary of war, unofficial reports of the taking of Pensacola circulated around the capital, and the Spanish minister pressed the secretary of state for explanations. "This, and other events in this Indian war, makes many difficulties for the Administration," Adams recorded on June 18. Soon the French minister was protesting, and the British minister demanded information on the executions of Arbuthnot and Ambrister. Regardless, the president left Washington on June 16 for his farm in Loudoun County, Virginia, thirty-three miles from the city. "Though the moment is very critical, and a storm is rapidly thickening," Adams confided in his diary, "he has not read many of the papers that I left with him, and he puts off everything for a future time."[25]

After two weeks, Monroe returned to the White House, having received Jackson's letter in the meantime. In a series of six lengthy cabinet meetings over seven days, the president's advisers discussed the administration's response to Jackson's conduct in Florida—particularly his taking of Pensacola. The president and all members of his cabinet except Adams agreed that Jackson had acted not only without authority but also against his instructions. Adams privately thought that Calhoun was personally offended that Jackson had disregarded the instructions from the War Department, and he reported that Crawford, fearing the public concern voiced in the press, favored a repudiation of Jackson and the restoration of Pensacola. Adams, however, argued that Jackson's actions were justified by his authorization to cross the Florida border and terminate the Indian war.[26]

Monroe and his cabinet, bar one, believed that the seizure of Pensacola constituted an act of war and that Pensacola must be restored to Spain. When Adams attempted to make a case for self-defense on Jackson's behalf, Calhoun led the rebuttal, insisting that it was a violation of the Constitution. Adams at first favored keeping Pensacola until Spain fulfilled its obligations to restrain the Indians from attacking the United States, but he came to accept the view of his colleagues that it could not be retained without an act of Congress. The cabinet spent hours discussing and amending Adams's draft of the note to be sent to the Spanish minister, Luis de Onís. In the end, Adams confessed, "the letter was modified so as to be made exactly conformable in substance to the President's original draft—the language only is mine."[27]

Once the cabinet decided to repudiate Jackson's aggression and return Pensacola to Spain, the president was charged with writing Jackson a friendly letter communicating the contents of the note to Onís and stating the constitutional ground on which Pensacola was to be restored. While the president was drafting this letter, Attorney General William Wirt was composing a piece for the press. In a diary entry on the cabinet meeting of July 18, Adams noted that "Mr. Wirt had also prepared the draft of an article upon the subject, to be published in the National Intelligencer, the discussion of which was continued till dinner was announced." At a cabinet meeting three days later, Wirt read what he called a second edition of his article for the *National Intelligencer.* Adams objected to several paragraphs but had little support among his colleagues and acquiesced in its publication. When Wirt gave the piece to Joseph Gales, one of the editors of the *National Intelligencer,* Gales asked about reports of a division of opinion in the cabinet. Wirt responded that there was diversity of opinion but that all had agreed on the result. Gales wanted to add that the opinion of the cabinet had been unanimous, but after Wirt conferred with Adams and found him unwilling to go that far, the piece appeared with no mention of unanimity. In his final revision Wirt struck out a paragraph to which Adams had objected.[28]

Without the help of Adams's diary, these details of how the Monroe administration managed the release of news to the press could not be reconstructed, though the process provides important insights into the operation of Monroe's administration and the role of the press. The *National Intelligencer* was widely recognized as having close contacts with the administration. Charles Jared Ingersoll, United States district attorney for Pennsylvania and former member of Congress, told Monroe that the foreign diplomats with whom he became acquainted at a Pennsylvania resort "look to the Intelligencer as religiously official, and take it for granted that every thing in the paper proceeds directly from your Secretaries."[29]

Though written by Wirt, there was nothing in the piece to suggest that it did not come straight from the newpaper editor. Appearing in the column under the masthead, normally used by the editor, it began: "The President of the United States has, we understand, decided, that Pensacola, and the other Spanish posts, which have been taken by General Jackson, in the Floridas, shall be restored to the Spanish authority; but with a requisition, that the King of Spain shall, hereafter, keep such a force in those colonies, as shall enable him to execute, with fidelity, the fifth article of the treaty between the United States and Spain."[30] The article cited obligated Spain to keep Indians within Florida from perpetrating hostilities against citizens or territories of the United States.

The bulk of the article was devoted to the Seminole attacks, and it was directed as much to Spain as to the American people. A paragraph relating to Jackson explained:

> In attacking the posts of St. Mark and Pensacola, with the fort of Barrancas, General Jackson, it is understood, acted on facts, which were, for the first time, brought to his knowledge, on the immediate theatre of war; facts, which, in his estimation, implicated the Spanish authorities in that quarter, as the instigators and auxiliaries of the war; and he took these measures on his own responsibility merely. That his operations proceeded from motives of the purest patriotism, and from his conviction, that, in seizing and holding those posts, he was justified by the necessity of the case, and was advancing the best interests of his country, the character of General Jackson forbids a doubt. Of the important facts alleged by him, satisfactory proof, it is understood, has already been furnished to the President, and proof of the other facts is confidently expected.[31]

The "editorial" went on to suggest that it was difficult to believe that the Spanish king would endorse the actions of his agents, but even so, only Congress could declare war. The president thus had decided to return the posts. It was supposed that the president, like most of his countrymen, recognized the great advantage to be gained from the possession of the Floridas, but not without the sanction of Congress. "To have retained these posts, under present circumstances, would *certainly* have had the *éclat* of being a *strong measure*: but we hope never to see a President of the United States disposed to be stronger than the Constitution of his country." The article closed with an expression of hope that a peaceful solution could be worked out.[32]

Wirt's piece, which filled two newspaper columns, has been quoted at length because it was a statement that had been discussed and approved by the president and his entire cabinet. Its main points were also repeated in Monroe's letter to Jackson informing him of the administration's decisions. In that missive, the president dealt more directly with the issue of Jackson's lack of authority. "In calling you into active service against the Seminoles, and communicating to you the orders, which had been given just before to General Gaines, the views and intentions of government, were fully disclosed in respect to the operations in Florida. In transcending the limit prescribed by those orders, you acted on your own responsibility," the president wrote bluntly. But he softened the indictment in language similar to that supplied by Wirt to Joseph Gales, acknowledging that Jackson acted "on facts and circumstances, which were unknown to the government when the orders were given, many of which indeed occurred afterwards, and which, you thought, imposed on you the measure, as an act of patriotism, essential to the honor and interest of your country."[33] Thus, though Monroe made it clear that Jackson had exceeded his orders, he did not impugn the general's motives.

In response to the president's letter, Jackson refused to accept the premise that he overstepped his authority and acted on his own responsibility—although his earlier letter of June 2 had implied that when he expressed uncertainty about whether or not his actions would be approved. Now, writing a confidential letter to Monroe from Nashville on August 19, Jackson argued that the orders to General Gaines restricting Gaines from attacking Spanish posts in Florida were not binding because his own orders had directed him to "terminate the Seminole conflict." The general reasoned, "How then can it be said, with propriety, that I have *transcended the limits of my orders* or *acted on my own responsibility*? My order was as comprehensive as it could be, and contained neither minute original instructions, nor a reference to others, previously given, to guide and govern me. The fullest discretion was left with me in the selection and application of means to effect the specified, legitimate objects of the campaign; and for the exercise of a sound discretion, on principles of policy, am I alone responsible."[34] Jackson asserted that he would not shrink from responsibility, if the common good required it; but it was clear from his letter that he did not expect to be asked to shoulder any blame.

Monroe received Jackson's letter while on his farm in Albemarle County, in the daily post sent from Washington. That express, he said, "keeps me informed of affairs there, and I continue the same direction over them that I should if I was present."[35] Hoping to give Jackson time to calm down, the president delayed answering the general's correspondence until returning to the city. Meanwhile, Monroe reflected on the administration's policy in a letter to George Hay in early September. Jackson's attacks at Pensacola and St. Marks had shown "the utter inability of Spain to maintain her authority there, much less fulfill her duties towards us. That attack may produce a good effect," he continued, "in promoting a cession, which the restoration of the posts enables her to do with honor." Had the administration turned on Jackson and brought him to trial, it would have created "internal feuds, of the most pernicious character, and told Spain that she had nothing to fear from us." He concluded that "by the course pursued, we have endeavoured to combine every interest, and the whole community, in support of the constitution, and of the rights of the country against Spain, while we put her in condition to do, with honor, what we wish; with a strong admonition, that she may risk much by not doing it."[36]

In late October, Monroe at last replied to Jackson's letter of August 19. In a conciliatory tone, he wrote:

> I was sorry to find that you understood your instructions, relative to operations in Florida, differently from what we intended. I was satisfied, however, that you had good reason for your conduct and have acted in all things on that principle. By supposing that you understood them as we did, I concluded that you proceeded on your responsibility alone, in which, knowing the purity of your motives, I have done all that I could to justify the measure. I well know also the misconduct of the Spanish authorities in that quarter, not of recent date only. Finding that you had a different view of your power, it remained only to do justice to you on that ground. Nothing can be further from my intentions, than to expose you to a responsibility, in any sense, which you did not contemplate.[37]

Expecting Congress to call for papers on the matter, Monroe suggested that Jackson write a letter to the secretary of war stating his views of the powers under which he had acted, and then Calhoun, "who has very just and liberal sentiments on the subject," would reply and affirm the administration's position. "Thus we shall all stand on the ground of honour, each doing justice to the other, which is the ground on which we wish to place each other."[38]

Monroe's letter received a prompt rebuff from the general. Jackson insisted that his correspondence on May 7 to the secretary of war already declared his position—that his actions had been taken "*in pursu-*

ance of your instructions under a firm conviction that they alone were calculated to ensure peace and security to the Southern frontier of Georgia." Jackson indicated that if the secretary of war wished to write to him, he would be glad to respond. But, he added, "I have no ground that a difference of opinion exists between the Government and myself, relative to the powers given me in my orders, unless I advert, either to your private and confidential letters, or the public prints."[39]

In the midst of this exchange, Monroe was composing his second annual message to Congress. Following the procedures employed in preparing his first message, he wrote the initial draft himself and by early November was reading various paragraphs of it to department heads.[40] Absent from the consultations was the newly designated secretary of the navy, Smith Thompson, who had accepted the appointment but had not yet assumed his duties.[41] When the cabinet reviewed the draft of the message, the issue of Florida and the Seminole war occupied little time, because the administration had agreed on its policy in July. Adams, however, saw the address as reflecting his own earlier defense of Jackson and reported that Calhoun thought the president had gone too far in justifying Jackson's actions. The principal subject of discussion in the cabinet related to South America, for the question of granting recognition to colonies declaring their independence from Spain remained a pressing issue.[42]

In his message to Congress, Monroe took up the status of relations with Spain near the beginning of a long address. He affirmed that the policy of neutrality in the contest between Spain and the colonies in South America would be continued. Promising to provide Congress with all documents relating to the Seminole war, the president made only brief observations on the recent conflict. He emphasized that in authorizing Jackson to enter Florida in pursuit of the Seminoles, "care was taken not to encroach on the rights of Spain." Monroe gave most attention to vindicating Jackson but also asserted that although the general's explanations were duly appreciated, the administration had no hesitation in ordering the return of Pensacola and St. Marks to Spain. Only the power of Congress to declare war could authorize the executive to occupy the Spanish posts, which would be restored to Spain upon the arrival of Spanish forces competent to control Indian aggression.[43]

In the House of Representatives, consideration of the section of the president's speech on the Seminole war was divided between committees on military and foreign affairs. Focusing on the trial of Arbuthnot and Ambrister, the military affairs committee reported a resolution disapproving of the proceedings in the trial and the execution of the two men. But the committee chairman, Richard M. Johnson, brought in a minority report praising Jackson's conduct. The committee on foreign affairs offered no resolution on the seizure of the Spanish posts, but one was offered from the floor that declared that the occupation of Pensacola was a violation of the Constitution of the United States.[44] On January 20, 1819, members of the Senate, foreign diplomats, and guests crowded the floor of the House of Representatives, and other visitors packed the gallery, to hear Henry Clay speak for three hours. Moved by Clay's powerful speech, Congressman Louis McLane called it "the most eloquent one I ever heard." Clay "came out strongly but decorously in opposition to Jackson, but supported the Executive," and McLane thought there was at least some possibility that Jackson would receive a vote of disapproval.[45] Margaret Bayard Smith, listening from the lobby, judged Clay's oratory "not only eloquent but amusing." She also observed that "every person had expected him to be very severe on the President and seemed rather disappointed by his moderation."[46]

As the debate on Jackson and the Seminole war entered its second week, McLane saw no end in sight. "The Lord knows when it will terminate," he confided to his wife, "since it seems to me that almost every man in Congress means to be heard in it."[47] While the general's actions were scrutinized, Congressman John Forsyth of Georgia judged that "among the prudent and reflecting and those who consider obedience to the laws of their Country and of humanity as the first duty of every Citizen, disapprobation is universal."[48] Yet after three weeks of animated speeches—during which Clay proposed to censure the general and Jackson himself arrived in Washington—all resolutions disapproving of Jackson's conduct were defeated.[49]

The influence of Monroe on the outcome of the House debates is difficult to judge. Federalist Louis McLane, observing that the administration had no talented spokesman on the floor to counteract Clay, remarked, "Mr. Monroe appears to be so destitute of active supporters that he has great need to fear the result of the next caucus."[50] Hugh Nelson, a supporter of the president, noted that some members considered the attempt to censure Jackson as "only a masked battery levelled at the President," but he himself believed that many who favored censure were not also opposed to the president.[51] Georgia's John Forsyth was convinced that the result would have been different had not Jackson's friends "succeeded in producing the impression that censuring the General was censuring the administration."[52]

When the smoke cleared, strong feelings remained. Members who thought the issue involved "principles of the first importance to the existence of our constitution" were soon forced to justify to their constituents their "vote *against* General Jackson."[53] One North Carolina congressman friendly to Jackson did not question his motives but pointed out that all officers took an oath to support the Constitution. "Permit this to pass unnoticed," he warned, "and some more ambitious and more designing General may seize it as an apology for more daring acts."[54] To Lewis Williams, another representative from North Carolina, "the question then, was simply this, 'shall Congress, to whom belongs exclusively, the power to make war, look with silence on such acts of usurpation; or shall they not rather speak out and vindicate the majesty of the Constitution?'. . . . Place the military above the civil authority, and in what respect would our government differ from the despotism of Bonaparte."[55]

Although Jackson escaped censure from Congress, he was insulted that anyone had even considered it and never forgave those who favored it. He became incensed when he later learned from Crawford that in the cabinet meetings Calhoun had been strongly opposed to his actions in Florida. After Jackson as president became alienated from Calhoun, his vice-president, the issue was reopened and became a subject of intense public controversy.[56] Jackson then claimed that he had received secret instructions to occupy Florida from Monroe through John Rhea (in accordance with Jackson's letter of January 6, 1818, to the president). When Calhoun relayed the charge to Monroe, the former president reaffirmed that he had never acted on Jackson's suggestion. Indeed, he remembered that he had been ill when Jackson's letter had arrived and had passed it on to Calhoun before even reading it. Though Calhoun had informed him it required his attention, the letter had been laid aside and never read until Calhoun reminded him of it after the war had ended. At that time, wondering whether Rhea might have misunderstood some conversation with him, he asked him in a general conversation if he had ever intimated to Jackson an opinion that the administration had no objection to his attack on Pensacola. Rhea assured him he had not.[57] Years later, Rhea, aged and with fading memory, wrote out a letter that followed a draft sent to him by Jackson, in which he stated that he had given Jackson a message from Monroe authorizing his actions in Florida. Jackson contended that he had burned the letter at Monroe's request.[58] In response Monroe signed a sworn affidavit declaring as utterly untrue that he had ever authorized Rhea to write any letter to Jackson to deviate from any orders from the War Department or that he had requested Jackson to destroy any letter written by Rhea to Jackson.[59]

The details of this later controversy need not be repeated here, but it should be noted that in none of the contemporary records is there any evidence to support Jackson's assertion as president that he had received authority from Monroe for his actions in the Seminole war. Nowhere in Monroe's or Jackson's correspondence during 1818 can anything be found implying that Monroe had sent a signal to Jackson through Rhea—or anyone else—to take Florida. In none of the long letters that Jackson wrote to the president and the secretary of war reporting and justifying his conduct in Florida was there a hint that he believed his actions had been authorized by a secret presidential directive. On the contrary, Jackson's tone suggested that he was aware he had gone beyond his orders. He went to considerable length to defend his decisions, presenting evidence to persuade the president that his actions had been necessary to end the Seminole hostilities.

Although he was not a party to Jackson's seizure of St. Marks and Pensacola, and though he disapproved of the general's methods, President Monroe was not unaware of how the events might be turned to the advantage of the United States. While the congressional debate on the Seminole war was in progress, he wrote to Madison that the administration had had three objects in view in reacting to Jackson's incursions in Florida: "first to secure the constitution from any breach, second to deprive Spain and the allies of any just cause of war, and third to turn it to the best account of the country."[60]

The last objective was evident in the actions of the secretary of state. While exchanging notes with Luis de Onís, the Spanish minister to the United States, over the taking of the Spanish forts, Adams had continued negotiations with him regarding the acquisition of Florida and the western border of the Louisiana Territory. In July 1818, as the cabinet was deliberating over the response to Jackson's movements, Adams asked the French minister Hyde de Neuville to carry to Onís a map marked with a western boundary line the United States would be willing to accept.[61] Spain, whose inability to maintain control over Florida had been demonstrated by Jackson's conquests, hoped to fix the western border to Spain's advantage, especially to include Texas. Between October 24, 1818, when Onís made a counteroffer to Adams's July proposal, and February 22, 1819, when they finally reached an agreement, Adams and Onís drew lines on a series of five maps. Each time, the lines—far apart on the first map—grew closer together until they at last agreed on a boundary.

The treaty signed on February 22 transferred the Floridas to the United States and provided that the United States would assume up to $5 million of claims by American citizens against Spain. It settled the Texas border to Spain's satisfaction and for the first time in official annals set the western boundary of the United States at the Pacific

Ocean.[62] "The acquistion of Florida has long been an object of earnest desire to this country," an exuberant Adams recorded in his diary. "The acknowledgment of a definite line of boundary to the South Sea forms a great epocha in our history." Adams took credit as the first to propose a line to the Pacific, noting that such a claim was in neither the treaty of independence nor the purchase of Louisiana.[63] The secretary of state may have been premature in his celebration, for the treaty had yet to be ratified in Madrid, but an equally pleased president sent it immediately to the Senate. Monroe was convinced that without his own policy—of not reprimanding Jackson while placing the blame on Spanish authorities—the cession of Florida would not have occurred.[64] On February 24, two days after receiving the treaty, the Senate approved it unanimously.[65] Coming only two weeks after the House voted down the resolutions that would have censured Jackson's conduct in the Seminole war, the Adams-Onís agreement provided a happy ending to a difficult period and closed the second year of Monroe's presidency.

6

WIDENING HORIZONS AND
DEEPENING PROBLEMS

Ever since his successful, if exhausting, tour of the northeast and northwest in 1817, Monroe had been planning a similar trip to other regions of the country. "I contemplate a journey in the spring," he wrote privately in late November 1818, "to the South, as far as Georgia, and thence westward to the Missouri territory, back home through Kentucky."[1] At the end of March 1819, the president left Washington accompanied by Secretary of War Calhoun, Samuel Gouverneur, his private secretary and future son-in-law, and Lieutenant James Monroe, his nephew and aide. Calhoun brought along his wife and two children, planning to accompany the president only on the southern portion of the tour and then to visit his home in South Carolina.

Departing Washington by steamboat, the party made its first stop at Norfolk, inspecting coastal defenses and viewing new sites for forts that would later become Fortress Monroe and Fort Calhoun. By way of inland waters, the group reached Edenton, North Carolina, on April 4, and the president and the secretary of war spent most of a week exploring the waters of the Albemarle and Pamlico sounds. On April 10, they visited New Bern and were in Wilmington by the fifteenth.[2] At every stop, welcoming ceremonies and public dinners followed precedents set on his northeastern tour. Reporting on Monroe's southern travels, *Niles' Weekly Register* observed, "He is every where received with great attention and respect, but there is much less pomp and parade than took place on his eastern journey."[3] Monroe's receptions in Edenton and New Bern, however, were elaborate. In New Bern, ringing bells and the discharge of artillery announced the president's arrival, cheering crowds thronged the streets, and a local observer reported that "such a burst of joy has not been manifested by our citizens since the memorable entry of the illustrious Washington," who visited New Bern in 1791.[4]

In Charleston, where the city council had prepared an elegant barge for the president's entrance to the city, the fanfare rivaled that of even larger eastern cities. After landing, Monroe was greeted by an elaborate military salute, welcomed by city officials, and accompanied by a procession of dignitaries and citizens to St. Andrews Hall for a reception.[5] The president spent a week in Charleston, inspecting fortifications and visiting sites in the city. The Charleston *Gazette* marveled that "every decent member of society has had (or could have had) access to him. The rich and the poor alike proffered their congratulations, and all were received with the utmost simplicity and republicanism of manner."[6] Monroe concluded his stay in the city by hosting a dinner for 150 people, paid for by the Charleston corporation. "The invitations were well arranged," he observed, "so as to satisfy all parties and will I have no doubt produce a good effect."[7] The city also commissioned Samuel F. B. Morse, then living in Charleston, to paint a portrait of the president to hang in the city hall beside John Trumbull's portrait of Washington, which had been commissioned to honor Washington's visit to Charleston in 1791. When Monroe could find no time while in Charleston to sit for Morse, the artist later traveled to the capital to take the president's portrait (fig. 8).[8]

The pace of the southern tour was less hectic than his eastern trip. On his last day in Charleston—a Sunday—Monroe had the leisure to write a seven-page letter to George Hay. Though he listed his various activities, the letter was less a report on his official duties than reflections stimulated by his experiences. Moved by the kindnesses of generals Charles C. Pinckney and Thomas Pinckney, once Federalist political foes, Monroe remarked on their past public service. He also related an affecting account of his first meeting with Thomas Pinckney, then a major, at the time of the fall of Charleston during the American Revolution. Monroe was then on a military mission to South Carolina for Virginia's Governor Jefferson. "In visiting this state, in my present office, I feel it a duty and I take a pride, in calling on these gentlemen and showing my respect for them," he wrote.[9] As Monroe continued, it was evident that some of his account was intended for publication in the press. Referring again to his visits with the Pinckneys, he told Hay:

It is possible that you may see the circumstances noticed, and even with censure. Whether it be with approbation or censure, you will decide how far it may be proper to make it the subject of a paragraph, merely from the interest such incidents, stated historically and concisely, tend naturally to excite. I am inclined to think that such a paragraph would have a conciliatory effect, in drawing the country together, shaking the foundation of party animosities, on just principles. But the incident should be stated as an editorial remark, without appearing to attach any consequence to it.[10]

The letter reveals that Monroe was concerned about his public image and sought to shape that image. After his lengthy reflections on the Pinckneys, he added, "Another incident merits attention, not precisely on the same principles, but as tending to prevent the fostering a party spirit of another kind." Then he reported that in Georgetown, South Carolina, he was commended for his services during the War of 1812 without any mention of Madison, so "I seized the opportunity to speak of him in the most respectful manner." In Charleston, when Jefferson's name came up in reference to the acquisition of Louisiana, "I spoke of him in terms as strong as I could find, expressive of his extraordinary service to his country and great merit."[11] Previously on the trip, Monroe had not found an opportunity to praise Jefferson without also mentioning someone else. "In this instance he stood alone, and I availed myself of the opportunity to do him all possible justice, and disarm those who would turn him, or his name, against me, of the power of doing it with success."[12] Ever the politician, Monroe missed few opportunities to bolster his political position.

Leaving Charleston, Monroe stopped at Beaufort, South Carolina, and continued on to Savannah, where, according to press reports, "he was received with splendid military honors, greeted with the approving smiles of beauty, and cheered by the universal acclaim of his fellow citizens." The editor of the Washington *National Intelligencer* commented that "the Southern cities appear to have engaged in a rivalship of courtesies and manifestations of respect towards their distinguished guest."[13]

From Savannah the president's party went by steamboat to Augusta, where public display lessened. A planned public dinner was canceled because of the brevity of the president's visit, but it was superseded by a ball in his honor. As the press reported, "The President was received in true republican simplicity. We had no other *show* to make, than the tender of a sincere respect and an unostentatious hospitality." At a small dinner in his honor in Washington, Georgia, "the President expressed himself highly pleased at the honest reception he met with," according to another press account, which added that "never was there any thing of the kind before more indicative of genuine republicanism: No ostentation—no pomp—no *aristocracy*. The *Chief Magistrate* of the greatest republic, not to say the greatest nation, in the universe, seated amid the rustic, though not less valuable citizens, as their friend, patron, father!"[14]

From Georgia, Monroe took the road through the Cherokee nation to Nashville—a route determined by his desire to visit an academy for the Indians.[15] Here he observed some sixty Indian children receiving instruction on the Lancasterian plan in a missionary school.[16] "After a very fatiguing journey though the Cherokee country, owing to continual rains, bad roads and accomodations," as Monroe explained to Adams, he arrived in Nashville exhausted. He spent a week there with Andrew Jackson at the Hermitage and in the city, where the mayor turned over his residence to the president and his party. A dinner, a ball, and other ceremonies again crowded the president's days and confirmed his decision not to proceed to St. Louis, as he had earlier planned, but to return home through Kentucky.[17] Although in poor health, Jackson not only accompanied Monroe on his visits in Tennessee but also traveled with him to Kentucky. With the Seminole war controversy quieted, the president felt at liberty to talk with the general about becoming governor of Florida once Spain ratified the treaty.[18]

From Nashville the entourage traveled north to Louisville, crossing the Ohio River southwest of the city to visit Corydon, Indiana's capital, before proceeding on to Louisville. After another public dinner and a ball, the president continued eastward to Frankfort, the Kentucky capital, and to Lexington. Among other greeters he was welcomed by the president of Transylvania College, Horace Holley, and by a member of the sophomore class, who pronounced a short address in Latin. Remaining in Lexington for the celebration of independence on July 4, Monroe told an enthusiastic audience that the growth of Kentucky "and of the whole western country, has surpassed what was ever seen before in any part of the world."[19]

Monroe's travels were widely reported in the press. The Washington *National Intelligencer* published a detailed account of Monroe's stay in Nashville and devoted nearly a full page to coverage of his visit in Lexington.[20] *Niles' Weekly Register* declared that his receptions at Louisville and Lexington were "very splendid—and almost as ceremonious as when he visited Boston."[21] Some observers noticed that Henry Clay was not present to welcome the president to his hometown, since Clay had not yet returned from a trip to New Orleans. Monroe, however, did meet with him at Greenville Springs near Harrodsburg, as he began his journey back to Virginia.[22]

The president had expected to meet Crawford in Wheeling and make his way to Washington by the Cumberland Road, but he learned from the newspapers that Crawford was already back in the capital. Weary from his travels and the summer heat, he decided to return home by way of the springs in Kentucky and western Virginia.[23] Monroe arrived at Highland in Albemarle County on August 2, "in good health, though much fatigued," and he wrote immediately to the secretary of state asking him to alert the cabinet that he would be in Washington within the week.[24] On August 8, he was back in the White House. A few days later he received a warm letter of praise from his friend Charles J. Ingersoll of Philadelphia assuring him that "whatever vestige of opposition there may have been in the east, or germ of it in the west, you have literally looked down, and rallied the whole country to your person as well as your government."[25] Ingersoll urged him to keep up his travels until he had visited New Orleans, St. Louis, and St. Augustine. Monroe, however, would not again attempt a presidential tour.

In his trips to the West in 1817 and 1819, Monroe demonstrated a genuine interest in that expansive region, and he combined that interest with policies designed to promote western development. Within his administration the key person in the formation of western policy was Secretary of War John C. Calhoun, whose department was charged with military defense and Indian affairs. While Calhoun appears to have been the principal initiator of western projects, he had the firm support of the president.

Three months after joining the cabinet, Calhoun began implementing a plan to locate a military post at the mouth of the Yellowstone River on the upper reaches of the Missouri River. Though the expedition to the Yellowstone attracted much western interest, it suffered numerous delays and setbacks, including the financial difficulties of 1819, and ultimately fell far short of attaining its objective. At the same time, the project indicated the administration's interest in establishing an American presence near the Canadian border and replacing English traders in the profitable fur trade. In asking American soldiers to serve at so remote a post, the secretary of war thought that "the glory of planting the American flag at a point so distant on so noble a river will not be unfelt." Writing a year before Adams negotiated the transcontinental treaty with Spain, Calhoun declared, "The world will behold in [the Yellowstone post], the mighty growth of our republic, which but a few years since, was limited by the Allegany; but now is ready to push its civilization and laws to the western confines of the continent."[26] Five months later Calhoun was inclined to think that the post should be situated some three hundred miles eastward at the Mandan villages, the point on the Missouri River nearest the British post on the Red River. This became the revised goal, but his purpose remained the same. "I am very desirous by taking strong and judicious posts," he wrote, "to break the British control over the Northern Indians."[27]

When the financial distresses of 1819 hampered the expedition's progress, friends and relatives of contractors for the project approached Monroe during his tour of Kentucky. He was quick to respond. From Lexington, the president authorized Calhoun to make a sizable advance to one of the expedition's major suppliers, James Johnson, who was also the brother of Congressman Richard M. Johnson. "The people of the whole Western Country take a deep interest in the success of the contemplated establishment at the mouth of the Yellow Stone river," Monroe wrote to Calhoun. "They look upon it as a measure, better calculated to preserve the peace of the frontier, to secure us the fur trade, and break up the intercourse between the British traders and the Indians, than any other, which has been taken by the government." In closing his letter, the president assured the secretary of war: "I take myself very great interest in the success of the expedition, and am willing to take great responsibility to ensure it."[28]

Although Monroe's commitment to the project was strong, he was not so immediately involved in its planning as President Jefferson had been in overseeing the Lewis and Clark expedition. In Monroe's administrative system, his approval was required, but it was Calhoun who, following Jefferson's example, added a scientific component to what had begun as an operation to establish a military post. If Calhoun's extensive papers are any indication, Monroe was less directly involved in military planning—despite his tours of military fortifications—than he was in the details of foreign policy. Although there are numerous notes and directives from the president in the papers of the secretary of state, the same cannot be said of the papers of the secretary of war, but it is possible that Calhoun—unlike Adams—did not keep all of the scraps of paper on which Monroe frequently scribbled notes.

To head the scientific expedition, Calhoun named Major Stephen H. Long of the Corps of Topographical Engineers, a Dartmouth graduate recommended by a superior officer as "the most skillful, industrious and enterprising officer I have known in that department."[29] During 1817 and 1818 Major Long had conducted military and topographical reconnaissance of the upper Mississippi River and in the Arkansas country. Soon after Monroe became president, Long had proposed to Monroe and the War Department an exploration of the western rivers and the Great Lakes by steamboat.[30]

In his instructions to Long, the secretary of war wrote that "the object of the expedition is to acquire as thorough and accurate knowledge as may be practicable of a portion of our country which is daily becoming more interesting but which is as yet imperfectly known. With this view you will permit nothing worthy of notice to escape your attention." Calhoun specifically directed Long to take precise readings of latitude and longitude of various geographical points—such as the extreme bend of the Missouri to the north—to ascertain more clearly the limits of British possessions. "You will enter in your journal everything interesting in relation to soil, face of the country, water courses and productions whether animal, vegetable or mineral." Information was also to be collected on the Indians, who were to be conciliated by kindness and presents. Calhoun expressed faith in the scientists in Long's expedition, confident that their performance would "add both to their own reputation and that of our country." Revealing the influence of Jefferson, Calhoun wrote in closing his letter: "The instructions of Mr. Jefferson to Capt. Lewis, which are printed in his travels will afford you many valuable suggestions of which as far as applicable you will avail yourself."[31]

The secretary of war also sent a copy of Long's instructions to Robert Walsh, Jr., of the American Philosophical Society, soliciting suggestions relating to the scientific objectives of the expedition. "The immediate object of the expedition is to acquire more accurate geographic knowledge of an interesting portion of our country; but it is also the desire of the government to render it extensively useful to the sciences," Calhoun wrote to Walsh.[32] In response, the American Philosophical Society promptly named a committee that prepared a series of papers and forwarded them to Calhoun. Walsh also reported that Thomas Cooper, a member of the committee, had already given a list of queries to a member of the expedition. "The Society has full confidence in the knowledge and sagacity of the men of science attached to the exploring party," Walsh replied to Calhoun, "and has therefore rather intended by what it offers, to testify its disposition to co-operate in the liberal aims of the Government, than expected to contribute any material aid."[33]

As word of the expedition spread, both Calhoun and Long received applications from members of the scientific community interested in accompanying the party.[34] In Philadelphia, Long gathered information, interviewed applicants, and made the final determination. Having supervised the construction of a steamboat, the *Western Engineer*, in Pittsburgh and assembled his scientific contingent, Long reported the final details to Calhoun on April 20, 1819. Dr. William Baldwin, a botanist and the physician and surgeon for the expedition, was to record descriptions of vegetation, investigate any diseases among the human inhabitants, and notice "any varieties in the anatomy of the human frame, or any other phenomena observable in our species." Thomas Say, a member of the Academy of Natural Sciences in Philadelphia and generally considered the most brilliant zoologist in the country, was charged with examining and describing "any subject in zoology and its several branches that may come under observation." Augustus Edward Jessup, a geologist and fellow member of the academy, was responsible for all that related to soils, minerals and fossils. Titian Ramsay Peale, son of Charles Willson Peale and an early applicant, was named assistant naturalist in all the fields and given the tasks of collecting and preserving specimens and sketching stratifications of rocks and soils.[35] Long, who had met the young Peale in Philadelphia, regarded him as "a valuable acquisition to the party; he paints with a good degree of execution, is well skilled in preparing birds and other animals, and collecting specimens of minerals, plants, etc."[36]

Samuel Seymour, an artist, was another member of the expedition. Long described his duties as "furnish[ing] sketches of Landscapes whenever we meet with any distinguished for their beauty and grandeur—he will also paint miniature likenesses or Portraits if required of distinguished Indians and exhibit groups of savages engaged in celebrating their festivals or sitting in council and in general illustrate any subject that may be deemed appropriate in his art." The official journal of the expedition was to be kept by Major Thomas Biddle, Jr., as an adjunct to his military responsibilities. Long instructed him to provide a full record of "whatever may be of interest to the community in a civil point of view," including the manners and customs of the inhabitants of the areas passed through and the histories of the villages and tribes of Indians visited. The attendant military personnel and the steamboat crew brought the roster of the expedition to twenty-four.[37]

As the *Western Engineer* prepared to depart from Pittsburgh for St. Louis, an enthusiastic press report appeared in the Washington *National Intelligencer*. No piece better illustrates the strong support during Monroe's presidency for the use of public funds for scientific endeavors. After explaining the purposes of the expedition, the reporter reflected on its significance:

> We anticipate much useful information from the result of this voyage; it appears to have been arranged by government with a great conviction of its importance, and the design bears a strong resemblance to the French expedition into Egypt, in which the cause of science was not lost sight of during their military operations. Although the Missouri is not embellished by such stupendous monuments of art as is

the Nile, her Indian mounds afford matter for much interesting disquisition; and although no Thebes, nor mutilated statues of a Memnon may be found, yet some clue may yet be discovered to assist our historical researches into the ancient manners of the Aborigines. At all events, the field of science may be much extended by the party. To this object government has been particular in its attention; and it is matter of no little pride that such gentlemen as Drs. Baldwin and Say, and Messrs. Jessup, Peale, and Seymour, have embarked in the enterprise. . . .

Undertakings of this kind do honor to a government; at the same time that they extend her own influence, the cause of universal science is advanced.[38]

Despite the careful planning, Long's expedition did not enjoy the success of the French venture into Egypt or the Lewis and Clark exploration. The scientific contingent suffered from the illness and early loss of Dr. William Baldwin, who had to be left behind at Franklin, Missouri, where he died in August 1819.[39] Though Calhoun thought the question of rank between the two majors had been clearly established, Biddle refused to perform all the duties Long assigned to him. Once aware of the contention, Calhoun intervened to support Long's authority. "The scientific expedition under Maj. Long has excited too much interest to fail, without producing unhappy consequences," he wrote privately.[40]

Problems with the newly constructed steamboat delayed the progress of the expedition and were compounded by "the extreme difficulty of navigating the Missouri, which has been far greater than the most exaggerated accounts had authorized us to expect," Long reported to Calhoun. "We were much retarded by grounding upon sand bars, and in some instances by want of a sufficient depth of water in the deepest channel, (which it was often difficult to find) to admit the passage of the boat." The mud in the Missouri River also caused unexpected problems, rising with the steam to create fine grit that fouled valves and other parts of the machinery.[41] The technology of steamboat building, though advancing rapidly, was still developing; indeed, Long's *Western Engineer* was far better designed for service in the Missouri River than the steamboats supplied by James Johnson for the military force that Long was accompanying. As it turned out, Long's party preceded the larger expedition up the river and had already established an encampment at Council Bluffs when the military personnel under Colonel Henry Atkinson finally arrived in September 1819. The military expedition had been slowed not only by steamboat problems but also by failures of supply, as the principal contractor, James Johnson, faced mounting financial difficulties and feverishly juggled his debts, paying off loans with monies advanced from the government.[42]

Finding a safe harbor for the *Western Engineer* in the vicinity of Council Bluffs, Major Long left his expedition there to extend their observations as far as practicable during the winter, while he returned to Philadelphia to make arrangements for the spring.[43] With the military objective stalled at Council Bluffs, Long proposed to Calhoun that his party explore westward by land to the source of the Platte River, from there southward to the source of the Red River, and down the Red River to the Mississippi. "The route here specified would embrace a region of which we at present have no certain knowledge," he wrote to the secretary of war, "and promises to be at least as interesting as any other within the limits of our Territory."[44] After consulting with Monroe, Calhoun informed Long that his plan had "met the approbation of the President"—further evidence of Monroe's active oversight of Calhoun's operations.[45]

Returning to Missouri with Captain J. R. Bell (replacing Major Biddle) and Dr. Edwin Jones (successor to Dr. Baldwin), Long reached Council Bluffs on May 12, 1820. After dispatching the *Western Engineer* down the Missouri River to St. Louis, the Long expedition ascended the Platte River to its source, and on July 14, Edwin James led a party of three to the summit of Pike's Peak. Returning eastward, part of the expedition began the descent of the Arkansas River, while the others pursued what was believed to be a stream flowing into the Red River. It led, however, to the Arkansas River, and both parties headed to Fort Smith, Arkansas, reaching there in September. The group dispersed at Cape Girardeau, Missouri, in October 1820.[46]

The scientific expedition, like the larger military one, had not lived up to early expectations, but the members returned with considerable information and numerous botanical and biological specimens. Long submitted to Calhoun a manuscript of 109 pages on the topography of the lands and rivers explored on the trek.[47] Edwin James, the botanist, prepared an extensive catalogue of the plants collected on the journey to and from the Rocky Mountains, which was published by the American Philosophical Society.[48] James also compiled a full account of the expedition, published in three volumes in Philadelphia in 1822–1823.[49] Titian Peale brought back enough quadrupeds, birds, fish, and reptiles to prepare nearly one hundred mounted exhibits for display at Peale's Museum in Philadelphia, where the War Department agreed to deposit them along with botanical specimens and over a hundred drawings from the expedition.[50] In forwarding sketches by Samuel Seymour to Calhoun, Long described them as illustrative of remote western landscapes, commenting that "the scenery exhibited is entirely of a novel character, tho not remarkably striking."[51] Peale's drawings and paintings also included Indian scenes and portraits of five members of the scientific corps.[52] The public attention that the explorations attracted revealed a widespread and growing interest in the western reaches of the nation during Monroe's presidency. With steamboats venturing up the Missouri River only thirteen years after Lewis and Clark descended it from their journey to the Pacific, the western expansion of the nation was racing to match the progress of its diplomats in pushing westward the boundaries of the United States.

In his annual message to Congress in November 1818, Monroe reported that "the fruits of the earth have been unusually abundant, commerce has flourished, the revenue has exceeded the most favorable anticipation."[53] Such was the president's view of the state of the Union on the eve of what would be recorded as the "panic of 1819," the first major depression in the economic life of the young republic. As the new year approached, many other Americans shared the president's optimistic outlook. Ethan Allen Greenwood, a Boston portrait painter and proprietor of the New England Museum and Gallery of Fine Arts, recorded in his private journal that "the year 1818 has been a happy and prosperous one to America and to the World. The U. States have had no check to the high career of national happiness, or the rapid progress of their advancement. The seasons have been delightful and productive. Commerce, Manufactures and Agriculture have shed their various comforts on the people. Industry has been everywhere crowned with success."[54]

Some alert observers of the nation's economy, however, were voicing concerns. "I expected something on the circulating medium, and perhaps the national bank," Charles J. Ingersoll wrote to Monroe from Philadelphia in acknowledging the receipt of a copy of the president's message. While praising Monroe for an "altogether American" state paper, he predicted that Congress would be turning to financial matters "so closely connected with the state of the union."[55]

In fact, signs of troubles ahead in the nation's banking system were already attracting the attention of Congress. Soon after the president's message, the House of Representatives appointed a committee to inspect the books and examine the proceedings of the Bank of the United States.[56] The committee traveled to Philadelphia and returned to expose "a series of improprieties on the part of the directors, not perhaps equalled in the history of any other moneyed institution," as one House member reported.[57] Another member described "a system of fraud, stock-jobbing, and speculation, which deserves severe reprehension."[58] Louis McLane of Delaware believed that "the abuses in the management of the Institution have been so gross" that "in applying the corrective, destruction rather than remedy will likely be the course."[59] A resolution to repeal the charter of the bank was introduced but defeated. The House finally settled on revising the manner of electing directors, hoping that a change of officers would relieve the situation.[60] When members of Congress returned home in the spring, they would find that economic difficulties went deeper than the mismanagement of the Bank of the United States.

Ten days after the House voted down the repeal of the charter of the second Bank of the United States, the Supreme Court rendered its decision in the case of *McCulloch* v. *Maryland*, upholding the constitutionality of the national bank. In one of the most important of the many influential opinions written by Chief Justice John Marshall, the unanimous court affirmed the supremacy of the national government and gave judicial sanction to the doctrine of implied powers. "The government of the Union . . . is emphatically and truly, a government of the people," Marshall wrote in a decision that went beyond the limited question of the constitutionality of the bank. "In form and in substance it emanates from them. Its powers are granted by them, and are to be exercised directly on them, and for their benefit." To summarize, "The government of the United States, then, though limited in its powers, is supreme; and its laws, when made in pursuance of the constitution, form the supreme law of the land." Regarding implied powers, he concluded that sound construction of the Constitution must allow discretion to the legislature respecting the means to carry out its enumerated powers. In words similar to those employed by Alexander Hamilton in 1791 in defending the constitutionality of the first Bank of the United States, Marshall affirmed: "Let the end be legitimate, let it be within the scope of the constitution, and all means which are appropriate, which are plainly adapted to that end, which are not prohibited, but consist with the letter and spirit of the constitution, are constitutional."[61]

Monroe did not share the hostility to Marshall's decision that found a strident voice in Judge Spencer Roane of the Virginia Supreme Court of Appeals. He told John Quincy Adams that his experiences in Madison's cabinet during the War of 1812 had convinced him of the absolute necessity of the national bank; as to constitutional objections, he considered them settled by twenty years of practice under the first bank.[62] At the same time, Monroe was slow to appreciate the impact of the bank's difficulties on the American economy. In a number of addresses delivered on his southern tour in the spring of 1819, he continued to refer to "the unexampled prosperity of our country" or "the spectacle of prosperity which is now exhibited to the admiring world by the United States" and to assert that he had seen on his trip "the most convincing proofs of the rapid growth and general prosperity of the country."[63]

Meanwhile, the Philadelphia Society for the Promotion of National Industry petitioned the president to call a special session of Congress, because "the calamitous situation of our agriculture, manufactures, trade, and commerce—the unfavorable balance of trade—the exhausting drain of specie—and the reduction of the prices of real estate, and the grand staples of our country, require the exercise of the wisdom of the legislature of the United States to apply an early and efficient remedy." In elaborating on these points and urging increased tariff protection, the society protested that "our markets are deluged with merchandise from foreign nations, while thousands of our citizens, able and willing to work, and capable of furnishing similar articles, are unable to procure employment."[64]

From Washington, Monroe's son-in-law George Hay wrote that "the complaint here about money is distressing. The fall in the price of property is ruinous." Hay was relieved that he had not purchased more than one lot in the city.[65] When Monroe reached Kentucky, he would be told firsthand what many had already relayed to Washington. Several letters from Congressman Richard M. Johnson arrived in Calhoun's office while he was traveling with the president. In one of them Johnson reported from Great Crossings, Kentucky, that "the times for money are alarming and frightful. I have never seen a time before but when I could raise $1000 with less difficulty than I can now raise $100."[66] Another letter was more urgent.

> It is impossible to describe to you the distress in this Country on account of circulating medium. Loans cannot be obtained from Banks or individuals—both are calling in their debts by wholesale, and nothing can be purchased on credit. This will produce much difficulty with all classes of the community; and those under contract with the Government will feel it to their disadvantage, and the Government also without very liberal policy as to the payment of money.[67]

The congressman's brother James Johnson, a primary supplier for the army, was one of many businessmen suffering from the contraction of credit; and Monroe himself heard James's case when he arrived in Kentucky. When he returned to Washington, the president found other letters reporting the western distress. As Worden Pope wrote from Louisville, "the people of the western states are now eating the bitter fruit of excessive Banking; and the people of Kentucky are in a dangerous and ruinous situation."[68] From Ohio, Thomas Worthington informed Calhoun about the drought and the poor crops there. "The times, *Hard* times, is the general complaint among us as elsewhere," he wrote.[69] While the president had been traveling, the June 19 edition of *Niles' Weekly Register* had issued an early warning, under the heading *Our manufactories*:

> We hear of the shutting up of several large manufacturing establishments. It is probable that during the present summer not less than 15,000 persons, and it may be many more, who subsisted by employment in those establishments, in addition to the great numbers already discharged, will be thrown from the productive into the consuming classes of the people. The political economist will estimate the effect of this on the national wealth.[70]

Niles, however, gave no support to the movement to summon Congress. "If Congress never shall meet until it meets to make paper money in a time of peace, we hope that it never will meet at all!" he exclaimed.[71] By October 1819, Niles was writing privately, "Tough times are everywhere—but they will become better. The foul system that chiefly caused them is giving way, and we shall get back to the old times of *honesty and leather breeches*."[72]

Monroe took no steps either to call a special session or to convoke Congress earlier than its scheduled date in December 1819. A month before Congress assembled, Jefferson wrote to John Adams, "The paper bubble is then burst. This is what you and I, and every reasoning man, seduced by no obliquity of mind or interest, have long foreseen. Yet its disastrous effects are not the less for having been foreseen. . . . Lands in this state cannot be sold for a year's rent."[73]

When Monroe sent his annual address to the Sixteenth Congress on December 7, 1819, he referred at the outset to economic conditions. Less blunt than Jefferson, the president stated that "a derangement has been felt in some of our moneyed institutions which has proportionally affected their credit." He then assured his countrymen that "the derangement in the circulating medium, by being left to those remedies which its obvious causes suggested and the good sense and virtue of our fellow citizens supplied, has diminished." In reporting an unusual drought in the middle and western states, he observed that agricultural production, though diminished, had still created a large surplus for export. When he directed attention to government finances, he noted that despite the difficulties, the Treasury would have sufficient funds to meet demands. At the same time, there was a drop in revenue from import and tonnage duties, and the president referred Congress to the reports of the secretary of the Treasury to determine if there was a need to raise additional revenue.[74]

Turning to manufacturing, Monroe used the word *depression* and said that "the pecuniary embarrassments which have so deeply affected the commercial interests of the nation had been no less adverse to our manufacturing establishments." In response to the growing demand for increased tariffs, he indicated that it was of great importance to promote domestic manufactures, but he left it to Congress to determine "how far it may be practicable . . . to afford them further encouragement, paying due regard to the other great interests of the nation."[75] When Monroe had read the draft of his message to his cabinet, Adams had observed, "On the pecuniary embarrassments of the country, the distressed and decayed state of manufactures, and the aspect of the Treasury Department, little was said, and I think the message will be found meagre by the public."[76] But neither Adams nor any other member of the administration urged any revisions on those subjects.

Monroe had based part of his address on the information furnished to him by the secretary of the Treasury, which indicated that current expenses would not outstrip available revenue. It would thus come as a shock to the president when Crawford informed Congress of a possible deficit of $5 million. Dismayed at Crawford's withholding information from him, Monroe suspected political motives. He was, however, aware that the First Congress had instructed the secretary of the Treasury to communicate directly with Congress, and since Washington's presidency they had done so without first showing their reports to the president.[77]

In preparing his annual message, Monroe did not have before him all the data that economic historians have subsequently compiled to show the extent of a depression that Monroe continued to minimize. Scholars today can calculate that the index of export staples fell from 169 in August 1818 to 77 in June 1819 and that imports fell from $122 million in 1818 to $87 million in 1819. They have also estimated that the total bank notes in circulation declined from $68 million in 1816 to $45 million by the end of 1819.[78] Even without such statistics, Monroe would have known that the prices of tobacco and cotton were plummeting. Farmers who sold tobacco at twelve dollars to thirty dollars per hundred pounds in 1816—and saw speculators push prices to the highest levels of the nineteenth century—would see tobacco quoted at four dollars to eight dollars in June 1819.[79] Cotton, selling as high as thirty-three cents a pound during much of 1818, had a top price of eighteen cents on the

Charleston market in the fall of 1819. The price of rice quoted at six cents to seven cents a pound in 1818 was below three cents a pound by the end of 1819.[80] Yet the only place in his address where Monroe referred to falling prices of products was in connection with the plight of manufacturers, where he admitted that the decline in prices and the lower cost of labor had "not shielded them against other causes adverse to their prosperity."[81]

The president had certainly learned on his travels about the bank failures in Kentucky, where forty banks set up in 1818 closed in 1819.[82] But he did not see government intervention as the answer to the nation's economic problems. Indeed, when he reported to the nation in his next annual message to Congress in November 1820, he looked back on the recent difficulties and declared that he could not regard those pressures "otherwise than in the light of mild and instructive admonitions, warning us of dangers to be shunned in future, teaching us lessons of economy corresponding with the simplicity and purity of our institutions."[83]

However much Monroe minimized the economic distress, that difficulty was not the only problem facing Congress in December 1819. John Adams, then in his eighty-fourth year, may have best summed up the state of affairs faced by the president when in late November he wrote to Jefferson:

> Congress are about to assemble and the clouds look black and thick, assembling from all points, threatening thunder and lightning. The Spanish treaty, the Missouri slavery, the encouragement of manufactures by protecting duties or absolute prohibitions, the project of a bankrupt act, the plague of banks, perhaps even the monument for Washington, and above all the bustle of caucuses for the approaching election for president and vice president, will probably produce an effervescence, though there is no doubt that the present president and vice president will be reelected by great majority's.[84]

7

THE MISSOURI COMPROMISE

Of all the problems confronting President Monroe as he approached the final year of his first term, none was more alarming and divisive than the question of slavery in Missouri. That issue would produce the most critical domestic crisis of his two terms as president and occupy his attention as did no other internal problem of his administration. With the Congress and the cabinet divided and leaders of his own state of Virginia pressing the slaveholding president not to compromise, Monroe faced a challenge unparalleled in his long political career.

The Missouri question was slow to build to a crisis. Early in 1818, Henry Clay, the Speaker of the House, and John Scott, the territorial delegate from Missouri, presented on separate days petitions from the Missouri Territory seeking permission to form a state government and be admitted as a state into the Union. Handled in a routine manner, the petitions were referred on March 16 to a select committee chaired by Scott. Less than three weeks later, Scott reported a bill authorizing the people of the Missouri Territory "to form a constitution and state government, and for the admission of such state into the Union on an equal footing with the original states." With the end of the session approaching, the House referred the bill to the Committee of the Whole and took no further action before it adjourned on April 20. Early in the next session, on December 18, 1818, Clay presented a petition from the Legislative Council and House of Representatives of the territory of Missouri, renewing the plea for permission to form a constitution and be admitted as a state.[1]

Although these steps were routine legislative procedures, close observers may have sensed an emerging controversy. On the day after Scott reported the Missouri enabling bill to the House in April 1818, Arthur Livermore, a representative from New Hampshire, proposed a constitutional amendment to prohibit slavery in any state thereafter admitted to the Union. The House promptly voted to not consider the proposal. Early in the new session, when the House was voting on the admission of Illinois as a state, New York Congressman James Tallmadge, Jr., opposed the bill because the constitution of Illinois, while not sanctioning slavery, did not sufficiently prohibit it. Meanwhile, in December 1818, the American Convention for Promoting the Abolition of Slavery held a special meeting in Philadelphia and appointed a committee to draft a memorial to Congress seeking the prohibition of slavery in all future territories and states created from them.[2]

On February 13, 1819, the House of Representatives took up the bill to authorize the people of the Missouri Territory to set up a state government. As the members worked to refine the details of the legislation, Congressman Tallmadge moved an amendment to bar the further introduction of slavery into Missouri and to provide for the gradual emancipation of slaves already within the proposed state. "This motion gave rise to an interesting and pretty wide debate," one observer recorded in reporting the opening exchanges, in which Tallmadge was supported by Livermore of New Hampshire and Elijah Mills of Massachusetts and opposed by Clay and Virginians Philip P. Barbour and James Pindall. But it was far more than an interesting debate. Tallmadge's amendment had suddenly transformed the routine business of admitting a new state into the Union into a dangerous dispute. It would produce the most important debate about slavery in the United States since the ratification of the Constitution; and its polemics would continue beyond the halls of Congress—in newspapers and pamphlets, on public platforms and pulpits, and in countless unrecorded exchanges throughout the country.[3]

As the congressional debate continued, two distinct opposing positions were advanced. On the one hand, some members insisted that Congress had no authority to prescribe to any state the details of its government except that it be republican in form. Such a power, if exercised, would be nugatory, they contended, because once admitted to the Union, the people of that state would have the right to amend their state constitution. On the other hand, it was argued that Congress was empowered to prescribe conditions for the admission of any new state into the Union and that slavery was incompatible with republican institutions. John W. Taylor of New York, in supporting Tallmadge's amendment, expressed what must have been in the minds of many: "Those whom we shall authorize to set in motion the machine of free government beyond the Mississippi will, in many respects, decide the destiny of millions. . . . Our votes this day will determine whether the high destiny of this region, and of these generations, shall be fulfilled, or whether we shall defeat them by permitting slavery, with all its baleful consequences, to inherit the land."[4]

When the House prepared to vote on Tallmadge's amendment, Arthur Livermore pleaded:

> An opportunity is now presented, if not to diminish, at least to prevent, the growth of a sin which sits heavy on the soul of every one of us. By embracing this opportunity, we may retrieve the national character, and in some degree, our own. But if we suffer it to pass unimproved, let us at least be consistent, and declare that our Constitution was made to impose slavery, and not to establish liberty. Let us no longer tell idle tales about the gradual abolition of slavery.[5]

These words and others voiced in the debate indicated that many members from nonslaveholding states were willing to see slavery as a national problem and to share the guilt and the burden. But southern members refused to debate the morality of slavery and vigorously opposed any restriction on constitutional grounds. Moreover, some privately expressed deep resentment. Writing from Washington, Congressman Hugh Nelson told a fellow Virginian:

> We have been for two or three days occupied on the Bill for erecting Missouri into a state. A warm and vehement debate was had in this Bill on an amendment prepared by the Yankees, to exclude slavery from that Country. The most outrageous doctrines have been advanced by these people, and no incident has occurred since the adoption of this Constitution, calculated to produce so much alarm with the slaveholding states—as the attempts of these Yankees to throw their arms around this vast region of Country in the West—and to exclude all the Southern people from migrating to this Country.[6]

Other influences besides the morality of slavery also were at work. Tallmadge himself brought up the clause in the Constitution by which three-fifths of the slave population was counted in the apportionment of representation in the House. The region west of the Mississippi River had no claim to such an unequal representation, Tallmadge contended. "Are the numerous slaves in extensive countries, which we may acquire by purchase, and admit as States into the Union, at once to be represented on this floor," he asked, "under a clause of the Constitution, granted as a compromise and a benefit to the Southern States which had borne part in the Revolution?"[7]

In the Committee of the Whole, the House voted 79 to 67 to agree to Tallmadge's amendment. When the bill was reported to the House, the debate was renewed, but the outcome was not altered. In the final vote, the two provisions of Tallmadge's amendment were separated. The clause to prohibit the further introduction of slavery into Missouri was agreed to by a vote of 87 to 76. The provision that all children born of slaves in Missouri after its admission into the Union would be free but could be held to service until age twenty-five was approved 82 to 78. The vote was strongly sectional; Willard Hall of Delaware was the only representative from a slaveholding state to vote for both provisions, and Samuel Smith of Maryland was the only other representative from a slaveholding state to vote for the second. Ten congressmen from the free states voted with the South against the first clause, and four others joined them in voting against the second.[8]

In the Senate the Tallmadge amendment was struck from the enabling act, but not without a debate. Rufus King argued vigorously that since the Missouri Territory was not within the confines of the original states, Congress ought to act on its right to bar slavery from the state of Missouri. "Freedom and slavery are the parties which stand this day before the Senate," he proclaimed, and based on its decision, "the empire of the one or the other" would be established in Missouri. When the House refused to concur with the Senate's action, the Senate would not reverse its decision, and the bill was lost.[9]

John Scott, the territorial delegate from Missouri, in a circular letter to his constituents, looked back on the session and wondered if greater political acumen on his part would have altered the outcome. But his report pictured events beyond his power to influence. Tallmadge's unexpected amendment "produced a greater sensation in Congress than was almost ever witnessed before," he wrote. "Mistaken motives of humanity and philanthropy governed some, while political and selfish views certainly had their weight with others." As to his own views, he said that he regarded slavery as wrong and regretted its existence in the United States, but he thought the people of Missouri had a clear right to decide the issue for themselves.[10]

By the time the next Congress met in December 1819, petitions against the extension of slavery into Missouri were streaming into Congress. Resolutions from a public meeting in Philadelphia, held at the statehouse on November 23, 1819, described slavery as "one of the greatest evils which exists in the United States—palpably inconsistent with the principles upon which the independence of this nation was asserted, and . . . at variance with the indestructible doctrines of universal liberty and right, upon which our constitution is erected." The memorial to Congress adopted at this meeting was printed and copies circulated by a committee of correspondence. Signed by inhabitants of the city and county of Philadelphia and sent to Congress, numerous copies of the memorial are preserved today in the National Archives of the United States. Some came from outside the city, as signers marked out "Philadelphia" and added the name of other towns or counties.[11] In "imploring the Congress of the United States, to exert all their constitutional powers for the prevention of slavery in states hereafter to be admitted into the Union," the petitioners stressed that "the highest modern authorities concur in representing it as incompatible with the genius, ends, and permanence of Republican Constitutions of government; as the lowest degradation and extreme misery of human nature."[12] The authors of the memorial took pains not to place the blame for slavery on the South and to assure slaveholders that they were not advocating the immediate repeal of slavery throughout the United States:

> Your Memorialists will not deny that most of the original slave holding states are free from blame with respect to the introduction of negro slavery, and its continuance until the present time, among them; that its immediate, total abolition is incompatible with their safety, and even with genuine benevolence to the blacks; and that, in permitting its admission in the new states of Louisiana, Mississippi and Alabama, Congress pursued a policy perhaps indispensable for the general security of our brethren of the south. But, for its toleration in the territories remaining to the Union, we cannot perceive that overruling necessity, upon which we would insist, as the only defence of which it is susceptible. . . .
>
> The extension of this moral pestilence over the vast countries beyond the Mississippi, so far from promising to contribute, as has been asserted, to its universal extinction in the end, would, in our opinion, have a tendency absolutely the reverse.[13]

The resolutions adopted at a public meeting at the statehouse in Hartford, Connecticut, on December 3, 1819, accompanied a memorial signed by concerned citizens. Lamenting the existence of slavery as an evil repugnant to the principles of republican government, the resolves summoned the language of the Declaration of Independence and affirmed that "the illustrious authors of that document never contemplated the farther extension of Slavery in these United States." The petitioners also asserted that "Congress possesses the clear and indisputable right to prescribe the terms upon which any territory may be admitted into the union as an independent state."[14]

A number of state legislatures took the Missouri question under advisement. The General Assembly of Delaware, a slaveholding state, passed a resolution supporting the constitutional authority of Congress to prevent the further introduction of slavery into a state as a condition of admission and insisting that the true interests of all states required the prohibition.[15] The legislature of Kentucky, a slaveholding border state, passed a resolution instructing its senators and requesting its representatives "to use their efforts to procure the passage of a law to admit the people of Missouri into the union as a state, whether those people will sanction slavery by their constitution or not." The Kentucky legislators prefaced this resolve by declaring that "the general assembly refrains from expressing any opinion either in favor or against the principles of slavery; but to support and maintain state rights, which it conceives necessary to be supported and maintained, to preserve the liberties of the free people of these United States." The states already in the Union had no right to deprive new states of equal privileges.[16]

The legislatures of Pennsylvania and New York instructed or requested their senators and representatives to vote against the admission of any territory into the Union unless slavery was excluded. The New York resolutions proclaimed "slavery as an evil much to be deplored; and that every constitutional barrier should be interposed to prevent its further extension; and that the constitution of the United States, clearly gives Congress the right to require of new States, the prohibition of slavery, as a condition of admission."[17] Resolves adopted by the New Jersey assembly asserted that the article of the Constitution restraining Congress from prohibiting the migration or importation of slaves before 1808 implied the general power of Congress over slavery "and concedes to them the right to regulate such migration and importation after that time into the existing or any newly to be created State."[18]

By the time Congress resumed consideration of the admission of Missouri, opposing sides had formed throughout the country, and contradictory interpretations of the constitutional powers of Congress were adamantly asserted. In the new Congress convening on December 6, 1819, the first matter to come before the House of Representatives—after organizing itself and receiving the president's annual message—was a petition from the district of Maine, presented by Congressman John Holmes of Massachusetts, seeking admission as a separate state on equal footing with the original states. The subject was immediately referred to a select committee chaired by Holmes. The Speaker of the House then recognized John Scott, who presented more petitions from the territory of Missouri seeking statehood. These were likewise referred to a select committee, which Scott was to chair. The next member to take the floor was James Strong of New York, who gave notice that on the following day he would ask leave to introduce a bill to prohibit the further extension of slavery within the territories of the United States. Though early moves had suggested that the Missouri question might be tied with the admission of Maine, Strong's announcement was a warning that the issue of slavery in the territories would remain central to any decision. On the next day, Scott reported from his committee the bill to authorize Missouri to form a constitution and state government, which was read twice and referred to the Committee of the Whole. Strong subsequently announced that, not desiring to embarrass the deliberations on the Missouri bill now before the House, he would defer his motion regarding slavery in the territories. This did not mean, however, that the slavery quarrel would subside from the Missouri debate.[19]

As the first week of the new Congress drew to a close, Congressman Livermore of New Hampshire reflected on the Missouri question: "It is certainly one of the utmost moment whether viewed in a religious and moral or a political light. A barrier against the further extension of slavery in North America is, in my opinion, indispensable for the security of all we have acquired by our federal and state constitutions."[20] Concerned with the deepening divisions, John W. Taylor of New York proposed, and was named to chair, a seven-member House committee to consider solutions. When Salma Hale, who had been a member of the House in the preceding Congress, learned of the move, he warned his former colleague against concessions.

> I am not, I allow, where I can take a view of the whole ground, but I see no necessity for a compromise. If we are firm for two years, changes of sentiment, and a new apportionment of representatives, will, I feel confident give us the victory. When that is obtained, all irritation will subside. . . . Are there not indications that slave labor, in consequence of the reduction of the prices of southern staples, will soon be of less value than heretofore?—and will not that tend to allay irritations?

By the time Taylor received Hale's letter, the committee had given up trying to reach a compromise and was discharged, at its request, on December 28.[21]

President Monroe did not mention the Missouri controversy in his annual message to Congress in 1819, but he closely followed developments and was not an inactive observer. After Congress postponed action until January, he told George Hay that the result was uncertain, "but I indulge a strong hope that the restriction will not pass." Those who wanted to bar Missouri represented, he thought, "a remnant of the policy, which sought in 1786, to shut up the mouth of the Mississippi." Monroe's private letter also reveals the president encouraging his son-in-law to write pieces for publication in order to influence the debates in Congress and throughout the country. "I think that your letters to the Edinburgh reviewers were useful, in placing important facts in a just light before the Eastern people, unknown to them before," he wrote, adding that he sensed in Boston "a more generous sentiment is manifested towards their southern brethren."[22] In the series "To the Edinburgh Reviewers" by "an American," Hay had replied to that journal's charge that the institution of slavery was the great curse of America. "It is not an American institution," he responded. "Slavery was introduced into America, our America, by you; by the merchants and traders of Great Britain." Identifying himself as a Virginian speaking only for Virginians, Hay argued that "the people of Virginia are not only not responsible for the introduction of slavery into this country, in its colonial state, but claim the merit of having done their best to oppose it." Published in the Washington *National Intelligencer* over a period of a week, the lengthy essays filled more than three large pages and included a long section of Biblical references to slavery.[23]

Monroe now urged Hay to direct his pen specifically to the Missouri question. "A paper showing that Congress have no right to admit into the union any new state on a different footing from the old, written with ability and moderation, would be eminently useful, if published immediately." He contended that the often-cited prohibition of slavery in the Northwest Territory "proves nothing," because that restriction was imposed by the Confederation and would be grounds for argument only if the Confederation had lasted.

> By the constitution, the states are incorporated together, in one body, for national purposes, and retain all the rights equally, each and all of them, not granted. The clause in the constitution applicable to the case recognizes no distinction, and it is absurd to suppose that the new states come in as equal members, and yet are not equal. . . . If the new states do not come in by complete incorporation, and equality, as to rights granted and reserved, you place the new on the footing of a league, governed by good faith, as in the case of ordinary treaties between independent powers.[24]

From Richmond, Hay promptly answered Monroe that he was taking precisely the same view of the subject as the president. "The first part (the constitutional question) is ready for the press, and will appear in the first paper published next week." The second part, already written, would soon follow. Though the final installment was not yet on paper, "the subject is arranged in my mind," he assured the president. Hay also reported that Senator James Barbour was talking to Thomas Ritchie, editor of the Richmond *Enquirer*, about a compromise. "I see not how a compromise can be made," he added. "I am very confident that none ought to be made. If the friends of the Constitution, of national honor, of *real* humanity and justice are firm, the scheme must fail."[25]

Writing to Hay a few days later, Monroe recalled when the Congress of the Confederation wrestled with the issue of slavery in the territories. He remembered that as a member at that time, "we were all inclined to extend the range of perfect freedom, as widely as we could, or rather to restrain that of domestic slavery as much as we could. It was a generous sentiment, which grew out of the revolutionary struggle." Now the president—who had been governor of Virginia at the time of Gabriel Prosser's abortive slave uprising in 1800—looked back to 1786 and reflected: "We had then no experience of the dangers menacing us from domestic slavery, and went the full length with our northern brethren. We have since had experience, and we expect, as we are equally attached to liberty with them, of which that fact is proof, that they will show some regard for our peculiar situation."[26]

As the new year opened, Monroe felt the pressure mounting. "The Missouri question has assumed its worst, and is producing all the mischief to which it can be made instrumental," he wrote hurriedly to Hay in Richmond on January 5, 1820, two days after the House passed a bill for the admission of Maine. "It is evidently an effort for power on the part of its authors, which is to be wielded, in every direction, for their benefit, without regard to its consequences on the southern states. Our members are enlightened and virtuous, but they want experience." He asked Hay to show this letter to Spencer Roane and get his advice on whether Hay should come to Washington immediately. Monroe thought that Hay would be very useful in the consultations going on in the capital, and he described the maneuvering in Congress:

> The object of Mr. King is to defeat any compromise applicable to unsettled territories, as the ground of the admission of Missouri; and the union of Maine with Missouri is producing the effect of alienating all the Eastern members from the Southern, on the question. They must vote for Maine, or destroy themselves at home, and thus separating from the friends of Missouri, their reunion will be difficult, if practica-

ble. If a compromise is made, it must be the ensuing week, so that your prompt decision and movement are indispensible. Should you come, however, nothing should be said about it, or done to attract attention.[27]

However difficult the situation in Washington, the pressures on Hay in Richmond seemed no less compelling. As a member of the Virginia assembly meeting in the presidential election year, Hay saw his presence there as even more vital than any advisory service he could perform in Washington.

Because Hay remained in Richmond, where Monroe could consult with him only by mail, historians have the opportunity to observe the president's thinking during the most critical domestic crisis of his administration. That the Missouri issue was uppermost in the president's mind was evident when he wrote to Hay on January 10, 1820. Noting that the Missouri question would take up the week, Monroe summarized his personal views.

> My own decided opinion is that new states cannot be admitted into the union, on other conditions than the old: that their incorporation must place them on precisely the same footing, as to rights granted, and retained. The Eastern people, who are so much pressed by their constituents, who have been moved by political men, for purposes of personal aggrandizement, want some ground on which to justify them in a measure of accomodation, to their constituents. They think, I mean those who have the public good only in view, that they may legislate more extensively over the territories, that is, that their power is more extensive there, than over the states, and under it, that they may prohibit slavery in a territory, leaving the state free, to admit it, after it becomes one. These seem to be willing, as I am told, to admit Missouri, and to make the northern boundary of that state, extending to the northern boundary of the US., the region over which the power of territorial legislation shall operate. I take of course no part in these concerns, tho' I am inclined to think that a difference exists in the two cases.

In closing his letter, Monroe added a postscript lauding Hay for the pieces he had urged him to write for the newspapers: "Your papers have certainly been well received, and produced a good effect. You have sustained the cause of the south and west, by arguments which have been much felt to the East and North, without producing any irritation."[28]

Although Monroe did not commit himself to support the proposal reported to Hay, his letter implied that he would not oppose it. Two days earlier, he had surprised John Quincy Adams by suggesting that he believed a compromise on the Missouri question would be found and agreed to. Adams thought "either there is an underplot in operation upon this subject, of which I had no suspicion, or the President has a very inadequate idea of the real state of that controversy, or he assumed an air of tranquillity concerning it in which there was more caution than candor, more reserve than sincerity."[29] Monroe's letters to Hay leave no doubt that the president understood all sides of the controversy but was proceeding cautiously, knowing full well that he could not openly take the lead in support of compromise given the strong opposition of Virginia.

When in late January 1820 Charles Pinckney called on the president carrying two issues of the Richmond *Enquirer* in which Hay's essays appeared, the proslavery congressman from Charleston made it clear that he was less than pleased with what he had read. The author had devoted too much attention to Rufus King's arguments and had "pushed the objection to the power of Congress, to make regulations for the territories too far." The details of Pinckney's complaint need not be examined here, but Monroe's response reveals his deep involvement in the Missouri issue. Though he had encouraged Hay to write the pieces, Monroe was persuaded by Pinckney that more was to be lost than gained by continuing the essays. "Being on the theatre of action, and knowing the disposition and sentiments of all the actors, much consideration is due to his opinion," Monroe advised his son-in-law. "If within your control, then, I think that you had better, prevent the publication of the paper heretofore alluded to."[30]

The president was, in fact, more actively engaged in discussions with members of Congress on the Missouri question than he disclosed to either Hay or Adams. He maintained particularly close contact with the president pro tempore of the Senate, James Barbour of Virginia. On February 3, Monroe began a letter to Barbour by saying that he had "reflected much on the subject of our conversation yesterday," and he ended by asking Barbour to dine with him that day. Also invited were representatives John Floyd of Virginia and Samuel Ringold of Maryland, along with "one or two more friends." The subject Barbour and Monroe had discussed was whether the admission of Maine should be made dependent on the admission of Missouri without restriction. In his letter to Barbour, Monroe gave his decided opinion that "the best course for our Union, and for that also of the Southern States, will be to separate the two questions at once, and to admit Maine." If delayed even for a few days, the opportunity would be lost, he warned, but if adopted immediately, it would put the southern members on high ground, reward the eastern members who had voted with the South against restrictions on Missouri, and "command the applause of the Union."[31] The movement of events, however, was outpacing the president. On the very day Monroe sent this letter to Barbour, Jesse B. Thomas of Illinois proposed in the Senate the prohibition of slavery in the unorganized area of the Louisiana Purchase north of 36°30', leaving Missouri as the only slave state in the territory north of that line.[32]

A week before, Henry Clay had observed that "the Missouri subject monopolizes all our conversation, all our thoughts and for three weeks at least to come will all our time. No body seems to think or care about any thing else. The issue of the question in the H. of R. is doubtful. I am rather inclined to think that it will be finally compromised."[33] After Thomas introduced his compromise proposal in the Senate, Clay reported a rumor that a caucus was to be held from nonslaveholding states to nominate some person for president in opposition to Monroe in the coming presidential election. "I hope there is no foundation for it," he wrote, "but if the question remains open I shall not be surprized at all at such an event." Clay then added that he thought a compromise might be reached "by agreeing on a line in the *uninhabited* territory which shall separate the Slave from the Free region."[34]

President Monroe no doubt had heard the same rumors as Clay, and he knew of the Thomas proposal when he wrote to George Hay on February 6. By this time the idea of an eastern conspiracy using the Missouri question to obtain power in the nation, which Monroe had hinted at earlier, seemed fixed in his mind. Some of the leaders were even willing to dismember the Union at the Allegheny Mountains, he suspected. He was convinced that the people of the eastern states were attached to the Union and were not involved in the scheme, but "the parties at the head of it, know that they risk every thing on the result, and have seemed to be resolved to push it to the greatest extremity."[35]

In view of Monroe's close contacts with James Barbour, it may be assumed that the Virginia senator had reason to believe the president would favor the Thomas compromise. Monroe would have been equally aware of the importance of Barbour's support, considering the determined opposition in Virginia to any concessions. Neither, however, may have anticipated the virulence of the reaction in Richmond that greeted the revelation of the developments in Washington.

On February 6, 1820, Barbour wrote a letter to Charles Yancey, a member of the Virginia assembly from Louisa County, indicating that he and James Pleasants, his Virginia colleague in the Senate, were inclined to accept the compromise embodied in the amendment proposed by Thomas. Barbour also reported that the president and members of the cabinet had advised acceptance of the compromise if rejection meant endangering the Union.[36] Barbour's letter arrived in Richmond on February 8, the day before the scheduled meeting of the caucus to nominate candidates for president and vice-president. As it was passed around, the letter "caused a high excitement here," Yancey observed in writing to Barbour the next day. Yancey also reported that a large majority of the House of Delegates was "for risking consequences" and would not assent to the compromise. "Many say they would not yield the 19th part of a hair," he wrote. "I can certainly say, if you wish to speak the voice of our present legislature, that you must stand stubborn in opposition to the compromise." Yancey expected the presidential nominating caucus, set for that evening, to postpone action. "It is said by many that the President and others in power think more of their *situations*, than the best interest of the people whose rights are involved in the Missouri questions—harsh expressions are used in relation to you all," he stated frankly, urging Barbour and Pleasants to stand firm in opposition to the compromise.[37]

By the time the Richmond caucus met on the evening of February 9, the contents of Barbour's letter to Yancey were widely known; and, as Yancey had predicted, the meeting adjourned until February 17.[38] "Should it be ascertained that Munroe from a fear of loosing his Station, advises the acceptance of the Compromise with a view of keeping himself in office, at the expense of the Constitution and the best interest of the slave holding states, we will show him that we are for principles and not men," Yancey declared privately.[39]

The following morning the Richmond *Enquirer* published a fiery editorial denouncing Thomas's proposal. "Can we compromise with the constitution of our country?" asked Thomas Ritchie. "We have witnessed popular excitement on several occasions. But we do not recollect any occasion in which the feelings of our citizens and of the Legislature were wrought up to a higher pitch." Rather than calm the situation, Ritchie sought to inflame his readers.

> And why yield? To save a Virginia President? Because these men tell us they will split the Union? And we are to yield in this panic—as we did in the embargo times. No, whatever be the consequence, let us do our duty. If they do put us under the ban of the constitution, it is far better for *them* to attempt it than for *us* to yield up our principles to our interests. . . . As to disunion, if our Eastern brethren have made up their minds to it, deeply, solemnly as we should regret it, we must bow to their resolution—but let us adhere to justice and the constitution. They may outvote us;—but let us not bind ourselves by our own votes.[40]

Monroe received his first account of the happenings in Richmond from Dr. Charles Everett, a member of the House of Delegates from Albemarle County, on February 11. He replied immediately, saying that he considered any attempt to set conditions on Missouri's statehood different from those imposed on the original states as unconstitutional and designed to dismember the Union. "My object has invariably been to defeat the whole measure, if possible, and in no event, even to save the union, to restrain Missouri in admitting her into the union, or any State hereafter to be admitted in any manner different from the other States." As to the proposed compromise, he stressed that it had not originated with anyone in Virginia or any southern state but "has been suggested by friends of the union elsewhere, who have voted with the Southern members, and who are anxious in that mode to defeat the object of those who wish to sever it. A crisis exists of which our friends at Richmond have no conception." The president emphasized that "with respect to this office, I did nothing to gain it. I will do nothing to keep it, a very slight injury would force me from it."[41] Monroe then asked Hay in Richmond to confer with Everett and decide how widely to circulate the letter's contents, and he reiterated to his son-in-law his insistence that his actions were not designed to promote his reelection. As to retaining office: "I hope that I am too well known not to be understood, to be ready to withdraw from it, without regret. The principles, on which I have, and shall invariably act, place me above all attempts to preserve it by measures of concession, either here or elsewhere. If the legislature prefer any one else, let them declare it. My own reputation is always under my own protection."[42] Writing to Hay again the next day, Monroe relayed reports that Rufus King disclaimed "all idea of compromise, his object being to push things to the worst. You may be satisfied, that I am under no pledge to anyone. However on this subject you had better say nothing."[43]

Before receiving this correspondence from Monroe, Hay had written to his wife concerning rumors of Monroe's willingness to compromise:

> This has excited great feeling here, and certainly would do your father great injury, if there was not a belief, that this is the very object which the northern people aim at. If your father does not stand compromitted on that point, I certainly should think his best course would be to let things take their course, and when the bill came to him imposing restrictions on Missouri (if it did come in that shape) to reject it, and also to reject any bill imposing restrictions on the territories, if he thinks Congress have no right to impose these territorial restrictions,

or that the right ought not to be exercised. No matter what the northern people may say. They will say and do any thing to effect their object; and they are only to be met with patience and firmness.[44]

Despite Hay's indirectly delivered advice, Monroe committed himself only to veto a bill for the admission of Missouri with restrictions. He continued to assert that the question of whether Congress had the constitutional power to restrict slavery in the territories was one that he had under study and on which he was still seeking advice, though at some point in his deliberations he made notes for a veto message directed against any legislation regarding slavery in the territories.[45]

Meanwhile, on February 13, James Barbour wrote a nine-page letter to Spencer Roane, detailing the recent history of the Missouri question, which he said had so entirely absorbed his time "as scarcely to have thought of any thing else." In reporting that he was the first to propose the junction of Maine and Missouri in any vote on statehood, he did not mention that Monroe had recommended separating the two questions, but he said there was no chance that Missouri would be admitted if Maine was detached. In regard to Thomas's proposal to prohibit slavery north of 36°30', he said that he had initially rejected any suggestion of that kind, but he became convinced that the southern members had "either to make the best of our condition by arrangement or dissolve the Union." He added that "in consultation with the President and Crawford, Clay, Lowndes and a host of others whose feelings were like mine, where the question was debated," it was decided that it was better to accept the compromise proposal than to dissolve the Union. Barbour outlined the likely scenario if the compromise was rejected: Missouri would not be admitted; a bill to exclude slavery from the territories would pass Congress and be vetoed by the president; Maine would then be admitted. "Missouri will be restricted and the whole territory of the West of the river will be interdicted to us. What then—we have no alternative but disunion. But the whole moral force of the government with a disproportionate force to our disadvantage will be against us. . . . If we dissolve the Union—and this now has become a common topic—how shall we divide—and how will it be effected. These are questions of the most serious character. It is not improbable that we shall have to answer them."[46]

On February 16, Monroe also drafted a letter to Spencer Roane declaring his firm conviction that all states must have equal rights. "Should a bill pass admitting Missouri subject to restraint, I shall have no difficulty in the course to be pursued," he wrote. But he also indicated that he was not as clearly decided on the question of the constitutional restraints on Congress regarding slavery in the territories. He invited Roane to offer his opinion.[47]

Monroe, however, did not send this letter to Roane but instead directed Hay to give it to him. The letter arrived in Richmond on February 17, the day on which the adjourned nominating caucus was to reconvene. By this time, Roane had already written to the president expressing his opinion "fully and strongly" against any compromise, and a copy of his letter was circulating in Richmond.[48] Hay thus immediately returned Monroe's letter, rejoicing that the president had sent it to him rather than to Roane. "In the present state of things, the effect of such a communication, indicating hesitation or doubt, would be fatal," he wrote. "I have never said how you would act, but simply that you would do your duty. The members have gone up to the Caucus under a conviction that you will put your veto on this infamous cabal and intrigue in all its forms and shapes. This I would certainly and promptly do. You may be injured in the N. and E. States, but you will be amply repaid in the gratitude and affection of the South."[49]

Thus the Virginia caucus met with an expectation that Monroe would veto any bill to restrict slavery in Missouri but with no further assurances. None of his letters to Hay or others had promised either a veto or approval of a compromise restricting slavery in the territories. As the caucus convened on February 17, it was not yet known in Richmond that on the sixteenth the Senate had passed the Thomas amendment. Hay reported the outcome of the meeting to Monroe in a brief paragraph, giving few particulars but stating that all had gone well.[50] The revolt against Monroe in Virginia had been contained.

Before Hay's letter reached Washington, the Senate passed a bill on February 18 to admit both Maine and Missouri and attached the Thomas amendment, but the House responded by rejecting all Senate amendments and passing its own Missouri bill with restrictions. "I have never known a question so menacing to the tranquility and even the continuance of our Union as the present one," Monroe wrote to Jefferson on February 19.[51] A conference committee was subsequently appointed to break the deadlock between the two houses. On March 2, John Holmes of Massachusetts presented to the House a conference report that proposed the admission of Maine and Missouri without restrictions and the exclusion forever of slavery in that part of the Louisiana Purchase north of 36°30' not included in the state of Missouri. By votes taken separately on the different parts of the report, the Missouri Compromise passed the House of Representatives on March 2. The crucial and closest vote was on the recommendation to strike the provision to prohibit slavery in Missouri, which passed by a vote of 90 to 87. Once the House accepted the compromise, the Senate agreed to the settlement. By an act of March 3, 1820, Maine, which prohibited slavery, was admitted as a state; and an act of March 6 authorized the people of Missouri to draw up a constitution and form a state government without any restriction on slavery.[52]

On March 3, Monroe summoned his cabinet to its first meeting on the Missouri question since the controversy arose. Monroe had purposely established sectional representation in his cabinet, and he was fully aware that his advisers differed on the issue of slavery. He well knew John Quincy Adams's opposition to slavery and understood Smith Thompson's silence. Before signing the bills to admit Maine and to enable Missouri to draft a constitution, Monroe asked the members of his cabinet for their opinions on two questions: (1) whether Congress had a constitutional right to prohibit slavery in a territory, and (2) whether the section in the Missouri bill interdicting slavery forever in the territory north of 36°30' was applicable only to a territorial state or remained in force after statehood. The president said that he wanted their individual opinions in writing to be deposited in the Department of State.[53]

According to the account of the cabinet meeting recorded by John Quincy Adams, there was unanimous agreement that Congress had the power to prohibit slavery in the territories. Considerable discussion took place over the second question, with Adams arguing forcefully that the prohibition extended to statehood. When it was evident that a consensus could not be reached, Calhoun suggested that the second question be restated to ask whether the section of the bill relating to the territories was consistent with the Constitution. Monroe readily agreed, and all members could now answer affirmatively, without appending any explanations or qualifications.[54]

As members of the cabinet and the Congress awaited the president's signing of the bills implementing the Missouri Compromise, some recorded their thoughts on the recent events. Congressman William Plumer, Jr., of New Hampshire, remarked to his father, who had been in Congress while Jefferson was president: "You can hardly conceive of the rage and fury which prevailed here on this subject. It was seriously proposed by the leading men on the other side, Lowndes, Clay, Barbour, and others, if we succeeded, that they would merely pass the appropriations bill, and then adjourn, to consult their constituents whether they should ever come back again! A dissolution of the Union was spoken of as certain, and hardly to be regretted." Plumer added that "the President will, no doubt sign the bill, though many think it will shake his popularity very much, particularly in Virginia. Few members from that state voted for the compromise."[55]

Reflecting on the long cabinet meeting on the issue and his own support of the administration's decision, John Quincy Adams wrote in his diary that he favored the Missouri Compromise, "believing it to be all that could be effected under the present Constitution, and from extreme unwillingness to put the Union at hazard." But he wondered if it might have been wiser, as well as bolder, to have persisted in the restriction on Missouri, until it led to a convention to revise the Constitution. "This would have produced a new Union of thirteen or fourteen States unpolluted with slavery, with a great and glorious object to effect, namely, that of rallying to their standard the other States by the universal emancipation of their slaves," Adams mused. He reckoned that "for the present, however, the contest is laid asleep."[56]

At Monticello, Thomas Jefferson also pondered the outcome of the Missouri controversy. "This momentous question, like a fire-bell in the night, awakened and filled me with terror," he wrote. "I considered it at once as the knell of the Union. It is hushed, indeed, for the moment. But this is a reprieve only, not a final sentence."[57]

James Monroe. *Oil on wood, 26 5/8 × 21 1/2 inches, by Gilbert Stuart, painted in Boston, July 1817, while President Monroe was on a tour of the Northeast. (Courtesy of the Pennsylvania Academy of the Fine Arts, Philadelphia; Pennsylvania Academy Purchase)*

James Monroe. *Oil on canvas, 26 ¹/₂ × 22 ³/₈ inches, by John Vanderlyn, 1816.*
(Courtesy of the National Portrait Gallery, Smithsonian Institution)

Elizabeth Kortright Monroe. *Oil on canvas, 28 ½ × 23 inches, by John Vanderlyn, ca. 1816. (White House photograph; courtesy of Thomas J. and William K. Edwards)*

Washington City, 1820. Watercolor, 5 11/16 x 9 3/8 inches, by Baroness Hyde de Neuville, wife of the French minister to the United States. (Courtesy of the Rare Books and Manuscripts Division, The New York Public Library, Astor, Lenox, and Tilden Foundations)

The north front of the White House is flanked on the left by the State Department (foreground) and the Treasury (background) and on the right by the War Department (foreground) and Navy Department (background).

The Old House of Representatives. Oil on canvas, 86 ½ x 130 ¾ inches, by Samuel Finley Breese Morse, 1822. (In the collection of the Corcoran Gallery of Art, Museum Purchase, Gallery Fund)

General George Washington Resigning His Commission to Congress as Commander in Chief of the Army at Annapolis, Maryland, December 23d, 1783. Oil on canvas, 144 x 216 inches, by John Trumbull, 1824. (United States Capitol Art Collection; courtesy of the Architect of the Capitol and the Library of Congress)

Painted and hung in the Capitol while Monroe was president. As a member of the Continental Congress in 1783, Monroe is shown seated, with legs crossed, at the end of the table to Washington's right.

West Front of the Capitol of the United States. *Watercolor on paper, 16 x 20 ¼ inches, by Charles Burton, 1825. (From* Tribute of Respect from the City of New York to General Lafayette, the Illustrious Friend of Civil Liberty; *Collection of The New-York Historical Society)*

James Monroe. *Oil on canvas, 94 ¼ × 59 ½ inches, by Samuel F. B. Morse, 1820. (Collection of City Hall, Charleston, South Carolina)*
    Commissioned by the City of Charleston to honor Monroe's visit there in 1819. By picturing Monroe in boots, wearing a sword, and holding a revolutionary hat, Morse reminded viewers of the president's military service.

8

TRANSITION TO A SECOND TERM

While the Missouri controversy dominated national attention, the issue of Florida remained unsettled. The Senate ratified the treaty with Spain on February 22, 1819, two days after it was signed by Secretary of State Adams and Spanish minister Onís, but the Spanish government failed to act within the six months stipulated in the agreement. Though Spain had promised to send a minister to the United States for clarification of certain provisions, no envoy had arrived in Washington before the president sent his annual message to Congress on December 7, 1819. Monroe thus asked Congress for discretionary authority to occupy Florida, thereby putting the treaty into effect as if it had been ratified by Spain. The United States would claim its rights under the treaty while also respecting the advantages secured to Spain by the agreement. Regarding South America, Monroe again expressed his sympathy for the revolutionists but promised to maintain "impartial neutrality."[1]

Such policies were too timid for some members of Congress, and one House committee reported a bill for the mandatory occupation of Florida. Henry Clay, long opposed to the president's South American stance and riled that Adams had given up claims to Texas in negotiating the Spanish treaty, vowed, "I mean to propose the recognition of the Patriots and the Seizure of Texas. Those two measures taken, and Florida is ours without an effort." In the course of the debates, Clay introduced resolutions that would have repudiated the relinquishment of the claims to Texas.[2] While the Missouri question monopolized the attention of Congress, the Florida issue was put aside. "All other business is suspended, and indeed so completely absorbed are all here, in that great question," Monroe remarked in February 1820, "that you never hear mention made of Florida, or any other subject, however interesting."[3] By the time the Spanish minister, General Francisco Dionisio Vives, finally arrived in Washington on April 9, 1820, the Missouri Compromise had passed Congress and been approved by the president. Attention again focused on Florida.

As conditions of ratification, Spain had sought a United States commitment not to recognize revolutionary governments in South America and a promise of stricter enforcement of its neutrality. In response, Monroe declared in a special message to Congress on May 9, 1820, that "it is manifestly so repugnant to the honor and even the independence of the United States that it has been impossible to discuss it." Word of liberal changes taking place in Spain reached the United States, however, and the president recommended to Congress that any decision on the matter be postponed until the next session of Congress.[4] Senator Waller Taylor of Indiana believed the true reason for this suggestion was that a considerable majority in both houses opposed adopting any measures that might lead to war with Spain and the president "thought it best to stifle the fact that the nation did not approve of what he had advised being done in his message at the opening of the Session."[5]

Before Congress reconvened, the least-contested presidential race since Washington's unanimous election was decided. In early April 1820 Congressman Samuel Smith of Maryland, who had presided at the nominating caucus of 1816, issued a call to all Republican members of Congress—and other members who thought it proper to attend—to meet on the evening of April 8 to select presidential and vice-presidential candidates. While no contender sought to challenge Monroe's incumbency, there was opposition to the renomination of Daniel Tompkins as vice-president, and Henry Clay was rumored to have his eye on the office. Nevertheless, on the scheduled evening, no more than forty members of Congress attended the caucus, which promptly adjourned after unanimously passing a motion that it was not expedient to nominate any candidates.[6]

In April 1820, the Columbus *Ohio Monitor* observed, "There appears no great excitement in any quarter, concerning the next presidential election. In most of the States the elections occur with great quietness, too great, perhaps, for the general safety of the Republic."[7] In New York and Pennsylvania, discontent with the Missouri Compromise did result in some organized opposition to Monroe's reelection. A rival slate of electoral candidates was presented to the New York legislature, but the Monroe ticket won by a vote of 72 to 54. In Pennsylvania, where presidential electors were popularly elected, the ticket pledged to De-Witt Clinton garnered the ballots of about a third of the voters in Philadelphia, but all electors chosen in Pennsylvania were pledged to Monroe. Elsewhere there was little electioneering activity.[8]

When the presidential electors cast their votes, only one did not vote for Monroe. William Plumer of New Hampshire unexpectedly cast his ballot for John Quincy Adams, while Monroe received the votes of 231 electors, including former Federalist president John Adams, who headed the Massachusetts electors. Plumer, a former Federalist senator who had been elected governor of New Hampshire as a Republican in 1812, refused to support Monroe because he disapproved of his economic policies and because Monroe had "conducted, as president, very improperly" and had "not that weight of character which his office requires."[9] Fourteen presidential electors, including Plumer, did not vote for the vice-presidential nominee, yet despite the low esteem in which he was held by many, Daniel Tompkins was reelected by 218 electoral votes.

By the time Monroe sent his fourth annual message to Congress on November 14, 1820, the Spanish government had approved the treaty and sent it to Washington, though that news had not yet reached the United States. The administration, however, was optimistic, and the ratified treaty soon arrived. When Monroe resubmitted it to the Senate, the treaty was ratified with only four opposing votes. A formal exchange of treaties was held at the Department of State on February 22, 1821.[10] Meanwhile, the president had asked Jackson to be governor of Florida, and the general had agreed to accept for a limited tenure.[11] "Had Congress determined, as was proposed at the last session, to occupy Florida, our situation might have been very different," one member observed. "It is true we could, at any time, have taken Florida by force, but it might have endangered the pacific relations between the two countries and eventuated in a war. The more prudent course of waiting a little longer was adopted, and recent events amply testify as to its correctness."[12]

In assessing the state of the Union in his 1820 message to Congress, the president said that "taking all circumstances into consideration which claim attention, I see much to rejoice in the felicity of our situation." He viewed the difficult economic times through which the country had passed as "mild and instructive admonitions," providing lessons of economy and warnings of dangers to be avoided. This was the shortest of all his annual messages, and Monroe detected no critical issues facing Congress. In regard to South America he reported the growing success of the revolutionists, noting that "the colonies have gained strength and acquired reputation, both for the management of the war in which they have been successful and for the order of the internal administration." He did not propose any change in American policy.[13]

Even as Monroe sent his temperate message to Congress, it was clear that all was not so harmonious as his words suggested. Two days later, he wrote to Madison that the contest for the speakership in the House indicated "a disposition to review the Missouri question in the temper displayed in the last session."[14] Having previously announced that he would not seek reelection to the House, Clay had resigned the speakership and was absent from the convening of the new session. In a sectional contest that required twenty-two ballots, the House elected John W. Taylor as Speaker. The choice of the New Yorker, who had been the leader of the antislavery forces in the House, initially alarmed many southerners, since their representatives had held the speakership in eight out of the ten Congresses since 1801. South Carolina's William Lowndes, who had run against Taylor, confided to his wife that "the election is the proof of a fact that I have been aware of for some time that the Northern States differing in every thing else are impatient to put the government in to the hands of Northern men."[15] But as Speaker, Taylor demonstrated exceptional impartiality.[16] His efforts were much needed, for the actions of the Missouri constitutional convention during the summer had reopened the controversy over the extension of slavery.

The constitution of Missouri, adopted July 19, 1820, by a convention assembled in St. Louis, was communicated to the Senate by the president on November 14, and delegate John Scott of Missouri laid a copy before the House on November 16.[17] Word had already circulated throughout the country that the proslavery constitution contained a provision mandating the Missouri legislature to pass any laws necessary to prevent free blacks and mulattoes from entering and settling in the state under any circumstances. In view of the fact that free blacks were considered citizens in some states, the mandate clearly conflicted with the United States Constitution, which guaranteed that the citizens of each state were entitled to all the privileges and immunities of the several states.

Congressman William Plumer, Jr., of New Hampshire, reasoned that the Missouri Compromise of the previous session could now be forgotten. "The act under which Missouri claims, contained conditions to be performed by her and by us,—she has failed to perform her part— she cannot therefore call upon us to perform ours—so that the act of the last session is in effect void—Missouri is still a territory." But Plumer himself did not believe that most members of Congress would take this view of the matter. "The subject no longer excites the same interest as it did last year," he confided to his father.[18]

The issue, however, did provoke considerable debate and consumed a large portion of Congress's time. When the day arrived to count the electoral vote in the presidential election, a wrangle developed in the joint session on February 14, 1821, as to whether the vote of Missouri—which had been cast—should be counted, although it was well known that it would make no difference in the outcome. A joint committee had agreed to Clay's proposal that the returns be reported with the vote of Missouri both excluded and included, but the accord almost vanished amid what John Quincy Adams described as "extremely violent and disorderly conduct" and the withdrawal of the members of the Senate from the House chamber.[19] Clay, who had returned to his seat in the House in January, used his skills to defuse the conflict, and the recording of the electoral tally resumed, with and without Missouri's three votes.[20]

The question of the Missouri constitution remained unresolved. Two weeks before Congress adjourned, one House member wrote that "this unfortunate subject of contention still hangs a dead weight on us, and impedes our progress to other subjects of immediate importance."[21] What alarmed many, in and outside Congress, was the fear that if Missouri was not admitted, the state might attempt to separate and attract some western states to join it.

On February 26, 1821, the House finally adopted a resolution admitting Missouri as a state on an equal footing with the original states. The resolve contained the condition that the article in the Missouri constitution prohibiting the immigration of free blacks and mulattoes should not be construed to allow the passage of laws by which any citizen of any state in the Union "shall be excluded from the enjoyment of any of the privileges and immunities to which such citizen is entitled under the Constitution of the United States."[22] Clay won wide acclaim for his role in working out the agreement. "The Country owes you much for the important services you have rendered. . . . The Constitution of the Union was in danger and has been saved," Langdon Cheves wrote to Clay. "It would have been a terrible spectacle to have seen Missouri independent and yet not a member of the Union."[23] Not everyone viewed the events in the same light. Congressman Lewis Williams of North Carolina regarded the objections to Missouri's admission as "altogether frivolous.—Any one of common sense and candour, ought to admit," he told his constituents, "that, if there was any thing in her Constitution repugnant to the Constitution of the United States, it would, upon receiving her into the Union be abrogated by the paramount authority of the Constitution of the United States. But our Northern and Eastern brethren have professed to think differently, and have caused this subject to consume an unreasonable portion of time."[24] The Missouri crisis was at last ended, but the underlying sectional tensions and the debate over slavery were merely shelved.

With the Missouri issue out of the way, Congress before adjourning passed an act to reduce the army—a move galvanized by the ratification of the treaty with Spain. The authorized strength of the army was 12,656, though the actual number in service, as reported by Secretary of War Calhoun to Congress, was 7,421 in December 1818.[25] Motivated by what Adams called the "penury of the Treasury" and "the passion for retrenchment," the House of Representatives in May 1819 had directed Calhoun to submit to the next session a plan to reduce the army to six thousand men.[26] Some members of Congress expressed particular concern about the high ratio of officers and noncommissioned officers to privates in the ranks.[27] Calhoun's proposal for a peacetime army, however, was designed to leave the leadership and organization in place so that in case of war, only the ranks of men had to expand to be ready for action.

In his report to the House of Representatives in December 1820, the secretary of war took it for granted that it was no longer necessary to defend the need for a standing army in time of peace.

> The great and leading objects, then, of a military establishment in peace ought to be to create and perpetuate military skill and experience, so that, at all times, the country may have at its command a body of officers, sufficiently numerous, and well instructed in every branch of duty, both of line and staff; and the organization of the Army ought to be such as to enable the Government at the commencement of hostilities to obtain a regular force, adequate to the emergencies of the country, properly organized and prepared for actual service.

Under this reasoning, the secretary of war put forward a plan for an army of 6,316.[28]

A few weeks after the House received Calhoun's report, Congressman David Trimble of Kentucky asked him to draft a bill in conformity with his recommendations. He told the secretary of war that he was not in favor of the whole scheme, but he preferred it to what had been submitted by a select committee on military affairs. Since it was his understanding that the chairman of the committee would not offer a bill based on Calhoun's report, he was "confident that one ought to be ready when the subject is pressed to a vote."[29] In a well-documented example of a member of Monroe's administration drafting legislation for Congress, Calhoun responded promptly to Trimble's urgent appeal. Two days later, the congressman returned Calhoun's draft of a bill with revisions for the secretary of war to incorporate.[30] Calhoun's efforts, however, were of little avail. The House committee on military affairs replaced Calhoun's plan to retain the officer corps and to organize an expandable force with a bill to reduce and consolidate the army. Senate changes moderated the final act of March 2, 1821; although reducing the army by 40 percent, the secretary of war was left some flexibility. While some dismissals would be necessary, Calhoun could make lateral transfers and lower the rank of officers as alternatives to destroying the army organization.[31] The reduction of the army to 6,126 men was expected to save $1 million a year.[32] "The act was the best which the Senate, though very sound, could obtain," Calhoun wrote to Jackson, "and although it makes a great reduction, avoids that disorganization, which the bill from the House, if it had become an act, must have produced."[33]

Despite the decreased strength of the army, the military reorganization that Calhoun had directed remained largely in place. Since his appointment by Monroe as secretary of war in 1817, Calhoun had revamped the army's central bureaucracy, appointed young officers to key positions, and encouraged the emerging professionalism of the officer corps. He also oversaw the transformation of West Point under Sylvanus Thayer, who became superintendent after Monroe visited West Point in the spring of 1817 and determined to replace the leadership there. Hezekiah Niles in his *Weekly Register* claimed in 1824 that "the order and harmony, regularity and promptitude, punctuality and responsibility, introduced by Mr. *Calhoun* in every branch of the service, has never been rivalled, and perhaps, cannot be excelled—and, it must be recollected, that he brought this system out of chaos." Calhoun's political ambitions were evident, but as a member of Monroe's administration, he was one of the most influential secretaries of war in the nineteenth century.[34]

In its retrenchment program of 1821, Congress also reduced the appropriations for military fortifications from $800,000 to $202,000 and withheld funding for some projects already under construction.[35] Building coastal defenses had been one of Monroe's cherished goals as president. With vivid memories of the War of 1812 when the vulnerable coast of the United States had left the nation exposed to British invasion, he had actively pushed an increase in coastal fortifications. "The President, who had formed this project, chiefly from the experience of the defenseless state of the country in that war," noted Adams, "had set his heart upon its accomplishment, and looks to it as one of the great objects by which his Administration may be signalized in the view of posterity." Monroe even held a cabinet meeting to consider whether surplus funds might be used to complete construction of a project that Congress had specifically refused to continue. While opinions on particulars differed, the cabinet agreed that funds should not be employed in this way.[36] Congress's recission of funding for projects so important to the president was a humiliating close to his first term, and it did not bode well for the future.

Three days after the army reduction act and a week after the resolution of the Missouri controversy, James Monroe took the presidential oath of office for a second time. March 4, 1821, was a Sunday, so the inaugural ceremonies were delayed to the following day. John Quincy Adams reflected that the Sunday was "a sort of interregnum, during which there was no person qualified to act as president; an event of no importance now, but which might be far otherwise under supposable circumstances."[37]

Much progress in rebuilding the war-ravaged city had been made since Monroe's first inauguration. The Capitol—called by more than one admirer a "magnificent building"—was the scene of the swearing-in ceremonies. While the House chamber, with its high dome, marble columns, and stone walls, was poorly designed for legislative debates, viewers were uniformly struck by its grandeur. "The Hall of the House of Representatives is a most magnificent room of a semicircular form, surrounded with a row of beautiful pillars of variegated marble, the floor elegantly carpeted," marveled Virginia Congressman William C. Rives upon taking his seat there in 1823.[38] Congressman Duncan McArthur of Ohio was equally impressed in counting the "twenty-six marble columns or pillars, richly varigated with very many colours, highly polished, of about 3 feet diameter and 25 feet high; 22 of them round and 4 square," supporting the dome.[39] On inauguration day in 1821, seats were reserved on the floor of the House for members of Congress, wives of cabinet members, and the diplomatic corps. Justices of the Supreme Court were seated in chairs immediately in front of the platform before the Speaker's chair.

At quarter of twelve on inauguration day, members of the cabinet assembled at the White House, their wives already having gone ahead to the Capitol. They departed immediately with Monroe for Capitol Hill. As Adams recorded, "The President, attired in a full suit of black broadcloth of somewhat antiquated fashion, with shoe- and knee-buckles, rode in a plain carriage with four horses and a single colored footman. The Secretaries of State, the Treasury, War, and the Navy followed, each in a carriage-and-pair." Adams observed that "there was no escort, nor any concourse of people on the way. But on alighting at the Capitol a great crowd of people were assembled, and the avenues to the hall of the House were so choked up with persons pressing for admittance that it was with the utmost difficulty that the President made his way through them into the House. . . . There was not a soldier present, nor a constable distinguishable by any badge of office."[40] The cabinet members also pushed their way through the crowd and followed the president as he entered the House to music played by the Marine Band.

A snow the night before had discouraged people from lining the streets to the Capitol but not from thronging the doors of the Capitol. Once the members of Congress and the invited guests were seated, the public was admitted without discrimination until the House chamber and the galleries were packed. The editor of the *National Intelligencer* estimated the number at not less than two thousand.[41]

After entering the chamber, Monroe took his seat on the platform, with the chief justice and the department heads on his right and the president of the Senate and the Speaker of the House on his left. Not present was Vice-president Tompkins, who took the oath of office in New York.[42] With the House and the galleries overflowing, there was some disorder and loud talking that did not completely cease even while the president was reading his address. In administering the oath of office, Chief Justice John Marshall "merely held the book, the President repeating the oath in the words prescribed by the Constitution," Adams observed. Afterwards, the president delivered his address, in "a suitably grave and rather low tone of voice." Several persons shook Monroe's hand as he left the chamber amid a cheering shout from the people in the galleries and music from the Marine Band.[43]

"There was not much form about this ceremony, which, in truth, requires no form but the forms of decency and decorum," the editor of the *National Intelligencer* observed, "but the scene was not the less impressive." Altogether, he thought it "characterized by simple grandeur and splendid simplicity" and a "truly Republican ceremony."[44] After the inaugural, the president received congratulations at a White House reception, and in the evening he and his family attended the inaugural ball at Brown's Hotel, though they left before supper was served.[45]

In his second inaugural address, which few heard but all could read in the *National Intelligencer* the next day, Monroe offered a general review of his four years in office. He had actually considered not delivering a speech at all, because some of his Virginia friends had suggested that it was antirepublican and not authorized by the Constitution. Sec-

113

retary of the Navy Thompson supported discontinuance, but no other member of the cabinet favored halting a practice that Washington had initiated in 1789.[46] In style and content the address was similar to his annual messages to Congress, though far briefer. Following his custom, Monroe had reviewed the speech with his cabinet and made some changes in the text. Hardly an eloquent or inspiring sentence graced the speech, though in closing he reflected movingly on the growth of the nation since the Revolution. "We now, fellow-citizens," he concluded, "comprise within our limits the dimensions and faculties of a great power under a government possessing all the energies of any government ever known to the Old World, with an utter incapacity to oppress the people."[47] But such moments were rare, and as far as is known, no entrepreneur printed the address on silk to be framed for display in the homes of admiring citizens—an honor bestowed on some of his predecessors.

In this speech, Monroe also surveyed Indian relations. He began by admitting the failure of past policies. "The care of the Indian tribes within our limits has long been an essential part of our system, but, unfortunately, it has not been executed in a manner to accomplish all the objects intended by it," he observed. "We have treated them as independent nations, without their having any substantial pretensions to that rank. The distinction has flattered their pride, retarded their improvement, and in many instances paved the way to their destruction." Pointing to the westward push of American settlements that constantly drove Indians from their lands, he asserted that the Indians had claims not only on the magnanimity but also on the justice of the nation. Urging Congress to adopt a plan to address the issue, he proposed that

> their sovereignty over vast territories should cease, in lieu of which the right of soil should be secured to each individual and his posterity in competent portions; and for the territory thus ceded by each tribe some reasonable equivalent should be granted, to be vested in permanent funds for the support of civil government over them and for the education of their children, for their instruction in the arts of husbandry, and to provide sustenance for them until they could provide it for themselves.[48]

Changes in Indian policy would come slowly, and before his second term ended, President Monroe would face the long-standing problem of the removal of Indian tribes from Georgia, to which the United States had become committed in 1802 when Georgia ceded its western lands.[49]

9

★★★★★

MONROE AS CHIEF EXECUTIVE

Before the end of his first term as president, Monroe had worked out the various practices and procedures employed in administering the presidential office, and he would continue to follow them throughout his presidency. When he took office, the structure of the executive branch had seen little change since the creation of the Navy Department during John Adams's term. The departments of State, Treasury, War, and Navy remained the principal executive offices, and their heads, together with the attorney general, composed the president's cabinet. No department of justice had yet been created, but since Washington's administration, the attorney general had sat with the department heads in the cabinet. The General Post Office also constituted a part of the executive branch, but the postmaster general was not a member of the president's inner circle.

The State Department in 1817 was only slightly larger than it had been during Jefferson's presidency, when seven clerks were employed. In the first year of Monroe's administration, eight clerks handled the business of the office of the secretary of state, while Dr. William Thornton and one clerk managed the Patent Office, also administered by the State Department.[1] The number of clerks in the office of the secretary of war had increased from five under Jefferson to thirteen at the beginning of Monroe's administration, and eleven clerks staffed other offices in the War Department.[2] In the Navy Department five clerks composed the staff for the secretary of the navy, an increase of only one since Jefferson's presidency, but three clerks had been added in the office of the commissioners of the navy.[3] During Monroe's two terms as president, the State, War, and Navy departments grew moderately. When he left office in 1825 there were two more clerks in the State Department than in 1817, eight additional clerks in the War Department, and four extra clerks in the Navy Department.[4]

The largest executive department at the time Monroe took office was the Treasury, as it had been since its establishment in 1789. Under Monroe it expanded considerably, in part because of the growth of the nation but also because of an act of Congress on March 3, 1817, the day before Monroe took office. By that legislation the offices of the accountants of the War and the Navy departments were abolished, and an additional comptroller and four new auditors were created in the Treasury.[5] The office of the secretary of the Treasury had seven clerks and remained small, but the staffs of the register, the two comptrollers, and the five auditors were considerably larger—the largest being under the third auditor, who handled the accounts of military expenditures. In all, the staff of subordinate officers and clerks in the Treasury Department totaled 146 in 1817 and increased to 165 by the time Monroe left office in 1825. This compared to 76 subordinate officers and clerks in the Treasury Department and the accounting offices of the War and Navy departments when Jefferson left office in 1809.

During Monroe's presidency the greatest growth in the bureaucracy came in the General Land Office, where the twenty-six clerks handling the affairs of that office in 1825 was twice the number in 1817. When Jefferson became president in 1801, a single clerk conducted the business of the land office.[6] The expansion of the General Post Office during Monroe's presidency nearly equaled that of the land office, with an increase from fifteen to twenty-seven postal clerks between 1817 and 1825.[7] These gains—in contrast to the modest growth in the State Department—reflected the internal growth of the nation, which looked inward to its development after the War of 1812.

The situation of the attorney general changed more during Monroe's administration than did that of any other cabinet member. In 1817 Monroe sought an appropriation from Congress to provide for the first time an office and a clerk for the attorney general. "The office has no apartment for business, nor clerks, nor a messenger, nor stationary, nor fuel allowed," Monroe had earlier explained to William Lowndes, chairman of the House Ways and Means Committee. "These have been supplied by the officer himself, at his own expense."[8] Despite some opposition on grounds of economy, Congress in 1818 appropriated funds authorizing the attorney general to appoint a clerk at a salary of one thousand dollars and a year later added five hundred dollars for contingencies.[9]

After more than four years in the office, Attorney General William Wirt wrote privately:

> I have never been a lazy man, but I never knew what work was 'till I came to Washington. I cannot find time to read any thing—not even the newspaper regularly—and I know little of what is going on in the world, out of the sphere of my own operations. My friends complain of me as a correspondent, but if they could be with me for a few days, so as to see my engagements, they would complain of me no more. I probably make my life more laborious than it need to be, but all the difficult questions of the departments are thrown upon me. The main current of their duties is so constant and so great, that if they were to take time to think, it would overwhelm them—so whatever requires thinking is thrown upon the Attorney General—and the contribution of this sent from the President and the four departments make an aggregate (mostly of new subjects) which imposes on me more labour in a week than used to fall on me in a month.[10]

Wirt's letter is revealing of not only his workload but also that of other department heads in a period when the country was expanding, the membership in Congress rising, and the business of all departments increasing. Wirt also disclosed that when he took office, he found "not one scrap of any opinion from the foundation of the government having been left in the office" by any previous attorney general. He thus began to keep a file of all his opinions for future holders of his office.[11]

The continuity in departmental subordinate officers and clerks that had prevailed since the establishment of the new government under the Constitution remained unbroken during Monroe's presidency. Among subordinate officers in the Treasury Department, Joseph Nourse, the register, and Richard Harrison, first auditor, had been in office when Jefferson became president in 1801. Peter Hagner, named third auditor in 1817, was chief clerk of the Treasury Department during Jefferson's administration. Thomas Tudor Tucker, the treasurer, had been appointed to the post by Jefferson in 1801. Edward Jones, chief clerk in the Treasury Department in 1817, had begun as a clerk while Washington was president. Daniel Brent, whom Secretary of State John Quincy Adams elevated to chief clerk in the State Department in 1817, had started his service in 1801. Numerous other examples could be cited, for subordinate posts and clerkships in the government had not been severely affected by the transfer of power from the Federalists to the Republicans in 1801, and there was even less turnover as Republican presidents continued to occupy the presidential chair.[12]

There was also little turnover in Monroe's cabinet, which was an unusually able group. Adams at the State Department, Crawford at the Treasury, Calhoun at the War Department, and Attorney General Wirt remained with Monroe throughout his two terms. Only in the Navy Department was there change. Smith Thompson replaced Benjamin Crowninshield—a holdover from Madison's administration—as secretary in 1818, and Thompson was succeeded by New Jersey Senator Samuel L. Southard, when Monroe named Thompson to the Supreme Court in 1823. Southard, who had once lived in Virginia and was a longtime friend of Monroe's, had long aspired to a federal post. Disappointed in being earlier passed over for attorney general and then for the Supreme Court, Southard accepted as promptly as decorum permitted, especially in view of the fact that Monroe's administration would be coming to a close in eighteen months.[13]

Monroe was a "hands on" president who devoted himself to his duties and held tightly to the final executive authority. From the outset Monroe instituted direct supervision over his department heads, but he gave closest attention to matters of foreign affairs. As noted previously, the papers of Secretary of State Adams are filled with memoranda from the president and copies of papers altered and revised by the president or by Adams following his directions.[14]

While the paper trail is less distinct in other departments, Monroe kept well informed about the operations of the War Department, as the inspections of military installations and coastal defenses on his tours of the country illustrated. The president and Secretary of War Calhoun worked closely together during the Seminole war, though he gave Calhoun a freer hand than Adams had in the State Department. Monroe was less immediately involved in financial management than in military matters and foreign affairs. This may be explained in part by his lack of interest in the details of Treasury business and by the requirements of Congress that the secretary of the Treasury report directly to Congress. But it may also be attributed to Crawford's having lost to Monroe in the nominating caucus of 1816.

Although the size of the Navy Department did not increase greatly while Monroe was president, his years in office witnessed substantial naval construction. In the final year of Madison's administration, Congress had appropriated $1 million a year for eight years to build ships, authorizing the construction of nine ships of the line, twelve forty-four-gun frigates, and three steam batteries. Much of this building would take place under Monroe, who annually reported steady progress in naval construction in his messages to Congress—even after Congress reduced the yearly appropriation for shipbuilding to half a million dollars. Congressman William Hendricks of Indiana reported to his constituents in 1820 that "the navy of the United States, since the late war, has been the peculiar favourite of the nation."[15] Less than two years after Monroe left office, his successor, John Quincy Adams, would declare that the intent of the 1816 act had largely been fulfilled and would praise the legislation as a message to posterity that it was the destiny of the United States "to become in regular process of time and by no petty advances a great naval power."[16]

The expanding operations of the navy also provide a prime example of President Monroe's initiative in policymaking. While reporting an increase in naval strength in his fifth annual message to Congress in December 1821, Monroe announced that it had been "necessary to maintain a naval force in the Pacific for the protection of the very important interests of our citizens engaged in commerce and the fisheries in that sea."[17] This brief announcement represented a major new policy that led to the establishment of the Pacific station—a permanent stationing of naval vessels off the Pacific coast.

In late August 1820 while Monroe was at Highland, Adams informed him of a report that some twenty vessels had been fitted out in New York ready to sail on seal-hunting and whaling voyages to a newly discovered island in the Pacific off the coast of South America. The discovery was Graham Land, the northern section of the Antarctic peninsula. Adams doubted whether American ships could reach the area before the British, but if they did, a confrontation could be expected. In his view,

> The British Government just now, have their hands so full of Coronations and Adulteries, Liturgy prayers and Italian Sopranos, . . . High Treasons, and Petty Treasons, Pains, Penalties and Paupers, that they will seize the first opportunity they can to shake them all off, and if they can make a question of national honor about a foot-hold in Latitude 61.40 upon something between Rock and Iceberg, as this discovery must be, and especially a question with us, they will not let it escape them.[18]

Far from shrinking from such a clash, the secretary of state suggested sending a navy frigate to take possession of the island. "The idea too of having a grave controversy with Lord Castlereagh, about an Island Latitude 61.40 South, is quite fascinating," he confessed.[19]

The president, less interested in a confrontation with Castlereagh than in expanding American influence, responded immediately that "the discovery of land in the Pacific, of great extent is an important event, and there are strong reasons in favor of your suggestion, to aim at its occupancy on our part." Requesting Adams to communicate the relevant documents to the secretary of the navy, Monroe said he would ask him to consider "how far it would be practicable to send a frigate there, and thence to strengthen our forces along the American coast."[20] The president's prompt actions to proceed in taking possession of the polar land and the subsequent establishment of the Pacific station contradict the view that Monroe was indifferent about American expansion to the Pacific.[21]

There was little turnover in departmental offices in Washington, where department heads appointed the clerks, but vacancies in numerous offices throughout the country and in diplomatic posts abroad required considerable attention from the president. The volume of papers relating to appointments to office that passed through Monroe's hands was huge, as attested to by the files preserved in the National Archives. Many letters were addressed directly to the president; others went to department heads who forwarded them to him. That Monroe personally reviewed these papers is indicated by his endorsements on many of them, sometimes with such specific notations as: "This recommendation is entitled to great consideration."[22]

Monroe's close involvement in the appointment process is well illustrated by the following letter addressed to the secretary of state, whose office was charged with preparing the formal appointment papers. In his own hand, the president wrote to Adams on November 23, 1819:

> From all the information obtained and much reflection on the subject, I am inclined to think that it will be advisable to appoint Mr. Skinner, judge for the western district of N. York, and Mr. Sutherland attorney in his place, Mr. Bland judge for the district of Maryland, and Mr. Forbes, agent of the U. States to reside in Chili. The judicial appointments, and that of attorney, had better be made without delay, and information given to Mr. Forbes of the arrangement in his favor, in which I take much interest, believing him to be from a long acquaintance with him, in the public service, an upright, well informed, discreet, and diligent public servant.[23]

Adams carried out the president's instructions, while recording in his diary that he had "opposed the appointment of Bland to the last moment; but, by the Constitution, the responsibility for appointments rests with the President and Senate. And when a head of Department is consulted upon a nomination which he disapproves, his duty of resistance ceases when the President has decided."[24]

After eighteen months at the State Department, Adams said that personally he "had been very cautious with regard to recommending persons for appointments. The President kept it very much in his own hands." Indeed, "there had not been a single appointment of any consequence, even in my own Department, made at my recommendation, nor one that I approved." The secretary of state pointed to Treasury Secretary Crawford as the principal manipulator behind appointments. He specifically blamed Crawford for the selection of Senator John Forsyth of Georgia as minister to Spain, despite Adams's assessment of him as "a man of some talent, but very indolent." Adams saw unsavory connections between Crawford and the Meigs—Josiah, the head of the General Land Office and Return Jonathan, Jr., the postmaster general. "These are both offices having extensive patronage scattered all over the Union," noted Adams, and Crawford was tied to "their little world of patronage and personal influence."[25] The fact that Forsyth's wife was Josiah Meigs's daughter and the niece of Return Jonathan Meigs, Jr., confirmed his suspicions.

Adams also blamed Crawford for the Tenure of Office Act passed in 1820 near the end of the congressional session and signed by Monroe along with thirty-three other acts on the day Congress adjourned. Members of his cabinet joined the president in the room reserved for him in the Capitol, and together they reviewed the bills before he signed them, yet none of them called his attention to this measure. It had passed quickly without debate or roll call and had attracted no notice in the press. Some years later Adams recorded in his diary that the legislation was "drawn up by Mr. Crawford, as he himself told me," and that it was introduced in the Senate by one of Crawford's devoted partisans, Mahlon Dickerson of New Jersey. The act specified that the term of office for principal officials concerned with the collection and disbursement of money was four years, though they could be reappointed. After he realized what he had signed, Monroe regarded the legislation as unconstitutional but saw no prospect of getting it repealed.[26] When he heard about the act, Jefferson suspected that it "must have been one of the midnight signatures of the President, when he had not time to consider, or even to read the law." Like Monroe, Jefferson saw the measure as "irrepealable but with the consent of the Senate, which will never be obtained."[27]

At the outset of his administration, Monroe had made it clear that he would not ignore party affiliation in making appointments.[28] Letters of recommendation commonly made reference to a candidate as "attached to the principles of Republicanism," or some similar comment. "By birth he is an American, and in principle a Republican," another correspondent wrote in support of his candidate.[29] Despite the demise of two-party competition on the national level and in some states, parties still persisted in many places. Nowhere was this clearer than in the scuffle for offices.

One of the major confrontations over appointments during Monroe's administration occurred early in 1822 regarding the appointment of the postmaster of Albany, New York. Though the selection of postmasters was in the hands of the postmaster general, Meigs cleared critical assignments with Monroe, since the postmaster general could be dismissed by the president. Monroe himself once advised a friend: "If you wish the Post Office at New Orleans, intimate it to the Post Master General, referring him to me for your character. By the law he makes the appointment, but in important cases he consults me."[30]

The Albany vacancy, created by the removal of Solomon Southwick for delinquency in his accounts, sparked intense political rivalry. New York Congressman Solomon Van Rensselaer, a former Federalist, secured the signatures of twenty-two members of the New York delegation in the House of Representatives in support of his own candidacy. With the application endorsed by members of both factions of New York Republicans and also by Federalists, Meigs moved promptly to appoint Van Rensselaer. But he had failed to consult the senators from New York—Martin Van Buren and Rufus King—and they were as quick to challenge the projected appointment. Writing to Meigs and to the president, they urged delay until New York constituents could be consulted. Vice-president Tompkins also joined in backing the senators' intervention.[31]

When Meigs informed the president that he intended to appoint Van Rensselaer unless Monroe objected, Monroe summoned his cabinet. He circulated the letters he had received and those to Meigs, who was called in for questioning. After Meigs withdrew, Monroe said he thought it problematic whether he ought to interfere in the case at all, and a spirited discussion followed. The president closed the meeting without announcing how he would decide, but he asked Navy Secretary Smith Thompson to remain behind. Thompson was a New Yorker and had strongly opposed Van Rensselaer from the outset. Two days later Monroe told Adams that he had informed the postmaster general that he would not interfere in the appointment of the postmaster at Albany.[32]

During Monroe's second term, appointments to office became increasingly entangled in the competition among rivals seeking to succeed Monroe as president. Referring to the contest among the members of his administration and their respective friends and advocates, Monroe explained the difficulties of his situation to Jefferson. "In the appointment to office, I have been forced either to distribute the offices among the friends of the candidates, to guard myself against the imputation of favoritism," he wrote, "or to take my own course, and appoint those whom I knew and confided in, without regard to them. Had I pursued the former, the office in my hands, for two or three years . . . would have sunk to nothing. I therefore adopted the latter, and have steadily pursued it."[33]

Monroe's administration of the presidential office was hampered by the lack of adequate staff. Congress provided no funds—not even for a secretary—and whether from lack of money or failure to attract talent, Monroe had trouble employing and retaining an efficient private secretary. After being turned down by William C. Rives, Monroe appointed his brother Joseph Jones Monroe as his private secretary in November 1817; and for several years the president depended heavily on members of his family to perform secretarial duties.[34] Calling at the President's House in the spring of 1818, when Monroe was too sick to receive company, a Washington visitor was greeted by his brother Joseph and his son-in-law George Hay, "who are his proxies."[35] Monroe appears to have employed Joseph as his secretary as much in an effort to help his brother—whose life needed purpose and direction—as to aid himself. In January 1818, Virginia Congressman Hugh Nelson wrote privately that "Joseph is I think doing well in his present situation, in fixing his reformation of bad habits, upon a confirmed foundation. The P[resident] keeps him closely occupied and is very regular and rigid in the rules of his house government."[36]

For a while Monroe's system may have worked. In the files of the State Department in the National Archives, there are a number of slips of paper with notes to Daniel Brent, the chief clerk, signed by Joseph Jones Monroe. One, for example, instructed: "The President wishes such of the documents as are ready, to be sent over immediately, to accompany his message. The sequel of them may go, at another time."[37] Another directed: "Will Mr. Brent have the goodness, to prepare and transmit to me, nominations of ministers to Madrid and Rio Janeiro, and any others, that are necessary to be laid before the Senate?"[38] At the same time, there are a number of similar notes in the president's own hand and others written by Samuel L. Gouverneur, Mrs. Monroe's nephew, who assumed the duties of private secretary in Joseph's absence and replaced him when Joseph left for Missouri in 1820. Gouverneur also accompanied the president on his tour in 1819.[39]

With insufficient staff, Monroe's days were full. Samuel F. B. Morse, who had been commissioned by the city of Charleston to paint Monroe's portrait in 1819, found the president as occupied in Washington as he had been in Charleston. The Monroes were gracious in allowing him to set up his easel in the White House and inviting him to dinner several times, but the artist often waited for hours for the president to sit—and then it was never for very long. "He cannot sit more than ten or twenty minutes at a time," the frustrated young artist wrote to his mother, "so that the moment I feel engaged he is called away again. I set my palette today at ten o'clock and waited until four this afternoon before he came in. He then sat for ten minutes, and we were called to dinner." It took Morse several weeks to complete the head of the full-length portrait (fig. 8).[40]

Samuel Gouverneur continued as presidential secretary after he married the Monroes' younger daughter Maria in a private ceremony in the White House in March 1820, but he left in late 1822 to study and practice law in New York.[41] He was succeeded by Dr. Charles Everett, a longtime friend of the president's from Albemarle County, Virginia. The position paid six hundred dollars per year, and Monroe told Everett, "You will have a good room and the allowance in other respects, which was made to my brother, and Mr. Gouverneur, which is the same, that was always made by my predecessors. I wish I had a better place to offer you, being sincerely your friend."[42] Although Everett yielded to the president's plea, he appears to have taken some long absences from the White House. In November 1823, as Monroe prepared for the convening of Congress, he wrote to Everett: "I have never thought of engaging any one to aid me here, since my conversation with you last spring. I have always wished that you would return, and remain with me while I was in office, and which I still do, and that it may suit you to come on at an early day." Telling him that others would copy his messages and that Everett would only have to present them to Congress, Monroe added that he was "so pressed with calls, and duties of the most urgent nature, that I have scarcely a moment to write to you."[43] With the turnover among his aides, Monroe never devised a well-functioning office. In the last year of his presidency, Adams referred to the "want of system in the multiplicity of business always crowding upon the President" and blamed it, above all, on "his want of an efficient private Secretary."[44]

Early in his presidency, Monroe established the practice of regularly assembling his cabinet for discussions of national issues and administration policies, and he maintained the practice throughout his two terms. Informality in calling cabinet meetings prevailed. The president frequently gathered his advisers by sending them notes to assemble at his office. Typical notes to members of his cabinet included the following addressed to Secretary of State Adams:

> J. M. will be glad to see Mr. Adams at 12 o'clock today, to meet the other heads of departments, on the subject of the war, with an Indian tribe, to the south.
> Dec. 26, 1817

> Mr. Calhoun, Mr. Thompson, and Mr. Wirt are here, in consequence of a suggestion that we would meet, on the subject of trade with British Colonies. Will you come over and intimate the same to Mr. Crawford?
> Monday   J. M.[45]

Numerous slips of paper with such notes in the president's own hand survive today, displaying the informality of Monroe's administrative procedures—in contrast to the formality of diplomatic etiquette. They also document the close involvement of and coordination between the cabinet and the president in the day-to-day executive operations of the government.

Individually the president's department heads gave him differing opinions and sometimes conflicting advice, and when the cabinet was divided, Monroe sought to find a consensus. If this proved impossible, he took the matter under advisement and made the final decision himself. On issues such as the Missouri controversy, where agreement was unlikely, he proceeded on his own to work with friends in Congress. In Latin American policy, for example, Monroe deviated from the recommendations of his secretary of state in order to counteract the efforts of Henry Clay in Congress to set the direction of American foreign policy by forcing recognition of the independence of Latin American republics.

Monroe consulted with his cabinet in preparing his first annual message to Congress but drafted the address himself. In later years he regularly gathered information and recommendations from them for his messages. After attending the meeting in which Monroe read to his cabinet the final draft of his fourth annual message to Congress, Adams observed:

> The composition of these messages is upon a uniform plan. They begin with general remarks upon the condition of the country, noticing recent occurrences of material importance, passing encomiums upon

our form of government, paying due homage to the sovereign power of the people, and turning to account every topic which can afford a paragraph of public gratulation; then pass in review the foreign affairs; the circumstances of our relations with the principal powers of Europe; then looking inwards, adverting to the state of the finances, the revenues, public expenditures, debts, and land sales, the progress of fortifications and naval armaments, with a few words about the Indians, and a few about the slave trade.[46]

Adams also noted that for the portions of the address relating to foreign affairs, the president usually called on him for advice and that he had from time to time written paragraphs that the president adopted with some alterations.[47] Monroe likewise requested information from other department heads, but he put the message together himself, revised it after hearing the comments of his cabinet, and determined the final text.

Monroe was very accessible to members of Congress, who were free to call at the president's office at will and were frequent guests at the president's dinner table. The influence of the administration on Congress was also exercised through department offices, for Congress furnished little in staff services to its members or even its committees. Thus Congress was heavily dependent on administrative offices for data, background information, and even recommendations for legislative remedies.[48] While there is no evidence that Monroe personally drafted bills for Congress, members of his cabinet did so.[49]

Even before Monroe's first term ended, the rival presidential ambitions of Crawford, Calhoun, and Adams made consensus building in the cabinet difficult. Adams thought Crawford always argued the opposite side of any position he took. Meanwhile, the decline of political parties left the president without a party base in Congress, where coalitions formed around friends of potential future presidential candidates. Early in 1820 Adams confided to his diary:

One of the most remarkable features of what I am witnessing every day is a perpetual struggle in both Houses of Congress to control the Executive—to make it dependent upon and subservient to them. They are continually attempting to encroach upon the powers and authorities of the President. As the old line of demarkation between parties has been broken down, personal has taken the place of principled opposition. The personal friends of the President in the House are neither so numerous nor so active, nor so able as his opponents. Crawford's personal friends, instead of befriending the Administration, operate as powerfully as they can, without exposing or avowing their motives against it. Every act and thought of Crawford looks to the next Presidency. . . . In short, as the first Presidential term of Mr. Monroe's administration has hitherto been the period of the greatest national tranquillity enjoyed by this nation at any portion of its history, so it appears to me scarcely avoidable that the second term will be among the most stormy and violent.[50]

Monroe's first term did not end so tranquilly as Adams expected, for Adams recorded these thoughts just before the Missouri crisis threatened the very existence of the Union. His prediction of the difficulties Monroe would face in his second term, however, was realized. Nor was Adams alone in making such projections. Only a few days after Monroe's second inaugural, Clay told Adams that although Monroe had been reelected with apparent unanimity, "he had not the slightest influence in Congress. His career was considered as closed. There was nothing further to be expected by him or from him." In fact, Clay argued that there "would not be a man in the United States possessing less *personal* influence over them than the President."[51]

As one who had pursued a course in Congress independent of the administration, Clay was hardly an impartial commentator, but his view was shared by others. Early in 1821, New York Federalist Senator Rufus King wrote privately, "Mr. Monroe is reelected unanimously or nearly so, and nevertheless the plans or measures of Government are without friends in Congress; by which I mean no one offers himself to explain or to support those measures which are supposed to have the recommendations and favor of the Executive."[52] A year later King avowed that President Monroe "though not yet buried is dead as respects direction, or control."[53] According to rumors in Washington during the same session in 1822, Federalist Senator Harrison Gray Otis delayed his contemplated resignation because he believed his vote in the Senate was necessary to carry some of the president's projects. Though Congressman Louis McLane found this hard to believe, he admitted "that this poor old President finds himself woefully beset; deserted by all his old friends, he is obliged to seek new ones, and it is not wonderful, if he should sometimes lean on broken reeds."[54]

As Adams and others had foreseen, rival presidential ambitions made it more and more difficult for the president to build consensus in the cabinet and support in Congress. Monroe himself increasingly felt the burdens of his office. After the Senate in 1822 rejected two of his nominations for military appointments, he told Madison:

I have never known such a state of things as has existed here during the last Session, nor have I personally ever experienced so much embarrassment and mortification. . . . The approaching election, though distant, is a circumstance that excites greatest interest in both houses, and whose effect, already sensibly felt, is still much to be dreaded. There being three avowed candidates in the administration is a circumstance which increases the embarrassment. The friends of each endeavour to annoy the others, as you have doubtless seen by the public prints.[55]

Madison, with whom Monroe corresponded regularly while president, acknowledged that "the aspect of things at Washington to which you allude could escape the notice of no one who ever looks into the Newspapers," but he ascribed it to "a peculiarity and combination of circumstances not likely often to recur in our Annals."[56]

The military nominations rejected by the Senate were particularly embarrassing to the president, because they had been interim appointments made during the recess of Congress. To compound the snub, resolutions were offered in the House of Representatives to censure the making of the appointments as not conforming to the mandate of the previous session to reduce the army. Despite Crawford's opposition in the cabinet, Monroe resubmitted the candidates, and they were again repudiated by the Senate. The opposition was led by Senator John Williams of Tennessee, brother of Lewis Williams, a member of the House from North Carolina—both devoted Crawford partisans.[57]

Crawford blamed Calhoun for the president's difficulties and accused him of leading Monroe to believe that Crawford was behind the Senate's rejection of the military nominations. Writing to Albert Gallatin in Paris, Crawford confided that he had taken no steps to counteract the suspicions of his role "because I believe it will not be injurious to me to remain in this state, or even to be removed from office." While insisting he was not seeking to be dismissed, he confessed, "I do not believe it would be injurious to me in a political point of view."[58] Monroe privately defended Calhoun, telling Madison that under Calhoun the staff of the army was "remarkably well organized" and its expense reduced to the minimum required. He saw the rejection of his nominees as designed "to raise up a new party, founded on the assumed basis of economy, and with unjust imputations against all those who are friendly to the system of defence."[59]

The tensions between Monroe and Crawford reached a new intensity when Crawford offered to resign in July 1822. "As my principal object in consenting to become a member of your administration was to be useful to you," he told Monroe, "I can have no inducement to continue in it, after it is ascertained, that, that object, cannot be affected."[60] In reply Monroe reaffirmed his commitment to "allowing to the Heads of Departments the utmost freedom of sentiment, without which their advice would be useless," but he stressed the necessity of their cooperation and support after his decision was made. He concluded:

> In performing the duties of the high office entrusted to me, I owe it to my country, as well as to the integrity of my own character, that its powers should not be paralized in my hands, but be preserved in their full force, to the last day of my service, in execution of the measures on which I have decided, and deem important to the public welfare. Knowing as you do, the embarrassments to which I have been, and may continue to be exposed, you can best decide, whether it comports with your own views to render me, the aid, which is desired and expected, and I refer it to your own candour to take the course which may be most consistent with the sentiment, which you have expressed in your letter.[61]

Crawford replied with a seven-page defense of his conduct, assuring the president that he agreed that once the president had settled on a policy, the heads of departments were bound to cooperate in carrying it out. "If the measure requires legislative sanction, the reasons in favor of its adoption ought to be offered by the proper department, and the other departments when a proper occasion offers should not withhold their aid. In no case ought their opinions or efforts to be employed against the measure." He insisted that out of respect for the independence of Congress he had abstained from any efforts to obtain legislation, beyond his official reports to Congress or invitations to appear before a congressional committee. "I have however never declined offering to individual members, who have introduced them as subjects of conversation, the reasons which have led the executive government to adopt any particular measures, whether it was connected with the Treasury or not." He promised the president that if he remained in the cabinet he would "render you the aid which you desire and expect." But in view of the president's letter, he declined to submit his resignation because it would imply that he had been deficient in his duty toward the president and that if he remained in office, he would continue to withhold the aid expected of him.[62]

The wearied president responded that he was not accusing Crawford of doing anything improper. He was gratified, he said, "to find that we agree as to the support which the Chief Magistrate has a right to expect on the principles of our Government from the Heads of Departments acting under him, and that it comports with your feelings and as well as with your views, to afford me that aid." In closing, he assured the secretary of the Treasury that he wanted him to continue in his administration.[63] Monroe thus sought to reassert command and improve harmony in his cabinet, but he was unable to restrain the competition among his chief advisers to be his successor.

Writing four months later to Richard Rush in London, Monroe expounded on the pressures and burdens of his office:

> My labours, during the session of Congress, are, as you well know, important, and very burdensome. The Executive of our government, by which is meant the chief magistrate, is in a peculiar degree the responsible party, in exclusion of the heads of the several departments. He is essentially responsible for the management of the concerns of every department, even where they act without his direction, which is seldom done. The whole movement takes its impulse from him, as well as its course. In the present state, proceeding from causes which will readily occur to you, I am compelled, to go into details, unusual for the person in this station, which proportionally increases my labours, and this will I presume, continue to operate during the residue of my term.[64]

Monroe could expect no help from his vice-president. Although Tompkins was reelected in 1820, he was little respected in Washington. He never presided with any regularity over the Senate, and his absence was a relief to many senators. When the vice-president left the city in February 1822, three months before Congress adjourned, Senator Waller Taylor spoke for many when he observed: "His habits became so notoriously debauched, that it was matter of much gratification to the Senate to get clear of him. He has become a confirmed sot." Recalling that Tompkins had appeared in the Senate intoxicated, Taylor judged him to be "morally and politically destroyed."[65] Six weeks earlier, at the opening of the Seventeenth Congress, Congressman Louis McLane had written to his wife that Tompkins had sought to join his mess at Strother's Hotel on Pennsylvania Avenue but everyone had looked for a pretense—which they evidently found—to exclude him. "He bears the most evident, and conclusive marks of a sot," McLane noted, "and the apprehension is that his habits may interfere with our pleasure."[66]

Recognizing the difficulties Monroe faced during his second term, his friends sought to give him encouragement. "Your labors are drawing to a close, but the part you have yet to act is difficult," Abner Lacock wrote to him in the summer of 1822.

> The members of your Cabinet are spoken of as rival candidates for your situation. They will all have their particular views and policy. For

you to act with them and decide between them, without being charged with partialities and a preference for some one, will be almost impossible. I know you will steer as far as possible a neutral course, but this will not exempt you from censure, in the storm of personal feelings and political discussions we are to pass through. Mr. Jefferson in one of his messages has spoken of the difficulty of closing an administration with the éclat that it commenced. You have that difficulty to encounter. You will meet it as you have others with firmness.[67]

10

★ ★ ★ ★ ★

LIFE IN MONROE'S WASHINGTON

During Monroe's presidency, administrative officials, members of Congress, diplomatic representatives, and visitors to the capital found an active social life in Washington, different from the Republican simplicity and informality of Jefferson's terms of office or the wartime capital of Madison's administration. As president, Monroe abandoned the familiar style adopted by Jefferson and returned to the formal diplomatic etiquette prevailing in the capitals of Europe. Anthony Merry, the British minister to the United States, had once felt insulted when Jefferson received him in casual dress, wearing slippers without heels.[1] Monroe did not follow Jefferson's example.

Dressed in a full black suit or a half military uniform and standing in the center of the drawing room, President Monroe received foreign ministers at formal audiences. The minister appeared in full court dress and, accompanied by the secretary of state, presented his letter of appointment to the president, who handed it unopened to the secretary of state. John Quincy Adams, who had served in several diplomatic posts in Europe, noted that all the sovereigns to whom he had delivered such letters had opened them and cast a cursory glance over them. In delivering his credentials to the president, the diplomat made a short address, to which Monroe had a standard reply—"the United States take a great interest in everything that concerns the happiness of their sovereign," making slight variations adapted to each case. This ceremonial exchange lasted less than five minutes, then the minister customarily withdrew. Adams noted that the Abbé Correa, the Portuguese minister, was an exception. After the formal etiquette was observed, he "doffs the diplomat aside, and opens a discursive field of conversation, upon which the President then readily enters," Adams remarked in 1819. "None of the others have the faculty or inclination for this, and their interviews are merely formal and dull."[2]

Though Jefferson's office door had been open to foreign diplomats whenever they chose to call, Monroe required appointments. For social contact they were invited to the evening drawing rooms that President and Mrs. Monroe hosted, usually fortnightly while Congress was in session.[3] No business, however, was to be conducted on these occasions. Citizens and Washington visitors, suitably dressed, were also welcome. These receptions were the successors to the levees that presidents Washington and Adams had held and that were revived during Madison's presidency, where Dolley Madison had been the center of attention.

Monroe's drawing rooms were generally crowded. After attending the last one of the congressional session in February 1819, Adams recorded that there was such a "choke-up of carriages in the yard" that it took nearly an hour to get to the door of the President's House. All the while, Adams feared being rammed by the pole of the carriage behind him.[4] Midway through his first term, Monroe began to question the wisdom of continuing the receptions. "The President mentioned several unpleasant disorderly occurrences at the drawing-rooms, and appeared to regret that he had not laid them aside altogether," Adams noted in his diary after a conversation with Monroe at the end of December 1819. Monroe mentioned a clerk in the Navy Department "who, having really no right to attend the drawing-room, had not only come himself but brought another person still more improper with him, who had abused and ill treated the servants in the house." Adams thought that at large parties, such incidents were to be expected. "I rather dissuaded the President from making any new regulations to exclude any one from the drawing-rooms, but advised him, if it should be found necessary, to employ one or two constables to keep order in the yard."[5]

By the beginning of his second term Monroe was seriously considering ending the functions completely. Monroe broached the matter to Abner Lacock, a former senator from Pennsylvania, and he strongly urged the president to do so. The drawing rooms, declared Lacock,

> do much harm and little or no good. At best what are those meetings, but a piece of miserable pageantry, in which the heart or head has little to do, every one present has to act a part in the farce or pantomime, some at the expense of their *healths,* all at that of their pockets,

and many of whom had better pay their honest debts. To see the President and his lady (two aged and grave persons for such they will generally be) standing on their feet two or three hours, acting the part of French dancing masters, and endeavouring to make fashionable bows, to a crowd of gaudy butterflies, would be considered ridiculous in the extreme by the honest yeomanry of our country, who are in reality the best hopes of our nation—and this is not all, the example become deleterious to the nation. The extravagance and prodigality of high dress exhibited at the drawing rooms spreads like an epidemic through the country, and the whole body politic becomes infected.[6]

There were fewer receptions during the last years of Monroe's second term, when Mrs. Monroe's health was poor, but the president rejected Lacock's advice and did not abolish the drawing rooms.

More frequent than these gatherings were the dinners that the president hosted for members of Congress, his cabinet, justices of the Supreme Court, foreign diplomats, and various citizens and visitors to the city. Monroe invited groups of congressmen to dine with him and gave large diplomatic dinners once or twice each winter. At first he invited the secretary of state to attend the diplomatic dinners, but other cabinet members thought they should also be included. This was unacceptable to the foreign ministers, who were willing to yield place to the secretary of state but not to four or five heads of departments and their wives. Jefferson had sought to avoid all such disputes by his solution of letting everyone find pell-mell a place at the table without any seating by rank. Monroe ultimately settled the issue by inviting only one department head and his wife to each diplomatic dinner, rotating through the cabinet. Seating problems also arose at dinners for congressmen. In November 1820 Adams reported dining with the president in a company of about thirty-five others, mostly members of Congress and all men, Mrs. Monroe's health not permitting her attendance. "There was a reappearance of the jealousies about precedence at this dinner," Adams observed. The president sat at the center of the table with the president of the Senate and the Speaker of the House on either side. Across from him was Nathaniel Macon, a senator from North Carolina who had been in Congress since 1791 and whom the president himself had asked to take the seat opposite him, apparently to the surprise of many.[7]

To reduce expenses, Monroe considered cutting down on the dinners that he hosted several nights a week while Congress was in session. After the reapportionment following the census of 1820, there were over two hundred members in the House of Representatives, and as steamboats eased travel to Washington, an increasing number of visitors arrived in the capital anticipating invitations to dine at the President's House. Expected to pay for all expenses out of his salary of twenty-five thousand dollars per year, the president became more and more concerned about the costs of hospitality. As Monroe's debts mounted, he began contemplating selling some of his land in Virginia. When he told Jefferson of his need to dispose of property in Albemarle County, the former president could sympathize with his plight. "I had had great hopes that while in your present office you would break up the degrading practice of considering the President's house as a general tavern and economise sufficiently to come out of it clear of difficulties," Jefferson said.[8] At one point, Monroe did decide to curtail his entertaining, but he was dissuaded from doing so by members of his cabinet, who argued that it would be seen as meanness to stop the custom now. When Monroe asked his old friend Charles Jared Ingersoll of Philadelphia his opinion, Ingersoll agreed that it was better to continue as he had been, but he added, "I had long said that it was a wrong system and that the Presidents would see the necessity of beginning a relinquishment of it. They must see company no doubt. But I should suppose that a dinner a month would do instead of 3 a week—perhaps they might have done with their promiscuous entertainments altogether and invite only their old acquaintances to occasional dinners."[9]

In December 1823, as Monroe approached his last year in office and with Mrs. Monroe in poor health, their son-in-law Samuel Gouverneur advised the president not to open the White House to the public during the winter. Having seen the pressures of presidential entertaining as Monroe's private secretary, Gouverneur suggested that "at the close of a laborious term of years in office," Monroe find as much repose as possible. He urged that the president "not hesitate to relieve yourself from the bodily and mental oppression, which must be imposed upon you by entertainment of a continual round of individuals, in whom except as public agents, you can feel no interest, and many of whom in fact are otherwise unknown to you."[10] The recommendation was not followed, and the New Year's reception of 1824 at the White House, with Eliza Hay standing in for her mother, was one of the most crowded receptions of Monroe's presidency.

During the winter season while Congress was in session, an active social life prevailed beyond the White House, but Monroe himself did not accept any invitations to attend functions at private homes or at the residences of foreign diplomats. Secretary of State and Mrs. Adams usually held an informal open house every Tuesday evening, receiving between fifty and a hundred visitors. The Adamses also hosted dinners and sometimes a ball during the Christmas season. They reportedly issued five hundred invitations to their party in the week after New Year's in 1822—a week in which Secretary of War Calhoun and Navy Secretary Thompson also held parties.[11]

Foreign ministers also contributed to the round of dinners and balls. Adams counted about two hundred members of Congress and others at a ball given by Hyde de Neuville, the French minister, in December 1817.[12] During the same social season, one member of Congress commented that "Mr. and Mrs. De Neuville, really are the life of this city, and their rooms being open every Saturday night, afford much more real entertainment than even the crowd at the Palace."[13] The following December, Hyde de Neuville expressed to the secretary of state his keen desire that President and Mrs. Monroe attend the ball he was giving. When Adams conveyed this information to the president, Monroe consulted one of Washington's former private secretaries to learn the first president's custom. Informed that neither Washington nor any president had ever been at the house of any foreign minister, Monroe decided not to depart from the established practice. In turn, Mrs. Monroe thought it inappropriate to attend any function it was improper for her husband to attend. Monroe then requested his daughter Mrs. Hay to accept the minister's invitation, and she agreed on condition that she be assigned no rank or station at the ball based on her father's position and that her name not be published in the papers as among the guests.[14]

Though declining invitations to private homes or ministerial residences, the Monroes did appear at some public functions. In the spring of 1824, Congressman William C. Rives saw "the President, with the *royal* family," Mr. Adams, and other *"great* folks," at "a great oratorio" at the Unitarian church, where a new organ—touted by the *National Intelligencer*—was dedicated. It turned out to be a "miserable" performance, in Rives's view. He described the notes of the organ as sounding like squealing pigs, and he reported hearing another listener compare it to the noise of a thousand jaybirds. "The best that can be said of the vocal music is, that it was a *fit accompaniment,"* he lamented.[15]

Few social customs aroused more controversy and ill feelings than the etiquette of making calls. By the time Monroe took office, the convention had been fixed in the minds of many senators that heads of departments should make first calls on them, while members of the House were to initiate calls on the secretaries. Secretary of State Adams insisted that this was not the protocol when he was in the Senate in the later years of Jefferson's administration, since he remembered that he had always called first on cabinet members. Although the custom often consisted of no more than leaving cards, it was time consuming, and Adams settled on the practice of returning only the visits of those who called on him. Heads of departments returned the first visits, and no others, of foreign ministers.[16] Wives of cabinet members were also caught up in the controversies over first calls. Ladies arriving as strangers in the capital expected cabinet wives to call on them, and some even presumed that Mrs. Monroe would call. The ebullient Mrs. Madison had indeed done so during the previous administration, but Mrs. Monroe neither paid nor returned visits. Mrs. Adams did not give precedence to strangers but returned all visits—a practice that, like her husband's policy, created resentment.[17]

Finishing a round of calls soon after becoming attorney general in 1817, William Wirt tried to make light of the duty, but he did not hide his lack of enthusiasm. Forewarning his wife of what would be expected of her when she arrived in Washington, he wrote:

> I have just returned from paying and returning a round of official and ceremonious visits—a business, you know, of all others the most congenial with my temper and habits. I set out at 10 o'clock—it is now one—I have been to the President's, the secretary of state's, the secretary of the treasury's, the acting secretary of war's, the British minister's, the British consuls and secretary of legation's, Commodore Decatur's, Walter Jones' etc., etc., etc. How do you think you will stand all this? and yet you will have to go through it all—aye and more, too. Why that sigh? It is nothing when you get used to it.[18]

Among the best contemporary commentaries on life in Monroe's Washington are letters written by congressmen to their wives, especially the letters of new members seeing the capital and the president for the first time. Most members of Congress came to Washington without their wives or families. They lived in boardinghouses on Capitol Hill, in Georgetown, and elsewhere in the city, clustered together with colleagues from their own state or region and members who shared their political outlook.[19] On December 5, 1817, five days after arriving in Washington, Congressman Louis McLane of Delaware, a Federalist, wrote to his wife, Kitty, about his first visit to the White House:

> I was presented to the President, with whom I was exceedingly pleased, because of the plain simplicity of his manners, and the easy dignity of his deportment generally. I found him alone, was received by him very graciously. . . . I had heard much of his imitation of the ceremony of foreign Courts and the ceremonious forms with which he was surrounded. I found none of it, beyond what was necessary and proper. By the servant who answered my first call the inquiry was made if I were a member of Congress, being answered affirmatively,

my name was entered upon his Book, and I was passed through the hands of one or two others, to the presence of his Excellency.[20]

Two weeks later McLane wrote to Kitty after returning from a party at the home of French minister Hyde de Neuville, where diplomats, heads of departments, government officers, members of Congress, citizens, and visitors—estimated by McLane to number more than 250—filled four rooms to overflowing. "Dancing, singing, rousing, eating, drinking, and wild wonder occupied the throng," reported McLane, who left the party at half past ten before the supper was served. McLane was much impressed with Madame de Neuville and charmed by Mrs. Bagot, wife of Sir Charles Bagot, the British minister, but he was shocked by the "dress, or rather want of dress" of many of the other women present. While most "put on some apology for a covering to the bosom," two "shameless fair ones," he exclaimed to his wife, "defied all such useless drapery and actually came without any."[21]

Attending his first New Year's reception at the White House, McLane was presented to Mrs. Monroe, whom he thought was "certainly the finest looking woman I saw" and appeared little older than her daughter Mrs. Hay. "The president was the same plain honest gentlemanly looking personage, which he at all times appears to be, and in the midst of the splendour by which he was surrounded, inspired every one with admiration for his country, and a love for its Chief Magistrate." He elaborated on the atmosphere of the White House:

> The splendour of this scene could not easily be surpassed, and it fully gratified the curiosity of all. Large and capacious as was the rooms allotted for the company, they were well filled. . . . The large Hall into which was the entrance, was the space for sauntering, and lounging, and taking breath after the ceremonies in the other apartments had been gone through. Here too was a band of excellent musick which played during the day. Immediately back of the hall were four rooms magnificently furnished, in which company were received, and supplied with refreshments. The taste and splendour of Europe have contributed to decorate and enrich these rooms: and have given them a splendour which is really astonishing. It would be difficult to pronounce which part of the furniture was most beautiful, though I think the mirrors and chairs were certainly most striking.[22]

Nearly four years later another first-term congressman, Job Durfee of Rhode Island, experienced reactions similar to McLane's upon meeting the president and encountering Washington society. Reporting his first visit to the president on December 4, 1821, Durfee told his wife that he had "this day spent half an hour with the president whom I visited and to whom I was introduced according to the custom of the place. He is a plain man—his countenance is expressive of a good heart and an amiable disposition. He is the most modest and unassuming man that I have seen."[23] Durfee's surviving letters do not provide any observations on the White House, but in commenting on social affairs, he sounded as shocked as McLane had been at women's party dresses. Offering his wife "a *touch of the times* here," he wrote:

> I the other evening attended a party at Mr. Thomson's secretary of the Navy. It was a party which I could not well decline accepting as it seemed to be of special nature and one that immediately followed the marriage of his daughter. As it was the first party of the kind that I have attended my curiosity broad awake, and I must confess that I never was more surprized than at the dress of the females—both comfort, and I might add decency (according to my ideas of it), were set at defiance. They resembled so many actresses with their bosoms and backs half bare.[24]

Serving his first term in Congress during Monroe's last two years as president, William C. Rives of Albemarle County, Virginia, sent a homesick letter to his wife on Christmas Eve 1823 and described his first dinner at the President's House:

> The President's dinner-party was as dull a scene as you can imagine. It consisted of about thirty members of Congress, drawn from every portion of the United States, scarcely any two of whom were acquainted with each other, and of course, there was very little conversation. The party assembled about 5 o'clock, and sat down to dinner by candle-light, in which, I think, there was as much policy, as fashion, for a dim light serves, in some degree, to hide the nakedness of the Presidential board. I scarcely ever saw a more scanty or meagre dinner. There were some ten or fifteen dishes only, scattered over an immense surface, at awful and chilling distances from each other. There were vacant spaces enough for a dozen plateaus, besides the large one which occupied the middle of the table.[25]

A plateau, Rives explained, was a long piece of table decoration, with gilt-framed, highly polished mirrors on the bottom, surmounted with gilt frames supporting flower baskets and candles. "It is a mere ornamental expletive, intended to fill up vacant space, of which there is an abundance on the President's table." The table was also so wide, he said, that it was inconvenient and unpleasant to talk to any person on the other side of it.[26]

140

Perhaps the food was better when Senator David Daggett of Connecticut dined at the President's House in 1818, since he came away with quite different impressions. Judging the president's dining table as "splendid enough for any *Republic*," he observed that "the plates are of beautiful French china, with the American coat of arms in the centre. The *plateau* (I believe they call it) is magnificent beyond anything I ever witnessed."[27]

Congressman Rives at first considered not going to the president's reception on New Year's Day 1824, having heard that the President's House was thrown open to everybody and people of all sorts and descriptions thronged there.[28] But he changed his mind and afterwards described the scene for his wife:

> As we approached the President's House, I saw with utter astonishment, and not without a feeling of admiration, an immense column of carriages, (more than a hundred), in front of the house, some just passing off, after having discharged their loads, while others were slowly advancing through the crowd to deposit their's. This gave us some intimation of the crowd we were to find within. We entered a very large Hall, where a band of music was playing fine patriotic airs, and groups of persons were collected all about, some conversing, some walking, and every one following the bent of his inclination without restraint. We then passed into another room, where Mr. Monroe, and Mrs. Hay, (who personated Mrs. Monroe, on the occasion), were receiving the salutations of their numerous visitors. This room was so much crowded that we found it almost impossible to *wedge* ourselves into it. Here were all the foreign ministers, in their splendid court-dresses, the military and naval officers, in full uniform, intermixed with the members of both Houses of Congress, and a large number of ladies elegantly dressed and arrayed in their *best looks.*[29]

Present at the same reception, Robert P. Henry, another first-term congressman, called it "the grandest spectacle" he had ever seen, with "all the beauty and taste and fashion of the city and the regions round about." To the thirty-five-year-old Kentuckian, the sixty-five-year-old president appeared as "a remarkably plain-dressed venerable old man." Henry was deeply moved by "the warm and voluntary effusion of regard and benevolence, which was paid, on this occasion, to that beloved fellow citizen, who wielded by popular will the executive energies of the strongest of all possible governments."[30]

Foreign guests were less likely to be impressed with White House receptions than Americans. Baron Axel Klinkowström of Sweden described the President's House as "not elegant but suitably and tastefully furnished as befits an officer of this rank in a country where the principle of equality prevails." But he said he had "often seen more lavish rooms in Europe in the homes of officials whose rank and station could not be compared with the President's." Attending a reception in 1819, he found Mrs. Monroe "charming and engaging. But from what I could tell," he added, "she did not seem especially to enjoy this affair."[31]

Visitors to the capital joined legislators and government officials in the social conventions of the Washington community—making calls, leaving cards, accepting invitations to parties, calling on the president, and attending receptions at the White House. When Horace Holley, a Boston Unitarian minister, visited Washington in the spring of 1818, en route to Kentucky where he had been offered the presidency of Transylvania College, Massachusetts Senator Harrison Gray Otis took him in his carriage to make morning rounds. They called first on the president, but he was ill and not receiving visitors. They called next on Henry Clay, the Speaker of the House, then Secretary of State Adams, and a number of senators.[32] As Holley explained in a letter to his wife, "The etiquette here requires that strangers should first call on the president, vice president, heads of departments, foreign ministers, senators, and the Speaker of the house first, and then they call upon the strangers, i. e., all of them but the president."[33]

Holley, who delivered a Sunday sermon in the hall of the House of Representatives, was pleased when Monroe regained his health and allowed callers. Visiting the president became the high point of his stay in Washington. Arriving at the President's House, he was ushered into Monroe's study, where Monroe greeted him with "kindness and courtesy, and his usual simplicity," he recalled. The visit was a leisurely one, and when Holley inquired about Mrs. Monroe, the president invited him to return for tea at seven in the evening to meet her and his daughters. Holley was so taken with the president and the day that he wrote his wife a fifteen-page letter describing the experience.[34]

Reconstructing his conversation with the president, Mrs. Monroe, and their daughter Eliza Monroe Hay, Holley reported at length on their discussion about Gilbert Stuart as a portrait painter, while they viewed the full-length portrait of Washington that Dolley Madison had saved from destruction by the British during the War of 1812. When Holley asked the president if he had received the portrait (fig. 1) that Stuart painted of him when he toured Boston the previous year, Monroe said that he had not but that it was not Stuart's "habit to finish a picture and send it home." Then he inquired if Holley had viewed the painting at the artist's studio, and the Bostonian replied that he had seen it several times.

"How far is it finished?" the president asked.

"Nothing but the head," replied Holley.

"Is it a good likeness?" Mrs. Monroe continued.

"A remarkably good one," Holley responded. "It is the general opinion that it is one of the artist's happiest efforts with his pencil. You will be pleased with it, but will observe immediately, when you see it, that your husband was sun-burnt as a traveller ought to be, and that the artist has been so long in the habit of copying faithfully what he sees that he has given this in the shading of the picture."

"I shall not like it the less for that. I think Stewart generally makes the color of the cheeks too brilliant, especially in the portraits of men, as in that of general Washington."

"The painting of Mr. Monroe then will meet your taste precisely."

"Have you seen Vanderlyn's portrait of Mr. Monroe?" the first lady inquired.

"I saw it in Vanderlyn's room in New York three summers ago, when Mrs. Holley and myself went to an exhibition which he had of paintings there."

"What do you think of it?" asked Mrs. Monroe.

"It is very inferior to Stewart's."

While they were talking, a servant brought in portraits by John Vanderlyn of Monroe (fig. 2) and Mrs. Monroe (fig. 3) and placed them on the piano.

"Yours, madam, I have never seen before," Holley observed. "The likenesses are about equally good, but neither does justice to the original. The ermine, thrown over your shoulders, is well painted, and becomes the wearer; but the spirit of the portraits is very different from that which Stewart gives."

"There is something remarkable in this head of Mr. Monroe by Vanderlyn," Mrs. Monroe said. "Cover up the eyes and the lower part of the face, and the forehead is a good likeness, cover the forehead, and all but the eyes, and the eyes are good. Let the mouth and chin only appear, and the likeness is still good. But look at the whole face and head, and the expression is defective. We are not then satisfied with the portrait. But the painting is very good, so far as mechanical execution is concerned."[35]

From painting, the president directed the conversation to agriculture. Holley then reminisced about Monroe's visit to Boston. After Mrs. Monroe referred to some of their experiences in France and England, her daughter brought up a recent book on France by an English author,

Lady Morgan, and said she thought it offered a remarkably correct picture of Europe and that a review of it in the London *Quarterly Review* was very scurrilous and disgraceful. The president appears to have remained quiet in the latter discussion, but

> when the manuscript from St. Helena was mentioned, the president said that he did not believe it was written by Bonaparte, but by a friend of his, and was designed to apologise for his errors. He then went on with an oration about Napoleon's character as a statesman and a general which was as animated as his speech at Cambridge. He said, that Napoleon had been overestimated; that his policy in Spain was miserable, his invasion of Russia madness, and his battle of Waterloo on a bad plan. Marshall Ney understood it, and gave a just account of it. Mr. Monroe knew Ney personally in France, and thinks very highly of his military judgment and character. History will not give Bonaparte, as Mr. Monroe thinks, the high station which his contemporaries appear even yet to be willing to award him.[36]

Holley's report, though stilted, provides an invaluable glimpse of an evening with the Monroes. The conversation revealed a widely traveled first lady and a daughter who was well read. Readers today, searching out the lengthy critique of Lady Morgan's *France* published in the *Quarterly Review,* a leading London journal, would likely agree with Mrs. Hay's estimation of the piece.[37] If Monroe seemed more eager to talk about agriculture and Napoleon than about Gilbert Stuart, he clearly shared the widespread interest in Stuart's portraits and in the artist as a person. His considered opinion about Napoleon's place in history also discloses a man not so consumed by the politics of the moment as he often appears.

Monroe's administration came at a crucial time in the history of the White House. The restoration of the building after its burning by the British in 1814 was nearing completion when Monroe took office in 1817, giving President and Mrs. Monroe the opportunity and challenge to direct the outfitting of the interior to match the splendor of the exterior.

Although Dolley Madison had saved Gilbert Stuart's portrait of George Washington from destruction, few other items survived to be returned to the mansion. The Madisons had gathered secondhand furniture and other items to furnish the house they occupied after the burning of the capital, but hardly anything was suitable for the renovated mansion. On the last day of President Madison's administration, Congress appropriated twenty thousand dollars to purchase furniture and furnishings for the President's House.[38]

Because it was expected that much of the interior decoration would be purchased in France, Monroe made available his own furniture, china, mirrors, and other objects from his house in Washington. Most of these pieces had been bought during his missions to France. After Monroe's furnishings were appraised at $9,071.22, he was advanced $6,000 from the funds earmarked for new furniture. He repaid this amount before the new purchases arrived from France, but later, after his household goods remained in use in the White House, he received payment for the appraised valuation.

The congressional appropriation stipulated only that the funds be administered as the president should direct. Monroe thus asked William Lee, second auditor of the Treasury, to handle the planning and purchasing, and he directed Samuel Lane, the superintendent of public buildings, to disburse the funds.[39] Monroe had known Lee since his first mission to France in 1796, when as minister to France he invited the young Massachusetts businessman to dinner. He later recommended Lee to President Jefferson, who appointed him as commercial agent, or consul, at Bordeaux in 1801. As one of his first appointments, President Monroe named Lee to the Treasury post in March 1817.[40] Lee's many years in France and his commercial ties and knowledge made him especially well suited for the assignment.

That President and Mrs. Monroe retained control over the furnishing of the White House can be seen in the following excerpt from a letter from Monroe to Lane in May 1818:

> We shall want for the Eastern room one chandelier, and perhaps silk to make the curtains, if not to cover the chairs. These articles had better be sent for to Mr. Russell. It may perhaps be better, to send them the height, and size of the windows, and have the curtains made in France for them. On these points Mrs. Monroe will decide. . . . The carpets must be obtained from Mr. Yard, for the bed rooms and East room. . . . The chairs, for the East room, and tables, and any other articles, for that room, and the mahogany benches, small tables, and chairs for the hall, will be made by Mr. Worthington and Mr. King.[41]

Unfortunately, in light of the later difficulties untangling Monroe's finances, Monroe also employed the services of Lane to manage his personal accounts. Among other matters, Lane handled all the expenses for the White House while Monroe was not in Washington. Numerous memoranda of Lane's activities, providing such details as disbursements for vegetables and other items for the President's House in his absence, can be found in the National Archives today.[42]

In November 1817 Joel Mead, the editor of *The National Register,* a Washington newsmagazine, investigated reports of the arrival at Alexandria of a shipload of furniture from France for the President's House. He found instead forty cases of "ornamental objects, such as looking glasses, chandeliers, clocks, sconces, china, and some silks for curtains; all of them articles which cannot be manufactured in the United States." He added that the items were "indeed, exquisite models of the arts; durable as well as beautiful and perfectly appropriate to the building and its style of decoration." He chided critics who might "delight in seeing the president's mansion decorated with furniture such as is to be found in a pawnbroker's shop in St. Giles." Reminding readers that Benjamin Franklin "was alike at home on a damask gilt settee as at his printing press," the editor added that "Franklin, like our present chief magistrate, was one of the most simple and unaffected men, but like him he shewed a dignity of deportment which so far from injuring the cause of republicanism created a veneration for it."[43]

The twenty-thousand-dollar fund for refurbishing the President's House proved insufficient for the "good quality, strong, massive, and durable" furniture needed in the spacious public rooms. In February 1818 Monroe asked Congress for an additional amount. "The furniture in its kind and extent is thought to be an object not less deserving attention than the building for which it is intended," the president told Congress. "For a building so extensive, intended for a purpose exclusively national, in which, in the furniture provided for it, a mingled regard is due to the simplicity and purity of our institutions, and to the character of the people who are represented in it, the sum already appropriated, has proved altogether inadequate."[44]

At the request of a congressional committee, William Lee prepared a report that showed expenditures had already exceeded the original authorization by ten thousand dollars. "The single article of linen for a house of this extent and of such extensive entertainment would form a very heavy item," Lee offered as an example of the need for more funds. "In the mere furniture for the dining room, such as dinner and desert sets of china, cut glass, ornaments, etc., a large sum would likewise be requisite." In closing his report, he observed:

> In furnishing a government house, care should be taken to purchase substantial heavy furniture, which should always remain in place and form as it were a part of the house, such as could be handed down

through a succession of Presidents, suited to the dignity and character of the nation.

In the end, this sort of furniture is the most economical. The most respectable furniture to be seen in the government houses in Europe has been made for a century; although fashion has quite altered the forms of private furniture, the convenience, solidity, and usefulness of the public furniture has a decided preference.[45]

Finding Lee's presentation persuasive, Congress appropriated an additional thirty thousand dollars.[46]

Even with the new purchases, Monroe's own furniture was still required to fill the spacious house, and the president's finances were such that he welcomed the money he received for it. When the furnishings were all in place, the White House had never looked more impressive. The mansion was widely admired by numerous visitors during Monroe's presidency. Most guests were likely to describe the president as plain and unassuming, but they depicted the White House as elegant, splendidly furnished, even magnificent.

11

★★★★★

THE MONROE DOCTRINE

Few events during Monroe's administration had more far-reaching impact than the wave of revolutions spreading through Spain's colonies in Latin America. As former British colonials who set the example of rebelling against European monarchs, the people of the United States were highly sympathetic to the revolutionary movements. Monroe well represented these feelings, having, as secretary of state under Madison, early contemplated granting recognition to the newly proclaimed states.[1] At the same time, the interest of the United States in acquiring Florida from Spain and in settling the issue of the southern boundary of the Louisiana Purchase dictated a cautious policy—one that expressed sympathy for the revolutionists but maintained a position of neutrality.

From the outset of his administration, Monroe was consistent in pursuing this course. In the draft of a letter that Secretary of State Adams prepared to send to Manuel H. de Aquirre, the Argentine agent at Washington, in August 1818, the president approved passages defining the administration's position of "impartial neutrality." Adams indicated that the United States considered the conflict a civil war, in which both parties enjoyed equal rights.

> The Government of the United States have extended to the people of Buenos Ayres all the advantages of a friendly intercourse which are enjoyed by other nations and every mark of friendship and good will which were compatible with a fair neutrality. Besides all the benefits of a free Commerce and of national hospitality, and the admission of

their Vessels into our Ports, the Agents of Buenos Ayres have, though not recognized in form, the freest communication with The Administration, and have received every attention to their representations which could have been given to the accredited Officers of any Independent Power.[2]

Endorsing this statement of United States policy, Monroe also instructed Adams to insert a paragraph:

The President is of opinion that Buenos Ayres has afforded strong proof of its ability to maintain its Independence, a sentiment which, he is persuaded, will daily gain strength with the powers of Europe, especially should the same career of good fortune continue in its favor. In deciding the question respecting the Independence of Buenos Ayres many circumstances claim attention, in regard to the colonies as well as to the United States, which make it necessary that he should move with caution.[3]

In revealing such sympathy for the revolutions in South America, Monroe went further than his secretary of state believed proper. As he reviewed the draft of the president's annual message to Congress in 1820, Adams observed that "Mr. Monroe's messages have always had a long paragraph upon the civil war between Spain and her Colonies, and there is one in the present message." Adams thought such passages were unnecessary. "My objection to it is, that, our system being professedly neutrality, any avowal of partiality for the South Americans was inconsistent with it, and liable to raise doubts of our sincerity." Yet Adams recognized that the president included the paragraph to counteract Henry Clay's efforts in Congress to raise an opposition by insinuating that Monroe's administration was predisposed against the South Americans; and Adams admitted that Monroe's tactic had been successful.[4]

While refraining from actions that might jeopardize the ratification of the treaty with Spain, Monroe continued to express publicly his affinity with the revolutionary movements in South America, as he did in his annual message to Congress in December 1820. Yet even after the exchange of ratifications of the Spanish treaty in late February 1821, Monroe took no immediate steps to change the administration's policy, ignoring the resolutions Clay had pushed through the House of Representatives that supported recognition of the Latin American republics. In his annual address in December 1821, the president merely stated his hope that the Spanish government would accept the impossibility of suppressing the revolutions in Latin America and recognize the new republics.[5]

Finally in March 1822, Monroe informed Congress of his intention to formally acknowledge the newly declared, independent republics of Latin America and asked Congress to concur by making the necessary appropriations to carry the policy into effect. The president indicated that the decisive success of the Latin American provinces in establishing their independence, with "not the most remote prospect of their being deprived of it," entitled the republics to nationhood.[6] The House of Representatives promptly passed a resolution in favor of recognition by a vote of 167 to 1.[7]

Congressman Lewis Williams told his North Carolina constituents that some able politicians thought the action should have been taken sooner. Still, he praised the recognition of the new governments of Mexico and South America as "an event calculated to distinguish the present as an important era in the history of our country. . . . The republics of the new world will now form a counterpoise to the monarchies of the old . . . and give additional impulse to the cause of freedom in every country."[8]

While President Monroe was focusing his attention on Latin America and the reactions of Europe to the movements there, Secretary of State Adams had simultaneously been watching Russian activities on the Pacific coast of North America, contemplating British claims there and developing the concept that the continents of North and South America were closed to further colonization. While waiting for Spain to ratify the transcontinental treaty he had negotiated with Spanish minister Onís, Adams declared at a cabinet meeting in November 1819 that the world should "be familiarized with the idea of considering our proper dominion to be the continent of North America."[9]

By 1821 Adams was telling Stratford Canning, the British minister to the United States, that while the United States would not encroach on British territory north of the Canadian border, Britain should "leave the rest of this continent to us." Adams was soon sending the same message to the Russians. In September 1821 Tsar Alexander I issued an imperial decree prohibiting foreign vessels from coming within one hundred miles of Russian-claimed land along the Pacific coast of North America north of the fifty-first parallel. This was a bald extension of Russian claims, which had previously stopped at the fifty-fifth parallel. In July 1823, Adams told the Russian minister at Washington that the United States would contest the right of Russia to any territorial possession on the continent of North America and would "assume distinctly the principle that the American continents are no longer subjects for *any* new European colonial establishments."[10] A few days later Adams, with the president's approval, instructed the American minister at St. Petersburg that "there can, perhaps, be no better time for saying, frankly and explicitly, to the Russian Government, that the future peace of the world and the interest of Russia herself, cannot be promoted by Russian settlements upon any part of the American Continent." Adams added that "with the exception of British establishments north of the United States, the remainder of both the American continents must henceforth be left to the management of American hands."[11]

As Monroe proceeded with the recognition of Latin American independence, Adams told the British minister to the United States that "the whole system of modern colonization was an abuse of government, and it was time that it should come to an end."[12] In November 1823 Monroe asked the secretary of state for a memorandum on foreign affairs for his annual message to Congress, and Adams suggested that in his report of negotiations with Russia regarding the northwestern coast, Monroe assert: "as a principle in which the rights and interests of the people of the United States are equally involved, that the American Continents, by the free and independent condition which they have assumed and maintain, are henceforth not to be considered as subjects for future Colonization by any European Power."[13]

At the same time Monroe was preparing his annual address, the administration was deep in deliberation on another major question of American foreign policy relating to the American continents. On October 9, 1823, Secretary of State Adams received from London a large packet of dispatches from Richard Rush, the United States minister to Great Britain. These papers revealed that George Canning, the British foreign secretary, had confidentially proposed to Rush a joint declaration regarding the Spanish colonies in America.[14] In a private note of August 20, 1823, Canning summarized their recent conversation and informed Rush that his government considered the recovery of the colonies by Spain to be hopeless and British recognition of their independence to be only a matter of time and circumstances. Britain did not aim at the possession of any portion of the provinces, Canning declared, and would not view with indifference their transfer to any power. "If these opinions and feelings are, as I firmly believe them to be, common to your government with ours, why should we hesitate mutually to confide them to each other; and to declare them in the face of the world?"[15]

While Rush was conferring with the British foreign secretary and studying his confidential memorandum, a French army was in Spain suppressing opposition to the Spanish monarchy. By the end of August 1823, Ferdinand VII was restored to power. After quelling revolution in

Spain, would French forces join other continental powers to subdue rebels in Spanish colonies? Such intervention in Spanish America would not be acceptable to Great Britain, and Britain had the naval power to thwart it. Indeed, before Rush's dispatches could reach the United States, Canning took steps to ensure that France would not be a party to European intervention by pressuring the French ambassador in London, the Prince de Polignac, to pledge in a memorandum that his government had no intention of intervening in Spanish America.[16]

Monroe and Adams, of course, could not know that Canning had abandoned the idea of a joint declaration with the United States even before his proposal reached American shores. As they contemplated the American response and worked on the draft of the president's message to Congress, Monroe sent Rush's communiqués to Jefferson and Madison asking their advice.

To Madison, Monroe described Canning's confidential overture as a plan of "cooperation between our two governments, in opposing, by reciprocal declaration, in the first instance, a project which he thinks exists, of the holy alliance, to invade the South American States, as soon as the business with Spain is settled." Monroe indicated that he was "persuaded that we had better meet the proposition fully, and decisively," because if the Holy Alliance of Russia, Prussia, Austria, and France succeeded in restoring the Spanish colonies, "they would, in the next instance, invade us." In conclusion, "Ought we not then to encourage Great Britain in the course she seems disposed to pursue, and avail ourselves, of any service she can render, in a cause which though important to her, as to balance of power, commerce, etc., is vital to us, as to government."[17] To Jefferson, Monroe confided: "My own impression is that we ought to meet the proposal of the British government and to make it known, that we would view an interference on the part of the European powers, and especially an attack on the Colonies, by them, as an attack on ourselves, presuming that, if they succeeded with them, they would extend it to us." But recognizing the complexity of the issue and the risk involved, the president was eager to hear from his trusted predecessors.[18]

Both former presidents advised Monroe to agree to Canning's proposal. Jefferson confessed that he had expected Cuba someday to be part of the United States, but he was willing to forego that possibility in order to obtain a British commitment never to intervene in the affairs of the American continents. "Great Britain is the nation that can do us the most harm of any one, or all on earth; and with her on our side we need not fear the whole world," Jefferson wrote. He emphasized that "our first and fundamental maxim should be, never to entangle our-

selves in the broils of Europe. Our second, never to suffer Europe to in-
termeddle with cis-Atlantic affairs."[19] Madison applauded a collabora-
tive statement with Britain expressing disapprobation of any European
intervention in Latin America and further suggested proposing to Britain "even to join in some declaratory Act in behalf of the Greeks" in
their war for independence.[20]

If Monroe had received the replies from Jefferson and Madison
when he held the first major cabinet meeting to consider Canning's proposal on November 7, he did not reveal them. In the meantime, the issue had become further complicated by a note delivered to the secretary
of state on October 16 by Baron de Tuyll von Serooskerken, the Russian
minister to the United States. The note communicated that the Republic
of Colombia had appointed a minister to Russia and that, in response,
Tsar Alexander had decreed he would receive no minister from any
South American government. Tuyll also reported the tsar's satisfaction
that though the United States had recognized the independence of the
new governments, it had declared its intention to remain neutral. Tully
did not indicate what the Russian response would be if the United
States swerved from neutrality.[21]

Present at Monroe's cabinet meeting on November 7 were Secretary
of State Adams, Secretary of War Calhoun, and Secretary of the Navy
Southard. Treasury Secretary Crawford was in Virginia, seriously ill
from a stroke suffered in September—or from improper medication—
though the condition of the potential presidential candidate was a
closely guarded secret.[22] Attorney General Wirt also was not in the city.
For two-and-a-half hours, the president and his advisers debated Canning's proposal, but there was no final decision.

In order to obtain Britain's pledge not to seize territory in Latin
America, Calhoun was inclined to agree to a joint declaration even if it
meant keeping hands off of Cuba or Texas. Adams disagreed with the
secretary of war, arguing that while the United States had no intention
of taking Cuba or Texas, the people of either, or both, might someday
seek a union with the United States. Secretary of the Navy Southard
supported the secretary of state. The president was opposed to any
course that had the appearance of subordination to Great Britain and
suggested sending a special envoy to protest against any intervention
by the Holy Alliance. Adams questioned the wisdom of a joint declaration. Referring also to the need to respond to the note from Baron de
Tuyll, Adams said that "it would be more candid, as well as more dignified, to avow our principles explicitly to Russia and France, than to
come in as a cock-boat in the wake of the British man-of-war."[23]

Nearly a week later, the president was still unsettled in his own mind as to the answer to be given to Canning, and Adams noted his alarm, "far beyond anything that I could have conceived possible," that the Holy Alliance was about to restore all of South America to Spain. Adams blamed Calhoun for stimulating the panic.[24] In a private conference in the president's office on November 15, Monroe showed the secretary of state the two letters he had received from Jefferson and Madison. At one o'clock in the afternoon the cabinet assembled, with Wirt and Crawford again absent. Wirt was in Baltimore and Crawford, though now in Washington, had sent a note saying that he was not well enough to attend but hoped to be out in a few days. As it happened, Crawford would not attend another cabinet meeting until April 1824.[25] Despite Crawford's lack of participation, the cabinet discussions took place against the background of the approaching presidential election of 1824 in which three members of the cabinet—Adams, Calhoun, and Crawford—were prospective candidates.[26] With Crawford out, the major sparring in the cabinet was between Adams and Calhoun.

In the cabinet deliberations, Adams saw further evidence that Calhoun was responsible for the president's despondency. "Calhoun is perfectly moon-struck by the surrender of Cadiz, and says the Holy Allies, with ten thousand men, will restore all Mexico and all South America to the Spanish dominion," Adams recorded in his diary. "I no more believe that the Holy Allies will restore Spanish dominion upon the American continent," Adams added, "than that the Chimborazo [a mountain peak in Ecuador] will sink beneath the ocean."[27]

On November 16 two more dispatches arrived from Rush in London. When Monroe stopped by the State Department the following morning, he seemed less worried to Adams. After reading Rush's reports, Monroe had concluded that Canning's alarm had dissipated and that the British minister's motivations had changed. He speculated that some inducement had been presented to Canning, after the triumph of the French in Spain, to quiet his apprehension. Adams suspected that Canning's earlier panic was affected to induce the United States to commit itself not to acquire Cuba.[28]

As Adams drafted instructions to Rush, he submitted them to Monroe for review, and the president suggested various amendments. At a four-hour cabinet meeting on November 21, Adams's instructions, Monroe's amendments, and Adams's proposed amendments to the amendments were discussed at length. "The President did not insist upon any of his amendments which were not admitted by general consent," Adams recorded, "and the final paper, though considerably varied from my original draft, will be conformable to my own views."[29]

At the meeting Adams also brought up the subject of the diplomatic note he was preparing to deliver to Baron de Tuyll. He planned to assert in a moderate and conciliatory manner, yet with firmness and determination, the principles on which the United States was founded. "And, while disclaiming all intention of attempting to propagate them by force, and all interference with the political affairs of Europe, to declare our expectation and hope that the European powers will equally abstain from the attempt to spread their principles in the American hemisphere, or to subjugate by force any part of these continents to their will."[30]

After approving the secretary of state's ideas, the president turned to the draft of his annual message to Congress. As he read his notes, members of the cabinet learned for the first time that the president intended to make a general declaration of principles regarding Latin America. Adams and other members of the administration had been thinking only in terms of diplomatic notes to Great Britain and to Russia.[31] Overall, Adams thought the tone of Monroe's draft too alarmist and too censorious in reference to the French invasion of Spain. It also contained an acknowledgement of Greek independence and recommended to Congress an appropriation for sending a minister to the new nation. Calhoun approved all of this; Adams urged the president to reconsider both the tone and the content. After further debate, Monroe said that he would draw up two drafts for consideration, presenting each view.[32]

The next day Adams called on the president privately to urge him "to abstain from everything in his message which the Holy Allies could make a pretext for construing into aggression upon them." In arguing his case, Adams appealed to Monroe to think about the legacy of his presidency. To deliver the government into the hands of his successor "at peace and amity with all the world" would ensure that Monroe's administration would be remembered "as the golden age of this republic," Adams suggested. "The ground that I wish to take," he concluded, "is that of earnest remonstrance against the interference of the European powers by force with South America, but to disclaim all interference on our part with Europe; to make an American cause, and adhere inflexibly to that."[33] Two days later when Adams stopped by the president's office, Monroe read him the revised paragraphs for his annual message. Adams was pleased to find them in accord with the views he had pressed at the last cabinet meeting and only hoped that the president would hold to the changes.[34] He did so, and the cabinet turned its attention to the note Adams was to deliver to the Russian minister.

At a meeting on November 25, Adams presented the draft of his note. "The paper itself was drawn to correspond exactly with a paragraph of the President's message which he had read to me yesterday," Adams recorded in his diary, while also observing that it conformed precisely with his own sentiments. Adams saw the note as being an answer to both Russia and Great Britain and also a broad statement of American policy, which he described as:

> essentially republican—maintaining its own independence, and respecting that of others; essentially pacific—studiously avoiding all involvement in the combinations of European politics, cultivating peace and friendship with the most absolute monarchies . . . but declaring that, having recognized the independence of the South American States, we could not see with indifference any attempts by European powers by forcible interposition either to restore the Spanish dominion on the American Continents or to introduce monarchical principles into those countries, or to transfer any portion of the ancient or present American possessions of Spain to any other European power.[35]

After Adams read his paper to the cabinet, a long and inconclusive debate ensued, Calhoun and Wirt being the principal discoursers. At five o'clock the president adjourned the meeting until the next afternoon.[36]

In resuming the discussion the following day, Monroe asked Adams to read a statement reviewing what had passed between the secretary of state and the Russian minister since October 16 and Adams's proposed response. "The president then read the draft of the corresponding paragraph for his message to Congress," Adams reported, "and asked whether it should form part of the message." Adams said his mind was made up that the United States should commit itself against the Holy Alliance by taking the proposed stance in relation to South America. William Wirt insisted that the country would not support the government in a war for the independence of South America. Calhoun responded that the principal object was to detach Britain definitively from the Holy Alliance; though there was always the possibility that the Holy Alliance would employ force, the United States should hold its ground even if it meant war. He was thus in favor of including the paragraph in the president's address. After Wirt and Southard found fault with many details in Adams's paper, the president held it for final determination the next day.[37]

In the morning Adams received a note from the president advising him to omit from his missive to Baron de Tuyll all paragraphs to which objections had been made in the cabinet. The secretary of state willingly gave up all parts except the one that he regarded as the heart of his paper and that Wirt had called "a hornet of a paragraph" in the cabinet debate.[38] Immediately following an opening statement that the government of the United States was republican, the disputed paragraph affirmed:

> The principles of this form of Polity are: 1 that the Institution of Government, to be lawful, must be pacific, that is founded upon the consent, and by the agreement of those who are governed; and 2 that each Nation is exclusively the judge of the Government best suited to itself, and that no Nation, can justly interfere by force to impose a different Government upon it. The first of these principles may be designated, as the principle of *Liberty*—the second as the principle of National *Independence*—They are both Principles of *Peace* and of Good Will to Man.[39]

Going directly to the president's office to plead his case to retain this paragraph, Adams persuaded Monroe to reconsider it, and in the course of the day the president notified Adams of his consent to its reinsertion. However, Monroe based his compliance on the importance that Adams attached to the declaration and expressed "apprehension that the paragraph of principles contained a *direct* attack upon the Holy Allies, by a statement of principles which they had violated."[40] The president indicated that "the illustration of our principles, is one thing; the doing it, in such a form, bearing directly, on what has passed, and which is avoided in the message, is another."[41] Still, he was averse to excluding anything that Adams deemed so material. With such a reluctant approval from the president, Adams omitted the paragraph when he read the note to Baron de Tuyll soon after receiving the president's memorandum.[42]

In 1902, Worthington C. Ford published the text of the document showing the deleted passages and suggested that Monroe's objection to Adams's paragraph revealed "the timidity of the President." This early student of the Monroe Doctrine opined that "we may wonder at the extreme susceptibility of the President in the matter."[43] Americans in the late twentieth century may perhaps judge Monroe's restraint in lauding the nation's virtues to the rest of the world, not as timidity, but as judicious maturity.

The note that Adams presented to the Russian minister concluded with the following paragraph:

> That the United States of America, and their Government, could not see with indifference, the forcible interposition of any European Power, other than Spain, either to restore the dominion of Spain over her emancipated Colonies in America, or to establish Monarchical

Governments in those Countries, or to transfer any of the possessions heretofore or yet subject to Spain in the American Hemisphere, to any other European Power.[44]

This was in accordance with what Monroe would announce publicly in his 1823 message to Congress, except for the addition of what would come to be called the "no-transfer principle." That principle did not originate with Adams but had been asserted in a joint resolution of Congress in 1811. After President Madison annexed West Florida—between the Mississippi River and the Perdido River—to the United States by presidential proclamation in 1810, Congress moved to prevent occupation of Florida east of the Perdido by any country other than Spain.[45] In secret session, Congress in January 1811 passed a resolution:

Taking into view the peculiar situation of Spain, and of her American provinces; and considering the influence which the destiny of the territory adjoining the southern border of the United States may have upon their security, tranquillity, and commerce: Therefore,
Resolved by the Senate and House of Representatives of the United States of America, in Congress assembled, That the United States, under the peculiar circumstances of the existing crisis, cannot, without serious inquietude, see any part of the said territory pass into the hands of any foreign power . . . .[46]

Less than three months after this resolve was adopted, James Monroe had joined Madison's cabinet as secretary of state. The declaration of 1811 applied only to territory contiguous to the United States, but after Monroe's message to Congress in 1823, it would be given wider application. The no-transfer principle would become a corollary to the Monroe Doctrine.

President Monroe's seventh annual message was read to both houses of Congress on December 2, 1823. After brief introductory remarks, Monroe turned to a review of foreign affairs. On the subject of negotiations with Russia over the northwestern coast of North America, he reported that it had been judged proper to assert "as a principle in which the rights and interests of the United States are involved, that the American continents, by the free and independent condition which they have assumed and maintain, are henceforth not to be considered as subjects for future colonization by any European powers."[47] These were almost the exact words that Adams had employed in the memorandum he had prepared for the president in response to Monroe's request for suggestions for his annual message to Congress.[48]

Near the end of his address Monroe returned to foreign relations.

He expressed a fervent hope that the Greeks would succeed in their "heroic struggle" to become again an independent nation. He also indicated his disappointment over the course of events in Spain and Portugal. Although Americans cherished "sentiments the most friendly in favor of liberty and happiness of their fellow-men on that side of the Atlantic," the United States had never taken part in the wars of European powers over continental disputes, nor was it American policy to do so. It was only when American rights were menaced that the United States made preparations for defense.

> With the movements in this hemisphere we are of necessity more immediately connected, and by causes which must be obvious to all enlightened and impartial observers. The political system of the allied powers is essentially different in this respect from that of America. . . . We owe, it therefore, to candor and to the amicable relations existing between the United States and those powers to declare that we should consider any attempt on their part to extend their system to any portion of this hemisphere as dangerous to our peace and safety. With the existing colonies or dependencies of any European power we have not interfered and shall not interfere. But with the Governments who have declared their independence and maintained it, and whose independence we have, on great consideration and on just principles, acknowledged, we could not view any interposition for the purpose of oppressing them, or controlling in any other manner their destiny, by any European power in any other light than as the manifestation of an unfriendly disposition toward the United States.[49]

For the most part, Monroe's message was warmly received in the United States. "Its general character is approved of at Washington, and from the prints appears to give general satisfaction," Congressman Benjamin W. Crowninshield wrote from the capital.[50] At the same time, some members of Congress were disgruntled that the president had not proposed stronger action in support of Greek independence. Noting that the president had taken "pretty high ground as to *this Continent,* and is afraid of the appearance of interfering in the concerns of the *other continent* also," Daniel Webster disagreed with Monroe's reasoning. "I think we have as much Community with the Greeks, as with the inhabitants of the Andes, and the dwellers on the borders of the Vermilion Sea," he wrote privately.[51] While Webster continued to promote the Greek cause in Congress, Monroe did not alter the administration's course.

On the foreign front, Henry Addington, the British minister to the

United States, reported to George Canning in London that Monroe's message was being acclaimed throughout the country.

> The explicit and manly tone, especially, with which the President has treated the subject of European interference in the affairs of this Hemisphere with a view to the subjugation of those territories which have emancipated themselves from European domination, has evidently found in every bosom a chord which vibrates in strict unison with the sentiments so conveyed. They have been echoed from one end of the union to the other. It would indeed be difficult, in a country composed of elements so various, and liable on all subjects to opinions so conflicting, to find a more perfect unanimity than has been displayed on every side on this particular point.[52]

The letters that President Monroe was receiving confirmed the British diplomat's assessment. From Frankfort, Kentucky, where copies of the president's message had arrived while the legislature was in session, John J. Crittenden informed Monroe that he had "never witnessed the publication of any state paper that was attended with so universal and so enthusiastic an expression of approbation and applause. . . . It has given us a more dignified and heroic attitude. It has made us the protector of the free governments of South America—And has arrayed us boldly against any attempt on the part of the Holy Alliance to extend to this Hemisphere that despotism and slavery which it has fastened upon Europe. Indeed, Sir, you have made me prouder of my country than ever I was before."[53] Another Kentucky correspondent told the president, "I have not heard a single dissentient to the principle expressed in it, nor have I heard of one."[54] Meanwhile, Governor John Adair forwarded to the president a copy of approbatory resolutions passed by the Kentucky legislature and sanctioned by the governor.[55]

The General Assembly of Pennsylvania also paid tribute in a resolution:

> That the magnanimous declaration of the President of the United States in defence of the cause of Liberty in this Western Hemisphere meets the entire approbation of the General Assembly of this Commonwealth. That whilst the Allied Sovereigns have manifested a determination that no free government shall exist in the Eastern Hemisphere it has afforded us the highest gratification to observe the President of the United States, expressing the sentiments of millions of freemen, proclaiming to the world that any attempt on the part of the Allied Sovereigns of Europe to extend their political systems to any portion of these Continents of America or in any other manner to

interfere in their internal concerns would be considered as dangerous to the peace and safety of the United States.[56]

Monroe, who received a copy of this resolution, could take satisfaction in such accolades, but he could not have been unaware of the reservations of some members of Congress. Willie P. Mangum, representative from North Carolina, commented that the president's message had "created some sensation" in Washington, but he "doubted exceedingly whether Congress will be found prepared to sustain the views of the Executive if it shall become necessary to try the question."[57]

Monroe's declarations on Spanish colonialism met with wide appreciation in the London press, but Canning responded by divulging the Polignac memorandum to the House of Commons to show that Britain had acted on the South American problem nearly two months before Monroe's pronouncement. In Russia, the official instructions to Baron de Tuyll declared that Monroe's statements merited "the most profound contempt," but the Russian minister was to preserve a passive attitude and remain silent. Austria's Metternich privately denounced Monroe's declaration as "a new act of revolt, more unprovoked, fully as audacious, and no less dangerous" than the Revolution of 1776, but he issued no public protest.[58]

Paris reaction was mixed. The ministerial press was critical; the opposition press, enthusiastic. Old friends of the United States were warm in their praise. Lafayette wrote to Monroe that he was "delighted with your message, and so will be every liberal mind in Europe and South America." In South America, where the position of the United States was widely regarded as less important than that of Great Britain, reaction to Monroe's message was restrained, though not unappreciative.[59]

Whatever its reception, neither Monroe nor Adams could claim full credit for a policy that had been evolving for some years. At the same time, the response of the United States to Canning's initiative was not predetermined by the past. Both Jefferson and Madison advised fuller cooperation with Great Britain than Monroe may have implied when he told them he was inclined "to meet" Canning's proposal. From the outset Monroe made clear his opposition to any course that had the appearance of subordination to Great Britain. After he sent Jefferson a copy of his message to Congress, Monroe told him:

> We certainly meet, in full extent, the proposition of Mr. Canning, and in the mode to give it the greatest effect. If his government makes a similar declaration the project will, it may be presumed, be abandoned. By taking the step here, it is done in a manner more concilia-

tory with, and respectful to Russia, and the other powers, than if taken in England, and as it is thought more credit to our government. . . . Had we moved in England, it is probable, that it would have been inferred that we acted under her influence, and at her instigation, and thus have lost credit as well with our Southern neighbours, as with the Allied powers.[60]

In sending Madison a copy of his message, Monroe noted that he had "concurred fully in the sentiments, expressed by you, and Mr. Jefferson, in regard to the attitude to be assumed, at the present interesting crisis . . . respecting the view of the allied powers towards South America."[61] Writing at greater length several weeks later, Monroe explained that the course taken was based on the idea that announcement of policy from Washington rather than from London "would place us on more independent and honorable ground, as a nation, . . . and with better effect with our southern neighbours, as well as with Russia and other allied powers. Had we moved first in London," he argued, "we might have appeared to take the course suggested there, as a secondary party, which by Great Britain would have had the principal credit with our neighbours."[62]

That Monroe proceeded cautiously to his final decision is evident from the prolonged cabinet meetings at which the replies to both Great Britain and Russia were debated. The influence of the secretary of state on the final outcome was significant, but it was Monroe who conducted the unrestrained cabinet deliberations and drafted—and redrafted—his message to Congress until he found a policy that he and his cabinet could support. While Adams influenced the content, it was Monroe who decided to announce the policy in his message to Congress, thus proclaiming it to the world. In view of the memorandum that Canning had pressured Polignac to sign, the immediate impact of the message abroad was negligible, but in the course of time the Monroe Doctrine would become the most lasting legacy of the presidency of James Monroe.

12

DOMESTIC CONCERNS

In his second inaugural address Monroe praised an energetic government, but no national consensus existed on the extent of federal powers. The president and Congress differed especially on the constitutional authority of Congress regarding internal improvements. Monroe had addressed the issue in his first annual message of 1817, and it continued to demand his attention throughout his two terms as president. Still, Monroe and Congress never reached agreement on the question. When Congress failed to act on his recommendation for a constitutional amendment, Monroe began drafting a paper on internal improvements and the need for such an amendment. At a cabinet meeting in December 1819, he stunned his colleagues by reading the treatise, which Adams described as long enough for two messages to Congress. The president proposed to confront the issue in his annual message of 1819 but was persuaded by his cabinet to omit it.[1]

Early in Monroe's second term, Congress passed a bill for the repair of the national road from Cumberland, Maryland, to Wheeling, Virginia, and for the establishment of toll gates and the collection of tolls.[2] Monroe promptly vetoed the measure, "under a conviction that Congress do not possess the power under the Constitution to pass such a law." He insisted that "a power to establish turnpikes with gates and tolls, and to enforce the collection of tolls by penalties, implies a power to adopt and execute a complete system of internal improvement."[3] He attached to his veto message a copy of the treatise that he had earlier composed.[4]

At the opening of the next Congress in December 1822, Monroe reiterated his support for a constitutional amendment. However, he added that should Congress reject that course, it had the authority to provide the funds to repair roads already built. "Surely if they had the right to appropriate money to make the road they have the right to appropriate it to preserve the road from ruin," he declared. The right of appropriation was distinct from "the right of jurisdiction and sovereignty over the territory in question."[5]

Monroe sent copies of the printed document containing his views on internal improvements to friends throughout the country, among them Justice Joseph Story and Chief Justice John Marshall. In thanking him for the favor, Story replied that he did not feel at liberty to express any opinion on the constitutional question because it might come before the Supreme Court.[6] Marshall, on the other hand, asserted that though intelligent men would differ on the issue, all would admit that the president's views were profound and that he had thought deeply on the subject. "To me they appear to be most generally just." He closed his note by observing: "A general power over internal improvement, if to be exercised by the Union, would certainly be cumbersome to the government, and of no utility to the people. But, to the extent you recommend, it would be productive of no mischief, and of great good. I despair however of the adoption of such a measure."[7]

Monroe repeated his position on internal improvements in his annual message of 1823 and proposed that Congress authorize the president to enter into arrangements with states through which the Cumberland Road passed to establish tolls to pay for repairs.[8] The House Committee on Roads and Canals reported its opinion that Congress already had complete power to set tolls on the Cumberland Road for the purpose of defraying the cost of future repairs. "This right in Congress has been solemnly declared by both branches of the Legislature on several occasions, and in particular by the passage of a bill for the erection of toll-gates on this road."[9]

Despite his restrictive view of congressional power in the area of internal improvements, Monroe in his 1823 message recommended funding for canals to connect Atlantic Coast rivers with the western country. "Congress possess the right to appropriate money for such a national object (the jurisdiction remaining to the states through which the canal would pass)," the president declared.[10] As the Erie Canal, under construction by the state of New York, neared completion, public support for canal building was mounting, and most members of Congress concurred. Before leaving office, Monroe would sign a bill authorizing the expenditure of $300,000 for the purchase of fifteen hundred shares of stock in the Chesapeake and Delaware Canal Company.[11]

While a majority in Congress rejected Monroe's interpretation of limited congressional authority over internal improvements, a minority was even more rigid than the president. They could do little more, however, than delay action. In 1824 Congress passed—and the president signed—the general survey bill, appropriating thirty thousand dollars to initiate surveys and procure estimates of roads and canals required for national military, commercial, or postal purposes.[12] A bill to extend the Cumberland Road from Wheeling, Virginia, to Zanesville, Ohio, with projected extensions westward to the Mississippi River, was reported in the House of Representatives in December 1823 but not acted on.[13] In the next session $150,000 was allocated for the construction of a road from Wheeling to Zanesville and signed by the president on his last day in office.[14] As Monroe's administration came to a close, Congressman George Tucker of Virginia complained to his constituents that "it has been decided that congress has the constitutional power of making roads and canals; and the majorities of both houses have been too frequent and too large to make a change of opinion probable."[15]

In the message of 1823 in which Monroe indicated his support for canal building, he also recommended "a review of the tariff for the purpose of affording such additional protection to those articles which we are prepared to manufacture, or which are more immediately connected with the defense and independence of the country."[16] After many long speeches, much debate, and a close vote of 107 to 102 in the House, a more protective tariff bill passed in both chambers and was signed by the president in May 1824.[17]

In 1824 the presidential election dominated the American scene as had no election since 1800. The contest indeed had been under way from almost the outset of Monroe's second term. Within Monroe's cabinet, the presidential aspirations of Crawford, Calhoun, and Adams—evident since the beginning of Monroe's presidency—intensified as his second administration drew to a close. In Congress Henry Clay's presidential ambitions likewise continued unabated. Monroe let it be known early on that he would follow the example of his predecessors and decline reelection to a third term.[18]

With attacks on the congressional nominating caucus spreading throughout the country, the competition for the presidency became more open and attracted increasing public attention. At the beginning of 1824, Calhoun was optimistic about his candidacy, but as political activity accelerated, he failed to arouse broad public support. While not withdrawing from the race, the secretary of war began to think in terms of the vice-presidency.[19] Despite Crawford's ill health—mainly kept secret—Crawford remained a contender. Meanwhile, John Quincy Adams retained solid backing in New England; and General Andrew Jackson, then a senator from Tennessee, emerged as an increasingly popular favorite. While the election campaign raged in the various states, the city of Washington was the scene of much political maneuvering. Monroe's last year as president was set against the backdrop of the most contested presidential election since Jefferson's defeat of John Adams in 1800.

"The Presidential question is here a topic of frequent, I might almost say, constant conversation," North Carolina Congressman Willie P. Mangum wrote from the capital in December 1823. "The principal movements of the members here is in relation to the next presidency—there is considerable effort and canvassing on that subject."[20] Mangum was soon reporting that "members of Congress instead of attending to those avocations exclusively for which they are elected, bestow in many instances both night and day upon intrigues connected with the subject."[21]

Meanwhile, a new congressman from Tennessee believed that Jackson was gaining support daily. "The General is calm, dignified, and makes as polished a bow as any man I have ever seen at court," Sam Houston noted. "But he has not forgot his Tennessee notions," he insisted, explaining that though Senator Jackson had been in Washington ten or twelve days, he had not yet visited the House chamber. "He will not do any thing out of his fixed course. He is much courted by the Great as well as the sovereign folks."[22]

After Monroe's New Year's reception at the White House in 1824, the Adamses opened the winter season with a large ball on January 8, the anniversary of General Jackson's victory at the battle of New Orleans. "There was an immense crowd of gentlemen and ladies, bowing and nodding at each other," Congressman Duncan McArthur wrote to his wife. "General Jackson attended in person, and received the nod of hundreds."[23] Louisa Kalisky, a young German visitor to the city, thought, "Mr. Adams is acting in a very diplomatic manner, thus to show honor to his rival before the world, for they certainly are rivals at this moment, for the Presidential chair will be vacated this year and the elections are beginning already."[24] The seventeen-year-old Miss Kalisky, attending a reception at the president's later in the month, found it very interesting to observe the differences among the various candidates for the presidency.

Adams receives formally in one saloon, Jackson in another and if the latter had not a very ordinary wife who smokes with him, he could certainly be nominated this time, but the ladies do not like to bow down to his wife, and they have great influence on the elections here. They would however far prefer to elect Mr. Clay another candidate, and a great ladies man. Jackson has a charming open hearted character, and great elegance of speech, says something agreeable to every one. Adams is silent and cold and has a disagreeable face but his wife is much beloved.[25]

At the time Miss Kalisky recorded these remarks, there was uncertainty in Washington as to whether or not a congressional nominating caucus would convene. The caucus system had been widely and vigorously criticized. "It is time to put an end to *Caucuses*," said Daniel Webster. "They make great men little, and little men great. *The true source of power is the People*."[26] A national nominating convention had been proposed to replace the caucus, but there was no political party organization capable of holding such a convention.

On February 6, 1824, an announcement signed by eleven members of Congress, all supporters of Crawford, issued a call for a caucus to meet on February 14.[27] An opposing group of 24 members published a declaration that 181 of the 261 members of both houses had given assurances that they would not attend, deeming it "inexpedient under existing circumstances" to hold the caucus.[28] On the evening of February 14, a packed gallery looked down on numerous empty seats on the floor of the House of Representatives, where only sixty-six members of Congress had assembled. The meeting, nevertheless, proceeded to vote. Crawford received 64 votes; Adams, 2; Jackson, 1; and Nathaniel Macon, 1. The tally included two votes cast by proxy.[29] The vote guaranteed that the congressional nominating caucus would remain an issue throughout the campaign of 1824, but the demise of the caucus was recorded with finality.

While Jackson was charming admirers in the drawing rooms of Washington, he was arousing strong feelings of alarm among others. Congressman Lewis Williams of North Carolina, writing in March 1824, pictured a potential despot whose popularity rested only on his military fame. "If Jackson is chosen," he wrote, "the government will be endangered or destroyed. . . . The peace of the country will be sacrificed and we shall be involved in wars, in debts, and Taxes, and finally perhaps in slavery all because Jackson won the battle at New Orleans." George Washington became president not because of his military fame but because of his civil virtue, Williams insisted. "Shall Jackson then with less military fame and no civil virtues at all be elected? . . . He has been a Tyrant in every situation in which he has been placed." Closing an expansive letter, Williams confided, "I do most conscientiously believe if Jackson is elected President that our government will not last a dozen years; that we shall be involved in war speedily and that a despotism will arise out of it."[30]

With such concerns diverting the attention of members of Congress away from Monroe's administration and with his own cabinet deeply involved in the competition, Monroe was careful to display no public or private preference for any of the candidates. While in Virginia during the summer of 1823, the president purposely avoided visiting James Barbour because Crawford was there, even though Crawford was ill. And he declined to attend the ball that Adams hosted in January 1824 to celebrate the victory at New Orleans, fearing that "if he should depart from his rule of not visiting at private homes, it might be thought he was countenancing one of the candidates for the next Presidency."[31] Throughout the election year Monroe maintained his neutrality in the contest for his successor.

Though he distanced himself from the election, Monroe's administration was impeded by the competition for the presidency. One of Monroe's greatest disappointments was his failure to gain Senate approval of a treaty with Great Britain to suppress the international slave trade. Negotiated by Richard Rush, the American minister in London, the treaty took the approach of condemning the slave trade as piracy, thus avoiding the issue of the right to search ships. Although Secretary of State Adams opposed the departure from the American position on the right of search, all members of the cabinet approved of Monroe's submission of the treaty to the Senate, which he did on April 30, 1824. Since the House of Representatives in 1823 had unanimously adopted resolutions in 1823 condemning the slave trade as piracy, the president expected prompt ratification by the Senate. Election politics, however, intervened, and the Senate approved only an amended treaty that limited the right of search to the coastal waters of Africa. As Monroe feared, the amendment was rejected in London and the agreement was lost, along with all hope for a general rapprochement with Great Britain.[32]

The visit to America by the Marquis de Lafayette diverted national attention from both the election campaign and Monroe's administration. Arriving in New York harbor on August 15, 1824, Lafayette began what would become a year-long celebration and farewell tour of the United States. In the course of his travels he would visit all twenty-four states and be greeted with elaborate pageantry and festivities wherever he went.[33]

Lafayette had been invited by Congress rather than by the president, and Monroe—concerned about the reactions of the European regimes of the Holy Alliance—was careful to maintain the distinction that this was not an official state visit. Lafayette, likewise well aware that he was a symbol of liberalism in conservative-dominated Europe, was circumspect in his own actions. He refused Congress's offer to send a United States naval vessel to transport him to America, and after arriving in New York, he did not proceed immediately to Washington. His reception in New York and everywhere he traveled was enthusiastic, warm, and generous, as local communities embraced the revolutionary hero as "the Nation's Guest."[34]

Pleased with his old friend's conduct and the public's welcome, Monroe greeted Lafayette warmly but unofficially when he arrived in Washington in October on his way to Yorktown for the anniversary celebration of the British surrender on the nineteenth. City officials had suggested that the president and the officers of the government join them in a public procession to meet Lafayette at the boundary of the District of Columbia. Monroe, however, objected to the plan, and city officials agreed to meet the general and conduct him to the Capitol, where he would be officially welcomed. The procession would then continue to the President's House, where the distinguished visitor would be privately greeted by the president, members of the cabinet, and other officers of the government.[35]

Despite the absence of public display at the White House, the president's welcome of Lafayette was sincere, and he assured the general that a plate would always be set for him at the White House dinner table.[36] As a nineteen-year-old officer, Monroe had been on the battlefield at Brandywine in 1777 when twenty-year-old major general Lafayette had been wounded in his first engagement in America.[37] Through the years, they had remained fast friends. Now the sixty-six-year-old president would observe of Lafayette that "time has produced less waste of his form . . . than it does on most men, and none on his mind."[38]

Monroe applauded the general's itinerary. "He did well by commencing with our constituents, and coming from them to the government," Monroe wrote to Madison. "It shows that the sentiment in favor of our republican principles is universal, and that he is respected and beloved by all for his devotion to those principles." The administration's policy was to offer Lafayette all possible courtesies but "to let the public demonstrations be those of our constituents only," Monroe explained. "By this the government is less compromitted with the holy alliance, with whom also the effect will be more imposing."[39] Presenting the argument to Jefferson, Monroe concluded that "the holy Alliance, and all the governments of Europe, must therefore look to us, as an united people, devoted to the principles of our revolution and of free republican government."[40]

After participating in the commemoration at Yorktown, Lafayette visited Jefferson at Monticello and Madison at Montpelier, and he was guest of honor at a dinner in the dome room of the still-unfinished Rotunda of the University of Virginia. In his last appearance at a public dinner, Jefferson sat between Lafayette and Madison. After a toast was raised to Lafayette, Jefferson himself was toasted as the founder of the university. Monroe had expected to be present for the occasion, but Lafayette's arrival in Albemarle County was delayed, and the president had to return to Washington to prepare for the convening of Congress. As he departed for the capital, Monroe confided to Jefferson, "I shall be heartily rejoiced when the term of my service expires, and I may return home in peace with my family, on whom, and especially Mrs. Monroe, the burdens and cares of my long public service, have borne too heavily."[41]

Sending his final annual message to Congress on December 7, 1824, President Monroe pictured a flourishing country where neither foreign nor domestic crises threatened the growth and prosperity of the young nation. He reported a reduction of the national debt from over $123 million to $86 million during his presidency and predicted that the entire debt could be discharged within ten years. In his first message eight years earlier, Monroe had perceived the nation largely in relation to Europe and South America, but in 1824, Monroe's horizon, like that of many of his countrymen, was more expansive. He proposed the establishment of a military post at the mouth of the Columbia River and recommended that the Pacific station naval squadron be maintained. "On the Pacific our commerce has much increased," he said, "and on that coast, as well as on that sea, the United States have many important interests which require attention and protection."[42]

Despite the earlier crisis over Missouri that had threatened the Union, Monroe expressed high optimism for the future and did not mention the issue of slavery. "There is no object which as a people we can desire which we do not possess or which is not within our reach," he insisted. "Blessed with governments the happiest which the world ever knew, with no distinct orders in society or divided interests in any portion of the vast territory over which their dominion extends, we have every motive to cling together which can animate a virtuous and enlightened people."[43]

In noting the expansion of the United States from thirteen to twenty-four states—five of the new states having been admitted during his presidency—the president appealed to Congress to develop some well-designed plan to rescue the Indians from the relentless westward expansion. He suggested that the land between the existing states and territories and the Rocky Mountains be divided into districts, by previous agreement of the tribes living there, and that civil governments be established in each "with schools for every branch of instruction in literature and the arts of civilized life." His hope was that all tribes within the limits of the United States might gradually be drawn to this region. The plan would necessitate considerable expense, he admitted, but only such a civilizing process could save the Indians from extinction.[44]

During his final year in office, Indian affairs had increasingly occupied the president's attention. Responding to mounting pressures from Georgia to empty the Indian lands in that state, Monroe sent a special message to Congress in March 1824. With it he transmitted papers relating to the compact between the United States and Georgia in 1802 by which the United States was committed to the removal of Indian tribes from that state. Monroe professed the inability of the executive to make any further progress in the expulsion of the Cherokees from Georgia without the special sanction of Congress. Reviewing his own actions and those of his predecessors in carrying out the compact with Georgia, he stated that he had been motivated by the hope that the relocation of the tribes west of the Mississippi River would promote "their improvement in civilization, their security and happiness." Such arguments had been pressed on the Cherokee chiefs who had come to Washington in January 1824 to plead their case, but the president reported their unqualified refusal to sell their lands in Georgia or to accept any exchange of lands. He concluded that at the present time the Cherokees could be removed only by force, to which the power of the executive was incompetent. Monroe also asserted that, in his opinion,

> the Indian title was not affected in the slightest circumstance by the compact with Georgia, and that there is no obligation on the United States to remove the Indians by force. The express stipulation of the compact that their title should be extinguished at the expense of the United States when it may be done *peacefully* and on *reasonable* conditions is a full proof that it was the clear and distinct understanding of both parties to it that the Indians had a right to the territory, in the

disposal of which they were to be regarded as free agents. An attempt to remove them by force would, in my opinion, be unjust.[45]

At the same time, Monroe believed that it would enhance the well-being of Indian tribes if they could be prevailed upon to move to the west and north of the states and territories of the United States on lands procured for them in exchange for those on which they then resided.[46] Meanwhile, the clamor from Georgia intensified. An angry letter from Georgia members of Congress charged the president with failing to execute the 1802 compact relating to the Cherokee lands. Monroe exclaimed to Jefferson that "such a [letter] I never received either in my public or private character."[47] Although he included the letter among other documents sent to Congress with his special March message, he did so without mentioning it.[48]

In his annual address to Congress in December 1824, Monroe reported that relations with the Indian tribes within the limits of the United States had not materially changed. He contended that many tribes had made "great progress in the arts of civilized life" and credited "the humane and persevering policy of the Government" for the advancements. Pointing to the establishment of thirty-two schools with 916 students, Monroe noted their instruction "in several branches of literature, and likewise in agriculture and the ordinary arts of life."[49]

Despite this optimistic summary, in another special message in late January 1825, Monroe recommended the removal of all the Indians east of the Mississippi River to a settlement west of Missouri and the Arkansas Territory. "Experience has clearly demonstrated that, in their present state, it is impossible to incorporate them in such masses, in any form whatever, into our system," he said. Without some change in policy, "their degradation and extermination will be inevitable."[50] As Congressman Joseph Gist explained to his South Carolina constituents, "It is not contemplated to force them to remove, but to induce them friendly to exchange their lands on the east, for the west of the river Mississippi."[51] With Monroe's presidency and the Eighteenth Congress both rapidly coming to an end, no action resulted from the president's message.

13

★ ★ ★ ★ ★

CLOSING A PRESIDENCY

Lafayette was in Washington when Monroe sent his last annual message to Congress in December 1824. Despite the attention the distinguished visitor attracted, Virginia Congressman William C. Rives sensed that he was more anonymous in the capital than elsewhere on his travels. Rives mused that perhaps Lafayette did not receive exclusive and undivided notice because the heads of departments, candidates for the presidency, and foreign ministers were "alike objects of curiosity" to be seen "amid the multitude of luminaries which blaze in the firmament of Washington."[1] Only one star, however, glowed when Congress welcomed Lafayette at a grand reception in the House of Representatives on December 10, 1824, three days after Monroe's address was read to Congress. Describing the event to his wife, Rives confessed that he sincerely believed it to be "the most august and impressive scene that the world has ever witnessed," In his detailed account of Lafayette's reception, the congressman wrote:

> He was conducted into the Hall by a committee of twenty-four members, one from each state. In the meantime, the Senate of the U.S. had, by invitation, taken their seats in the Hall—the sofas, in the recesses of the colonnade around the Hall, were occupied by ladies, and the corridor, behind the Speaker's chair, was also filled with ladies, foreign ministers and distinguished citizens, and the galleries were crowded and *packed*, almost to suffocation. The moment the General entered, all the members rose from their seats and stood uncovered—

175

the rest of the immense crowd, animated by one common impulse, rose likewise. He was conducted to a seat in the area immediately in front of the Speaker's chair. After a momentary interval, the Speaker [Henry Clay] rose and addressed him in his happiest and most impressive manner, the General standing all the while, and manifesting deep sensibility. The General then, and all the company resumed their seats, for a moment; when he rose, the whole assembly rising with him, and delivered a handsome and eloquent reply, the effect of which was greatly enhanced by his foreign accent and imperfect enunciation. During all this ceremony, there was the most profound attention and awful silence. There was, indeed, a *religious solemnity* in the whole scene, which none of us, who witnessed it, can ever forget.[2]

In his annual message to Congress, President Monroe made reference to the warm and enthusiastic welcome the general had received everywhere he visited. He also urged that the nation show its appreciation for Lafayette's "very important and disinterested services and sacrifices" in a grant worthy of the character of the American people. Though the president made no mention of Lafayette's circumstances, it was widely known that the general—who had served without pay and supported his own staff and aides during the American Revolution—was financially strapped.[3] Monroe did not propose a specific appropriation, but privately he suggested $200,000. Henry Clay thought that a sum between $100,000 and $150,000 and a township of land was adequate.[4] After the impressive and moving reception for Lafayette, Congress responded with a grant of $200,000 and a township of land (23,040 acres), although some members thought this was too generous.[5]

The president departed from his normal practice of not appearing at social functions in Washington outside the White House by attending the dinner for Lafayette given by the members of Congress. The dinner was held at Williamson's Hotel on Pennsylvania Avenue at four o'clock on January 1, 1825, and John Quincy Adams counted about 150 members of both houses and about 30 civil and military officers of the government in attendance. Among the sixteen toasts given was one offered to "*The President of the United States*—Our respectability abroad and prosperity at home are the best eulogy of his administration." Monroe responded with what Adams described as "a short address of thanks."[6] Other commentators were less generous. Though he had not attended, Federalist Congressman Louis McLane reported to his wife that some resented "the trick practiced to extort the expression of some approbation of Mr. Monroe's administration." Insisting that had he been present he would have abstained from the toast, McLane sneered that "the old dotard . . . forgetting all the dignity of his station, rose and made the company a speech, thus holding out to the nation that the representatives of Congress had thus complimented his political course."[7] This critic was the same congressman who, as a freshman member attending his first reception at the White House in 1817, had been "exceedingly pleased" with the president and had admired "the plain simplicity of his manners, and the easy dignity of his deportment generally."[8] Monroe was as ready to leave Washington as McLane was to see him go, but the state of Monroe's finances was not much better than Lafayette's, and he too was hoping for some generosity from Congress.

Lafayette would remain in Washington during January and February 1825, but the presidential election overshadowed his presence, as it did the thoughts of nearly everyone in the capital. For months many members of Congress had been convinced that no candidate could win a majority in the electoral vote and that the final election would be decided by the House of Representatives. In February 1824, before the congressional nominating caucus met, North Carolina Congressman Willie P. Mangum had predicted: "Unless the caucus shall produce considerable effect I am satisfied that an election cannot be made by the people and that the election will ultimately come to the House of Representatives, as much as it is to be deprecated."[9] The day after the caucus, Daniel Webster was also convinced that the House would determine the election. As evidence of how widely this view was shared, he pointed to how "very civil towards *Federalists*" all the candidates had become.[10]

In May 1824 supporters of Henry Clay issued a printed circular letter assessing the current strength of the candidates in the various states. They projected the electoral vote as Adams, 51; Crawford, 48; Jackson, 47; and Clay, 46. "The election must, in any and every event that can be anticipated, come into the House of Representatives," Clay's strategists believed. Their estimates would have eliminated Clay from the expected showdown in the House of Representatives, where—as required by the Twelfth Amendment—the House must choose from among the three candidates with the largest number of electoral votes. But Clay's advisers saw several possibilities that might alter the predicted outcome and place him among the top three contenders. They urged all his friends to remain steadfast in their support.[11]

On December 8, when Andrew Jackson arrived in Washington, Congressman Joseph Johnson of Virginia reported that the prevailing opinion in the capital was that Jackson would be elected president. "All is uncertainty yet with regard to the race between Clay and Crawford. The state of Louisiana it is presumed will decide which of them will come into the House."[12] When news reached the capital on December

14 that Louisiana's vote was divided between Jackson and Adams, Clay's hopes were shattered.[13] The final electoral tally was Jackson, 99; Adams, 84; Crawford, 41; and Clay, 37. In the vice-presidential contest, Calhoun decisively won with 182 electoral votes.

With Clay eliminated from the presidential competition, political maneuvering and speculation quickened. "The report of the last hour is contradicted by the rumour of the next," Congressman Robert P. Henry of Kentucky wrote to his brother on January 3, 1825. In Henry's opinion, "It *is certain*, that the final struggle will be between Jackson and Adams. It *is certain*, that the friends of Crawford still delude themselves with calculations which the result will prove to be, *entirely visionary*. It *is certain*, that intrigue is *up and doing*, but the scope and design of her machinations are yet unknown."[14] As a representative from Clay's home state, which had voted for Clay in the election, Henry belonged to a key delegation whose members were divided. He counted a majority for Adams but was inclined to support Jackson. Liking Jackson better than Adams—and believing him to be the choice of his constituents—Henry refrained from committing himself either way. Concerning the rumor that Adams was to be elected president and Clay was to become secretary of state, Henry said, "All that I know about it is, that the propositions have been made to Clay from that quarter, that *he is inclined* to embrace them, and that an effort has been made to obtain the vote of Kentucky, for Adams."[15] Clay himself was courted by all sides, and he remarked that "really the friends of all the three Gentlemen are so very courteous, and affectionate, that I sometimes almost wish that it was in my power to accommodate each of them."[16]

Clay spent the evening of January 9, 1825, with Adams. They discussed the possibility of an Adams administration with regard to, as Adams recorded in his diary, "some principles of great public importance, but without any personal considerations for himself." Before leaving, Clay indicated that his preference was for Adams.[17] But Clay made no public announcement of his position. A few days later, it was reported around Washington that the legislature of Kentucky had instructed its representatives to vote for Jackson for president. Although members of Congress were not bound by instructions from any source, the news was seen as "a heavy blow for Clay."[18]

On January 23, Senator Waller Taylor of Indiana wrote to a Virginia friend that "it has been circulated here for a week, and not contradicted, that Mr. Clay has agreed to support Adams's election with all the influence he possesses."[19] While Taylor doubted the rumor, Clay's support of Adams became public knowledge the next day. "There is at this moment a very high state of excitement in the House," Adams wrote in his diary on January 25, "Mr. Clay and the majority of the Ohio and Kentucky delegations having yesterday unequivocally avowed their determination to vote for me. . . . The impression almost universal, made yesterday, was that the election was settled in my favor."[20] At the same time, Jackson's forces were said to be courting Crawford supporters. Few were ready to admit that the contest was over, and after two more weeks of talking, scheming, and pressuring, the outcome was still in doubt.

At noon on February 9, 1825, in a joint session of Congress meeting in the House of Representatives, the certificates from the electors in each state were opened, and the ballots counted. Confirming the result already known unofficially, the returns gave no candidate a majority of the electoral vote. The senators then withdrew, and the House proceeded immediately to conduct the election. When the clerk called the roll by states, only one member of the House was absent. Each state delegation then received a ballot box in which individual members deposited their ballots.[21] The majority vote of each delegation determined that state's vote, and the concurrence of thirteen states determined the election.

When the votes were counted, the six New England states and New York—carried by Adams in the electoral college—stayed with him. The three states won by Clay in the electoral vote—Kentucky, Missouri, and Ohio—cast their ballots for Adams. Of the eleven states that had supported Jackson, four deserted him in the House election. North Carolina voted for Crawford, who kept the three states he had won in the electoral vote—Delaware, Georgia, and Virginia. Maryland, Louisiana, and Illinois switched from Jackson to Adams, giving Adams the victory. The final vote was Adams, 13; Jackson, 7; and Crawford, 4. To the surprise of many, only one ballot was required to elect John Quincy Adams the sixth president of the United States.

No one could accuse Monroe of being involved in the intrigues to choose his successor, either in the general election or in the House vote. When the competition began, he had said that he expected some blows would be aimed at him, but "deeming it improper, on principle, to take any part . . . in the election, or even to be suspected of doing it, I keep myself as abstracted from it, as I possibly can."[22] Indeed, the retiring president was more concerned about his own immediate future than about the person who would follow him in office. In addition, his wife's health was a source of great anxiety. In late August 1824, William Lee, second auditor of the Treasury and longtime friend of the president's, wrote privately: "Mrs. Monroe is very ill. I fear she will die. If she does, the President will not survive her long."[23] Monroe was also deeply concerned about his worsening financial circumstances.

On January 25, 1825, two months before his term of office ended, Monroe sent a brief message to Congress asking the members to review his financial accounts with the government.

> I have been long in the service of my country, and in its most difficult conjunctures, as well abroad as at home, in the course of which I have had a control over the public moneys, to a vast amount. If, in the course of my service, it shall appear, on the most severe scrutiny, which I invite, that the public has sustained any loss by any act of mine, or of others, for which I ought to be held responsible, I am willing to bear it. If, on the other hand, it shall appear, on a view of the law, and of precedents, in other cases, that justice has been withheld from me, in any instance, as I have believed it to be in many, and greatly to my injury, it is submitted whether it ought not to be rendered.[24]

The president indicated that he did not expect Congress to take any final action on the matter while he remained in office. At the same time, he was willing to furnish any information and testimony that Congress might request while he was still in Washington and accessible.

A few days later Samuel D. Ingham of Pennsylvania, a friend of Monroe's, moved that the president's appeal be referred to a select committee with instructions to review and report to the House any evidence or explanation of Monroe's claims he might think it proper to present. Named to chair the committee, Ingham informed the president on January 17 that the committee was prepared to hear from him. Monroe had been assembling records and refining his arguments for some time, and he sent the documentation to the committee the next day. With the end of the session approaching, the committee moved promptly and submitted its report to the House on February 21, 1825. When printed, the report, which included all the materials submitted by the president, comprised 286 pages.[25]

Monroe's financial difficulties had been pressing on him for some time, and it had become clear that he would be forced to sell part of his land and property to meet his debts. Two years before the end of his second term, Monroe unburdened himself in a confidential letter to Fulwar Skipwith, a longtime Virginia friend who had accompanied Monroe on his mission to France in 1794 and served as secretary of the legation until appointed consul general at Paris in 1795. Skipwith had also been in Paris in 1803 when Monroe returned on the mission to purchase Louisiana.[26] As one familiar with the foreign service and the economy of Virginia—both of which Monroe blamed for his impoverishment—Skipwith could be expected to understand. In his letter, Monroe candidly reviewed his situation.

You know well, that all the offices which I held abroad were all allowed salaries, which, with the greatest economy which I could practice, were incompetent to my support; and you know equally well,
that I had no other resource to meet expences but my salary, disdain-
ing all kind of speculation, and other means of raising money. In my
absence, my plantations, instead of affording me funds on my return
to meet debts incurred abroad, had actually run me in debt to some
amount. In this state I came here, and in the six years I held the departments of state and war, especially in the latter, when our country
was overwhelmed with difficulties and my whole mind was absorbed
with the heavy duties which pressed on me, the neglect of my private
affairs increased in the degree, and my debts in like manner. The
present office found me in this state, from which no saving that I can
make will rescue me. I shall owe much money on my retirement; and
my object now is to make such an arrangement of my affairs as will afford me the greatest aid and relief that may be practicable.[27]

In counting his assets, Monroe began with his slaves, who had increased in number to about sixty or seventy, "having been kindly
treated" during his long service, he said. His land-holdings in Albemarle and Loudoun counties were once very valuable, "but all such
property has of late declined much in value, and for the reason that our
produce sells for nothing." It would be necessary to sell some of his assets, and he had decided to put his house and lands in Albemarle
County on the market.[28] Senator Henry Johnson of Louisiana and some
other friends had suggested that he move his slaves to land that could
be bought cheaply in Louisiana and paid for in installments from a good
income to be derived from the cotton produced. Monroe had been told
that he could probably sell the land and the slaves at a handsome profit
within a few years. "If I sell my slaves in Virginia, in families, they will
sell for almost a trifle; and I would not separate them," he wrote. "If I
send them down the Mississippi, they will be kept together in families,
and if I should ever sell them, they would be sold in families." Monroe
sought Skipwith's advice on the proposal.[29]

In early June 1823, Monroe wrote his son-in-law Samuel Gouverneur that he had advertised his landed property in Albemarle for sale in
the two Richmond newspapers and in the Washington *National Intelligencer*. Although he thought the outlook for selling it was very unfavorable, "it will bring the subject before the public, and as I offer credit, it
is probable that propositions may be made to me for it." The Albemarle
slaves were not included in the offering.[30] Meanwhile, Monroe informed
the Washington branch of the Bank of the United States, which held a
mortgage on thirty-five hundred acres of the land, that he would "not

sell one acre of that tract, without doing it in harmony with the bank, equally as to the price and the application of the money."[31] In September 1823 Monroe believed he had a prospect of selling a part of his lands in Albemarle, but no transaction occurred before he left office.[32] Less than six weeks after retiring from the presidency, Monroe would again advertise his Albemarle property for sale.[33]

During the summer of 1823 Monroe had gathered documents and marshaled arguments in support of claims for past service on two diplomatic missions to Europe, for which he believed he had not been fully compensated. In October 1823—before he became absorbed in the issues that would lead to the enunciation of the Monroe Doctrine—he sent off a bundle of papers to his son-in-law Samuel Gouverneur in New York. In a long letter accompanying the documents, Monroe indicated that he was considering sending a message on the subject to Congress. He asked Gouverneur's opinion on the advisability of the plan and the timing—if it should be done in the approaching session or in the final one of his presidency. Monroe personally favored presenting his claim at the coming session. If the matter was postponed until after he retired, he argued, the claim would have to be brought forward by petition, introduced by a friend in Congress, or settled by his successor. By not waiting, Monroe thought he would demonstrate that he was inviting inquiry, "that I look to character, as well as to compensation and dread no scrutiny."[34]

Gouverneur's lengthy response was supportive of Monroe's case. "The papers you have enclosed to me, afford the strongest evidence, that in an account fairly stated, between the country and yourself, the former would be brought considerably in your debt," he wrote. But Gouverneur also counseled his father-in-law to seek the advice of his friends and not to decide immediately on any course; Gouverneur could then confer with him again in person.[35] Whether because of Gouverneur's advice or because of the press of national affairs, Monroe delayed raising the issue with Congress until the end of his presidency.

Some of the specific suggestions that his son-in-law offered in November 1823 were followed by Monroe in January 1825. Gouverneur recommended that the president not transmit all of the papers to Congress at once but send a short message and wait for his friends in Congress to request further information. He also stressed the importance of asking for the payment of interest, which would amount to a sum greater than the principal.[36] Monroe, however, rejected Gouverneur's admonition not to include with his claims any papers relating to funds for furniture for the President's House or his personal accounts with Colonel Samuel Lane. Though some had insinuated that the president was connected with the shortage of public money in the accounts of Samuel Lane, late commissioner of public buildings, Gouverneur argued that "it is of no manner connected with the public—and I think it would show a sensibility to the mean and contemptible inventions and gossiping stories of a few men, who are totally beneath your notice."[37] When he tendered his documentation, Monroe nevertheless included these papers along with his claims.

Although Gouverneur had discouraged Monroe from making a speedy application to Congress, he thought it highly advisable that the president communicate with Congress on the subject before he left office. His claim should show that a considerable balance had been due him for some years and should state the reasons why it had not been previously settled. "This is particulary desireable with a view to the question of interest, which will be important to you, and which under all the circumstances of the case, I do not think they could refuse, cheerfully to allow."[38]

The claims Monroe submitted to Congress in 1825 reached back to his first mission to France beginning in 1794. They derived also from the second period of his European service, which included the negotiations in Paris for the purchase of Louisiana in 1803, appointment as minister to England from 1803 to 1807, and a special mission to Spain in 1805.

On December 6, 1796, Monroe had received notice of his unexpected recall as minister to France from President Washington's secretary of state, Timothy Pickering. In accord with state department regulations, Monroe's salary ceased on that date, though diplomats were allotted a quarter salary for returning home. Monroe received that payment. But diplomats were also normally allowed to choose the date of their recall, and Monroe's dismissal from office denied him that advantage. In 1816 he had obtained a continuance of his salary until January 1, 1797, the date he officially took leave of the French Directory. Monroe now sought salary for the period from January 1 until he sailed for home on April 20, 1797. "It was impossible for me to leave the country, without exposing my family to the dangers of a winter's voyage," he told Congress, adding that, in any case, he doubted he could have obtained earlier passage because of the British blockade and French restrictions. Monroe asked for $2,750 in additional salary and $3,515 in contingent expenses.[39]

Monroe's claims regarding his second mission to Europe were more extensive. He noted that at the time of his appointment as a special envoy to France in 1803, he had been denied an outfit allowance. When he settled his account in 1810, he was compensated for that expense, but he now sought interest from 1803 to 1810 on the $9,000 allowance. In relation to his missions to Great Britain and Spain, he applied for contingent expenses of $2,000 and extraordinary expenses of $10,500. The reimbursements claimed for all missions totaled $23,570, and the interest was calculated at $30,266.[40]

The salaries and allowances that American diplomats abroad received from a frugal American government were rarely adequate to enable them to live in the style expected in the capitals of Europe. In living beyond his means, Monroe was not exceptional. Nor was it unusual for claims for additional expenses to be filed or for accounts to remain unsettled for years. Still, Monroe's claims were extraordinary in their scope, and his arguments were often labored. That he was driven to put them forward was surely impelled by his financial plight as he approached retirement. That Congress was receptive to considering the claims was undoubtedly influenced by his lifetime of public service. Monroe's report and the detailed documents accompanying it were carefully examined, and some amounts rejected or reduced. In the end Congress in 1826 allowed the former president $29,513 of the $53,836 submitted in principal and interest. Monroe was disappointed with the payment. Although he accepted it in satisfaction of all his claims, he never saw it as the final settlement that it became.[41]

14

THE END OF AN ERA

The enunciation of the Monroe Doctrine in December 1823 and its warm reception in the United States marked the zenith of Monroe's presidency. As the praise he received for that policy faded and the election to choose his successor increasingly dominated the political scene, Monroe became a common target for criticism. Editor Hezekiah Niles, writing in his *Weekly Register* in May 1824, remarked: "I am not one of those who 'fell and worshipped' Mr. Monroe, when the sun of his greatness was at its meridian, nor will I be among his enemies *because* his political power is about to pass into other hands. He was praised without decency, and now is abused without shame."[1] As the election contest drew to a close, however, and Monroe prepared to return to Virginia, amicable feelings revived.

As was his custom, Monroe sent copies of his annual message of 1824 to friends throughout the country. Among those acknowledging the favor was Chief Justice John Marshall, who wrote congratulating the president "on the auspicious circumstances which have attended your course as chief magistrate of the United States, and which crown its termination." Between Monroe and the Virginia Federalist who had dominated the high court for twenty-four years there was never the gulf that had divided Marshall and Jefferson; and Marshall assured the retiring president, "You may look back with pleasure to several very interesting events which have taken place during your administration, and have the rare felicity not to find the retrospect darkened by a single spot the review of which ought to pain yourself or your fellow citizens."[2]

The wave of American nationalism that followed the end of the War of 1812 had brought an awakening of historical consciousness. In 1817 Congress, for the first time, began the systematic publication of congressional records beyond that of the journals of the two houses. In the following year Congress authorized the printing of one thousand copies of the journal of the Constitutional Convention at Philadelphia in 1787, which heretofore had remained secret.[3] When John Binns of Philadelphia published an engraved print of a facsimile of the Declaration of Independence—certified as accurate by Secretary of State Adams—two copies were hung over the fireplaces at the front of the House chamber. Displayed in handsome gold-decorated frames with the American eagle at the top, they were included in the painting of the House of Representatives by Samuel F. B. Morse in 1822 (fig. 5). The prints remain today above the preserved fireplaces in the old hall of the House of Representatives.[4]

In January 1817, in the closing weeks of Madison's presidency, Congress passed a joint resolution authorizing the president to employ John Trumbull to compose and execute four paintings commemorative of the most important events of the American Revolution. Trumbull had appealed to Jefferson to back the project, and President-elect Monroe had served as a conduit for communicating Jefferson's support to key members of Congress. Monroe later informed Jefferson that he had wielded Jefferson's influence "with the best effect, to the purposes for which it was intended." Monroe, who did not share Jefferson's friendship with Trumbull, told the former president that he was convinced Trumbull owed his success in getting the commission "principally to your favorable opinion of his merit."[5]

Soon after Monroe took office as president, Richard Rush, acting secretary of state, drew up the articles of agreement specifying the commissioned paintings. They were to depict the adoption of the Declaration of Independence; the surrender of the British to the American forces at Saratoga; the surrender of the British at Yorktown; and the resignation of General Washington as commanding general at Annapolis. The paintings, no less than eighteen feet by twelve feet with the figures as large as life, were to be hung in the Capitol Rotunda, then under construction.[6] In 1819, when Trumbull delivered his first painting—the large version of his earlier *The Declaration of Independence*—the Rotunda was far from complete, and it would still be unfinished when Trumbull presented the last of his four works in 1824.[7] By the time Trumbull's paintings were finally hung in the Rotunda in 1826, John Quincy Adams would be president. Meanwhile, the paintings were displayed in the

Senate chamber and in the meeting room of the military and naval committees.[8]

Monroe was pictured in the last of Trumbull's four paintings (fig. 6). As members of the Continental Congress in December 1783 when Washington resigned his commission as commanding general of the army, Monroe and Jefferson were among those who witnessed that moving and historic scene. Some younger members of Congress, along with John Quincy Adams, thought Trumbull's talent as an artist had waned.[9] But when Adams as president viewed Trumbull's works in the Rotunda for the first time in 1826, he observed that they were placed "in such a favorable light that they appear far better than they have ever done before."[10]

As Monroe left the presidency, the revolutionary generation of Americans was passing from the scene. It was thus fitting that Trumbull's scenes of the American Revolution were put on display in the Capitol during Monroe's administration and found their final placement in the Rotunda after his terms had ended. As the last president of the United States to have borne arms against the British in the revolutionary war, Monroe closed an era that had given birth to a new nation.

As a political figure, Monroe aroused neither the adulation nor the detestation that Jefferson stirred in his admirers or detractors. Indeed, as president, Monroe excited less public controversy and fewer strong feelings than any of his predecessors in the first office. Horace Holley, visiting the capital early in the second year of Monroe's administration, wrote of the president that "it is astonishing to find how little one thinks of him here, notwithstanding he is the principal man of the country. But he does not make the community feel him."[11]

Although Monroe restored formality to the White House, reversing Jefferson's casualness, visitors remarked repeatedly on the plainness of the president. They described him as "a plain man" with "a good heart and amiable disposition," and as "the same plain honest gentlemanly looking personage, which he at all times appears to be."[12] On his travels, the president impressed his fellow citizens with his graciousness and lack of pretensions. Monroe had neither the learning nor the intellect of Jefferson or Madison, and he suffered by comparison to them. But he recognized his limitations and compensated with hard work, devotion to the duties of his office, and supplementary activities, such as his two extended tours of the country.

President Monroe was willing to take advice, and he engaged his cabinet in his decision-making process. When his cabinet was divided by conflicting opinions—as it frequently was—he heard all sides. He gave strong support to his capable secretary of state, yet Adams frequently modified his own position after hearing the president's views. Weighing the evidence, the relevant circumstances, and other considerations, Monroe decided his policy. Nowhere was this better demonstrated than in his handling of the crisis over slavery and the admission of Missouri as a state and in his declaration of the doctrine that would bear his name. As chief executive, Monroe was cautious and more inclined to delay action when unsure of his course than to make precipitate moves. Neither an ideologue nor a leader with a grand vision, he was a political person who sought to achieve specific, attainable objectives.

Monroe never had the influence in Congress that Jefferson enjoyed, and political rivalries in Congress increased the difficulties of implementing his initiatives. Members of Congress did not wait for direction from the president nor hesitate to oppose him on matters about which they disagreed. With no dominant political party in Congress to rely on—as Jefferson had had through much of his presidency—Monroe was forced to build coalitions of support.

Once he set a course for his administration, Monroe was resolute in pursuing it. He withstood pressures to recognize the republics of Latin America until he thought the time and circumstances were right. He adroitly handled the difficulties with General Jackson in the First Seminole War. He tolerated Spanish delays in ratifying the Adams-Onís treaty, which ceded Florida and defined the boundary of American claims across the continent to the Pacific. Monroe's presidency was thus important in strengthening the power of the presidency in the conduct of foreign affairs. This can be seen in his resistance to congressional calls for early recognition of Latin American independence, in the acquisition of Florida, in the extension of territorial claims of the United States to the Pacific, and in the formulation and proclamation of the Monroe Doctrine. In the occupation of Amelia Island and the prosecution of the Seminole war, Monroe's administration was also influential in advancing the war-making role of the presidency, though such a consequence was neither sought nor favored by Monroe.

The label "era of good feelings" that a Boston newspaper used to describe the advent of Monroe's administration has created images that distort and mask both the problems and the accomplishments of Monroe's presidency. Even the limited application of the harmonious description to partisan politics is misleading. Although the Federalist party vanished as a national entity, Federalists did not disappear. Monroe began his administration believing that all divisions could be eliminated, and throughout his presidency, he continued to assert that political parties were not necessary to republican government. "Surely our government may get on and prosper without the existence of parties," he wrote to Madison in 1822. "I have always considered their existence as the curse of the country." He believed that the conditions that fostered parties in other countries did not exist in the United States, where "we have no distinct orders." At the same time, in making appointments or in deciding policies, Monroe never ignored past Federalist allegiances or stances. He refrained from appointing Federalists to office on the grounds that the president should not act against his own party. "The charge of amalgamation is not correctly levelled at me," he insisted.[13]

Many members of Congress praised the decline of parties in Congress, but the demise of two national political parties did not eliminate partisanship. Blocs within the dominant Republican party formed to compete for places, policies advantageous to their constituents, and influence in electing the next president of the United States. Although Monroe continued to envision a political world without parties, the factions within Republican ranks and the competition among members of his cabinet to succeed him compounded the difficulties of his presidency during his last years in office.

In the developing market economy of the young republic, Monroe's presidency was a time of transition. Monroe's approval of a national bank, his hesitant and only partial acceptance of internal improvements, and his signing of the tariff bill of 1824 reflected the shifting power of economic and sectional interests. In a symbolic recognition of changing times, Monroe visited the first exhibition of American manufactures held in the Rotunda of the Capitol in late February 1825, in the final days of his presidency. The display of textiles was the most extensive, but also on view were a variety of metal works and numerous other articles, including umbrellas, brushes, watch chains, and even two pianofortes from New York and "one superior coach" from Baltimore. Hezekiah Niles enthusiastically reported in his *Weekly Register* that the exhibition was "sufficient to *astonish* many who had not reflected on the quantity of labor and amount of capital employed and vested in the manufacture of wool, cotton, iron and other metals, and wood, etc." Niles reported that the Rotunda was "crowded by a succession of individuals of both sexes, for three days."[14] The president himself even sent a cloak of American manufacture that he had recently received to be placed on exhibit.[15]

In a printed letter to his constituents, Congressmen James B. Reynolds of Tennessee relayed his optimism:

> There is no country on the globe, with a dense population, better cal-
> culated for manufactures, than our own; and nothing can establish
> the opinion more clearly than the pleasant and elegant exhibition of
> the different specimens of manufactures, from all parts of the Union,
> now displayed at this moment in the Rotundo of the Capitol. I have
> hastily examined some of the articles, and particularly the broad-
> cloths, and judges inform me that some of them are as good and of as
> fine a quality as any imported, and for nearly one half the price.[16]

While picturing a future in which there would be flourishing American manufactures rivaling those of Europe, Congressman Reynolds assured his Tennessee constituents that, at the present, the policy of the government ought to be to keep manufactures subordinate to agriculture.

President Monroe, in encouraging manufactures, did not add such a qualification. Declaring in his inaugural address in 1817 that American manufactures "require the systematic and fostering care of the Government," he repeated similar assertions in most of his annual messages to Congress.[17] In the first message of his second term, Monroe predicted that "under the protection given to domestic manufactures by existing laws we shall become at no distant period a manufacturing country on an extensive scale."[18] In his message of 1823, the president recommended additional aid for manufactures, and he signed the bill for tariff increases in 1824.[19] As long as Monroe was in office, the potentially explosive issue of protective tariffs remained under control. When the debate arose again in the next administration, Monroe told John C. Calhoun that his views on the promotion of manufactures expressed in his inaugural address of 1817 and repeated in subsequent messages to Congress had not changed but had "gained strength by subsequent events."[20]

As the last of the Virginia dynasty of presidents, which had begun with Jefferson in 1801 and continued under Madison in 1809, Monroe's administration closed an era in which southern leadership had been national leadership. When, on March 4, 1825, Monroe followed president-elect John Quincy Adams into the House of Representatives for Adams's inauguration, the seat of national power had begun its passage from the South to the North. And, as Monroe watched John C. Calhoun take the oath of office as vice-president, he was also witnessing the shift of southern leadership from Virginia to the Lower South. To thoughtful citizens who remembered the difficulties that Monroe had faced in reconciling Virginia to the Missouri Compromise of 1820, fear of future sectional conflict may not have been easily suppressed. There is no record that such concerns weighed on the retiring president, for his confidence in the abilities of both Adams and Calhoun was high and his respect for the good sense of his countrymen had been confirmed by the two extensive national tours he had undertaken as president.

Reflecting on his eight years as president, Monroe probably recalled the controversy over slavery and the admission of Missouri as his most trying crisis, for it had threatened the very existence of the Union. His memories also must have been vivid of the Seminole war and the controversial actions of General Andrew Jackson. He would not have expected his most-remembered legacy to be the Monroe Doctrine, but the revolutions in Latin America and their repercussions in the United States and Europe had certainly been a recurring concern throughout his presidency. The recollection of the problems created by the presidential ambitions of members of his cabinet would have been fresh in his mind as Monroe retired from the executive office. But his own public career had often taken a partisan course, and he could derive satisfaction from having assembled and retained in his cabinet so able a group of assistants and advisers. While Monroe's vision of a nation extending to the Pacific Ocean was less sharp than that of Secretary of State Adams, his continental vision was clearer than often recognized.

If President Monroe could claim no success so glowing as Jefferson's purchase of Louisiana (in which Monroe himself had played a role) or so exciting as the Lewis and Clark expedition to the Pacific, he had no disappointment so severe as the failure of Jefferson's embargo or the conspiracy of Aaron Burr. Monroe's greatest personal experience may have been associating with his fellow citizens on his two extensive tours of the country and at the same time proving to himself his own endurance and abilities. His deepest private concerns as president were about his wife's health and the deteriorating state of his personal finances.

As he left office, Monroe could find gratification in the expressions of appreciation that reached him. Among them were the resolutions passed by the legislatures of a number of states. The General Assembly of Maryland praised "his wise impartial and dignified administration of the General Government."[21] The legislature of Louisiana, declaring the "highest veneration of James Monroe, who by his administration of Government has preserved the purity of Republican institutions and the honor of the nation abroad," also thanked him for his earlier role in effecting the union of Louisiana with the United States.[22] Joining other states in commending "the public services and long tried patriotism of James Monroe, President of the United States," the people of Maine expressed the hope "that their best wishes for his prosperity and happiness will ever accompany him in his retirement from the arduous duties of the highest office, which was within the power of a great people to bestow upon him."[23] The General Assembly of New York thanked Monroe for his "many highly important services, which have been rendered to the republic," and declared that "his administration of the General government for eight years just past has been eminently calculated to promote the permanent prosperity and honor of his country." New York also voiced "its ardent wishes that he may long live to enjoy with his fellow citizens the blessing of that liberty and independence, for the attainment of which he shed his blood, and for the perpetuation of which he has so long and faithfully labored."[24]

Long life would not be accorded to Monroe, whose death came on July 4, 1831. While not so astounding as the deaths of both Thomas Jefferson and John Adams on the fiftieth anniversary of the Declaration of Independence five years earlier, it was nonetheless a remarkable coincidence that the last president of the United States to have fought in the American Revolution should also die on that memorable date.

NOTES

CHAPTER 1
THE ROAD TO THE PRESIDENCY

1. Monroe was born in Westmoreland County, Virginia, on April 28, 1758. The records are sparse relating to his life before the Revolution. The best biography of Monroe is Harry Ammon, *James Monroe: The Quest for National Identity* (New York: McGraw-Hill, 1971); see pp. 2–33. See also Monroe to Jefferson, June 26, 1780, in Stanislaus M. Hamilton, ed., *The Writings of James Monroe*, 7 vols. (New York, 1898–1903; reprint ed., New York: AMS Press, 1969), 1:3–8.

2. Dumas Malone, *Jefferson and His Time*, 6 vols. (Boston: Little, Brown and Company, 1948–1981), 1:410; Ammon, *Monroe*, pp. 34–39, 43.

3. Ammon, *Monroe*, pp. 38, 45–47, 52–53, 61–63.

4. Jack N. Rakove, *The Beginnings of National Politics: An Interpretive History of the Continental Congress* (Baltimore: Johns Hopkins University Press, 1979), pp. 346–47, 349; Monroe to Madison, Dec. 28, 1784, July 26, 1785, and Monroe to Jefferson, Apr. 12, June 16, 1785, in Hamilton, ed., *Monroe Writings*, 1:59, 68, 80–82, 97–99; Madison to Monroe, Mar. 19, May 13, 1786, in William T. Hutchinson et al., eds., *The Papers of James Madison*, 22 vols. to date (Chicago: University of Chicago Press, and Charlottesville: University Press of Virginia, 1962–), 8:505, 9:55; Ammon, *Monroe*, pp. 50–51, 59–60.

5. Monroe to Madison, Oct. 13, 1787, Feb. 7, 1788, and Madison to Jefferson, Apr. 22, 1788, in Hutchinson et al., eds., *Madison Papers*, 10:193, 481, 11:28; Monroe to Jefferson, Apr. 10, July 12, 1788, in Julian P. Boyd et al., eds., *The Papers of Thomas Jefferson*, 25 vols. to date (Princeton: Princeton University Press, 1950–), 13:50, 351–53; Ammon, *Monroe*, pp. 68–69.

6. Ammon, *Monroe*, pp. 68–70; in Hamilton, ed., *Monroe Writings*, 1:307–43.

7. Monroe to Madison, Aug. 12, 1789, in Hamilton, ed., *Monroe Writings*, 1:205–6; W. P. Cresson, *James Monroe* (Chapel Hill: University of North Carolina Press, 1946), pp. 104–5.

8. Linda DePauw, ed., *Documentary History of the First Federal Congress of the United States of America* (Baltimore: Johns Hopkins University Press, 1972–), 1:535–36; *Annals of Congress*, 1 Cong., 3 Sess. (Jan. 20, 1791), p. 1791; *Journal of William Maclay, United States Senator from Pennsylvania, 1789–1791* (New York, 1890; reprint ed., New York: Frederick Ungar, 1965), p. 357.

9. Boyd et al., eds., *Jefferson Papers*, 20:556–57.

10. Ammon, *Monroe*, p. 89; Noble E. Cunningham, Jr., *The Jeffersonian Republicans: The Formation of Party Organization, 1789–1801* (Chapel Hill: University of North Carolina Press for the Institute of Early American History and Culture, Williamsburg, Va., 1957), pp. 8–12, 21–23.

11. Ammon, *Monroe*, pp. 79–80, 131.

12. *National Gazette* (Philadelphia), Nov. 14, 24, Dec. 12, 1791; Ammon, *Monroe*, pp. 87–88, 594 n.23.

13. Cunningham, *Jeffersonian Republicans*, pp. 46–49, 57–60.

14. Ammon, *Monroe*, pp. 112–14.

15. Monroe, address to the National Convention, Aug. 14, 1794, in Hamilton, ed., *Monroe Writings*, 2:13–14; Stuart Gerry Brown, ed., *The Autobiography of James Monroe* (Syracuse, N.Y.: Syracuse University Press, 1959), pp. 64–65; Ammon, *Monroe*, pp. 115–16, 119–20.

16. Madison to Monroe, Dec. 4, 1794, in Hutchinson et al., eds., *Madison Papers*, 15:405.

17. Ammon, *Monroe*, pp. 151–52; Gerard H. Clarfield, *Timothy Pickering and American Diplomacy, 1795–1800* (Columbia: University of Missouri Press, 1969), pp. 53–56.

18. Gallatin to his wife, June 28, 30, 1797, in Henry Adams, *The Life of Albert Gallatin* (Philadelphia, 1879; reprint ed., New York: Peter Smith, 1943), pp. 186–87; Noble E. Cunningham, Jr., *In Pursuit of Reason: The Life of Thomas Jefferson* (Baton Rouge: Louisiana State University Press, 1987), p. 210.

19. James Monroe, *A View of the Conduct of the Executive, in the Foreign Affairs of the United States, Connected with the Mission to the French Republic, During the Years 1794, 5 & 6* (Philadelphia: Benjamin Franklin Bache, 1797). The introduction is reprinted in Hamilton, ed., *Monroe Writings*, 3:383–457.

20. Jefferson to Monroe, Dec. 27, 1797, in Paul L. Ford, ed., *The Works of Thomas Jefferson*, Federal edition, 12 vols. (New York: G. P. Putnam's Sons, 1904), 8:350.

21. Wolcott to George Washington, Jan. 30, 1798, in George Gibbs, *Memoirs of the Administrations of Washington and John Adams, Edited from the Papers of Oliver Wolcott, Secretary of the Treasury*, 2 vols. (New York: n.p., 1846), 2:12; Pickering to Washington, Jan. 20, 1798, in Hamilton, ed., *Monroe Writings*, 3:385n; Ammon, *Monroe*, pp. 165–67.

22. Ammon, *Monroe*, pp. 170–73; Cunningham, *Jeffersonian Republicans*, pp.

120–23; Ralph Ketcham, *James Madison: A Biography* (New York: Macmillan, 1971), p. 388.

23. Noble E. Cunningham, Jr., "Election of 1800," in Arthur M. Schlesinger, Jr., and Fred L. Israel, eds., *History of American Presidential Elections, 1789–1968*, 4 vols. (New York: McGraw-Hill, 1971), 1:131–33.

24. Monroe to Jefferson, Jan. 18, 27, 1801, in Hamilton, ed., *Monroe Writings*, 3:256–57.

25. Monroe, message, Dec. 7, 1801, ibid., pp. 316–17.

26. Ibid., p. 306.

27. *Enquirer* (Richmond), June 25, 1805, quoted in Ammon, *Monroe*, p. 175.

28. Jefferson to Monroe, Jan. 13, 1803, in Ford, ed., *Jefferson Works*, 9:418–19; Alexander DeConde, *This Affair of Louisiana* (New York: Charles Scribner's Sons, 1976), pp. 161–75; Ammon, *Monroe*, pp. 203–24.

29. Bradford Perkins, *Prologue to War: England and the United States, 1805–1812* (Berkeley and Los Angeles: University of California Press, 1968), pp. 114–37; Noble E. Cunningham, Jr., *The Process of Government Under Jefferson* (Princeton: Princeton University Press, 1978), pp. 57–58.

30. Randolph to Monroe, Sept. 16, 1806, and Monroe to Randolph, June 16, Nov. 12, 1806, in Hamilton, ed., *Monroe Writings*, 4:460, 466–68, 486–91; Noble E. Cunningham, Jr., *The Jeffersonian Republicans in Power: Party Operations, 1801–1809* (Chapel Hill: University of North Carolina Press for the Institute of Early American History and Culture, Williamsburg, Va., 1963), pp. 228, 232.

31. Creed Taylor to unknown recipient, Dec. 21, 1807, Creed Taylor Papers, University of Virginia.

32. Cunningham, *Jeffersonian Republicans in Power*, pp. 110–11, 183–84.

33. Jefferson to Monroe, Feb. 18, 1808, in Ford, ed., *Jefferson Works*, 11:10–11.

34. Ibid.; Monroe to Jefferson, Feb. 27, 1808, in Hamilton, ed., *Monroe Writings*, 5:26.

35. Undated memorandum, James Monroe Papers, Library of Congress (hereafter, LC); "The following interesting correspondence between the President of the United States and Mr. Monroe, is published by consent of the president, at the request of Mr. Monroe," Richmond, Oct. 27, 1808, circular, James Madison Papers, LC; Cunningham, *Jeffersonian Republicans in Power*, pp. 234–35; Ammon, *Monroe*, p. 277.

36. Jefferson to Madison, Nov. 30, 1809, in Ford, ed., *Jefferson Works*, 11:126–28; Ammon, *Monroe*, pp. 280–86.

37. Irving Brant, *James Madison*, 6 vols. (Indianapolis: Bobbs-Merrill Company, 1941–1961), 5:22–25, 275, 278, 282–87; Cunningham, *Process of Government Under Jefferson*, p. 133; Ammon, *Monroe*, p. 287; Madison to Monroe, Mar. 20, 1811, and Monroe to Madison, Mar. 23, 29, 1811, in Hamilton, ed., *Monroe Writings*, 5:181–84.

38. Ammon, *Monroe*, pp. 292–93, 298–99.

39. Ibid., pp. 301, 313–19.

40. Ibid., pp. 323–24, 328–30.

41. Ibid., pp. 331–34; Brant, *James Madison*, 6:298–302; Donald R. Hickey,

The War of 1812: A Forgotten Conflict (Urbana: University of Illinois Press, 1969), pp. 197-98.

42. Ammon, *Monroe,* pp. 335-37; Brant, *James Madison,* 6:330-32; C. Edward Skeen, *John Armstrong, Jr., 1758-1843: A Biography* (Syracuse, N.Y.: Syracuse University Press, 1981), pp. 199-200.

43. Monroe to the Military Committee of the Senate, Feb. 22, 1815, in Hamilton, ed., *Monroe Writings,* 5:325-26; Ammon, *Monroe,* p. 345.

CHAPTER 2
THE ELECTION OF A PRESIDENT

1. Jonathan Fisk to John W. Taylor, Dec. 31, 1815, John W. Taylor Papers, New-York Historical Society.

2. Morgan Lewis to Taylor, Dec. 22, 1815, ibid.

3. Robert V. Remini, "New York and the Presidential Election of 1816," *New York History* 31 (1950): 308-23; Ray W. Irwin, *Daniel D. Tompkins: Governor of New York and Vice President of the United States* (New York: New-York Historical Society, 1968), pp. 205-10.

4. George Hay to Charles Everett, Feb. 1816, Hugh Nelson Papers, LC.

5. John W. Taylor to John Taylor, Feb. 18, 1816, and J. W. Taylor to Esek Cowen, Mar. 4, 1816, Taylor Papers, New-York Historical Society.

6. Fisk to Taylor, Feb. 29, 1816, ibid.

7. Hay to Everett, Feb. 1816, Hugh Nelson Papers, LC.

8. *Niles' Weekly Register* 10 (Mar. 25, 1816): 59; John W. Taylor's note on his invitation to the March 12, 1816, caucus, Taylor Papers, New-York Historical Society.

9. *Niles' Weekly Register* 10 (Mar. 25, 1816): 59-60; John W. Taylor to Jane Taylor (wife), Mar. 17, 1816, Taylor Papers, New-York Historical Society.

10. Remini, "New York and the Presidential Election of 1816," p. 319; Harry Ammon, *James Monroe: The Quest for National Identity* (New York: McGraw-Hill, 1971), p. 356; Lynn W. Turner, "Elections of 1816 and 1820," in Arthur M. Schlesinger, Jr., and Fred L. Israel, eds., *History of American Presidential Elections, 1789-1968,* 4 vols. (New York: McGraw-Hill, 1971), 1:305.

11. *Exposition of Motives for Opposing the Nomination of Mr. Monroe for the Office of President of the United States* (Washington, D.C., 1816), p. 11.

12. Gideon Granger to DeWitt Clinton, Mar. 27, 1816; Clinton to Jabez D. Hammond, Apr. 19, 1816; Clinton to Roger Skinner, Nov. 14, 1816; Roger Skinner to Clinton, Nov. 21, 1816, Taylor Papers, New-York Historical Society.

13. King to Christopher Gore, Nov. 5, 1816, in Charles R. King, ed., *The Life and Correspondence of Rufus King,* 6 vols. (New York: G. P. Putnam's Sons, 1894-1900), 6:32.

14. Rufus King to William King, Apr. 22, 1818, quoted in Robert Ernst, *Rufus King: American Federalist* (Chapel Hill: University of North Carolina Press for the Institute of Early American History and Culture, Williamsburg, Va., 1968), pp. 351-52.

15. *National Intelligencer* (Washington), Feb. 12, 14, 1817.

16. Jackson to Monroe, Nov. 12, 1816, in Sam B. Smith, Harriet C. Owsley, and Harold D. Moser, eds., *The Papers of Andrew Jackson*, 4 vols. to date (Knoxville: University of Tennessee Press, 1980–), 4:75 (spelling corrections made).

17. Monroe to Jackson, Dec. 14, 1816, in Stanislaus M. Hamilton, ed., *The Writings of James Monroe*, 7 vols. (New York, 1898–1903; reprint ed., NewYork: AMS Press, 1969), 5:342–43.

18. Ibid., pp. 344–45.

19. Ibid., pp. 345–46. On Monroe and political parties, see also Richard Hofstadter, *The Idea of a Party System: The Rise of Legitimate Opposition in the United States, 1780–1840* (Berkeley and Los Angeles: University of California Press, 1969), pp. 188–203.

20. Monroe to Jackson, Dec. 14, 1816, in Hamilton, ed., *Monroe Writings*, 5:347.

21. Monroe to Jefferson, Feb. 23, 1817, ibid., 6:4.

22. Nelson to Charles Everett, Dec. 21, 1816, Hugh Nelson Papers, LC.

23. Merrill D. Peterson, *The Great Triumvirate: Webster, Clay, and Calhoun* (New York: Oxford University Press, 1987), p. 50.

24. Crawford to Albert Gallatin, Mar. 12, 1817, in Henry Adams, ed., *The Writings of Albert Gallatin*, 3 vols. (New York: Antiquarian Press, 1960; orig. pub. 1879), 2:24–25; Irving Brant, *James Madison*, 6 vols. (Indianapolis: Bobbs-Merrill Company, 1941–1961), 6:412.

25. Monroe to Jackson, Mar. 1, 1817, in Hamilton, ed., *Monroe Writings*, 6:5.

26. Monroe to Shelby, Feb. 20, 1817, ibid., pp. 1–2.

27. Monroe to Jefferson, Feb. 23, 1817, ibid., p. 4.

28. Carl J. Vipperman, *William Lowndes and the Transition of Southern Politics, 1782–1822* (Chapel Hill: University of North Carolina Press, 1989), p. 153.

29. Monroe to Wirt, Oct. 29, 1817, and Wirt to Elizabeth Wirt (wife), Nov. 13, 1817, William Wirt Papers, Maryland Historical Society, microfilm edition.

30. Henry Adams, *History of the United States of America During the Administrations of Thomas Jefferson and James Madison*, 9 vols. (New York: Charles Scribner's Sons, 1889–1891), 9:173.

31. Douglass C. North, *The Economic Growth of the United States, 1790–1860* (New York: W. W. Norton, 1966; orig. pub. 1961), pp. 63–64.

32. *Historical Statistics of the United States: Colonial Times to 1970* (Washington, D.C.: Bureau of the Census, 1975), pp. 8, 805; *Biographical Directory of the American Congress, 1774–1971* (Washington, D.C.: Government Printing Office, 1971).

33. *Historical Statistics of the United States*, p. 1118.

34. North, *Economic Growth of the United States*, p. 62.

35. House Document 45, 24 Cong., 1 Sess., Mar. 4, 1836, p. 51.

36. *Niles' Weekly Register* 8 (1815): ii.

37. Frances Wright, *Views of Society and Manners in America*, ed. Paul R. Baker (Cambridge: Harvard University Press, 1963; orig. pub. 1821), p. 212.

38. Russel Blaine Nye, *The Cultural Life of the New Nation, 1776–1830* (New York: Harper and Row, 1960), pp. 255–57.

39. Noble E. Cunningham, Jr., *Popular Images of the Presidency: From Washington to Lincoln* (Columbia: University of Missouri Press, 1991), pp. 28–29, 36–38, 61–62, 147–48.

40. Noble E. Cunningham, Jr., *In Pursuit of Reason: The Life of Thomas Jefferson* (Baton Rouge: Louisiana State University Press, 1987), pp. 338–39.

CHAPTER 3
FIRST MONTHS IN OFFICE

1. *National Intelligencer* (Washington), Mar. 5, 1817.

2. Monroe to Marshall, Mar. 1, 1817, and Marshall to Monroe, Mar. 1, 1817, John Marshall Papers, College of William and Mary; *National Intelligencer* (Washington), Mar. 3, 1817.

3. *National Intelligencer* (Washington), Mar. 4, 1817; Clay to James Barbour, Mar. 3, 1817, in James F. Hopkins, Mary W. M. Hargreaves, Robert Seager II, Melba Porter Hay, and Carol Reardon, eds., *The Papers of Henry Clay*, 10 vols. (Lexington: University Press of Kentucky, 1959–1992), 2:320.

4. *National Intelligencer* (Washington), Mar. 5, 1817.

5. Ibid.

6. Sally Otis to William Foster, Mar. 12, 1817, in Samuel Eliot Morison, *The Life and Letters of Harrison Gray Otis*, 2 vols. (Boston: Houghton Mifflin, 1913), 2:205.

7. Ibid., p. 206.

8. *National Intelligencer* (Washington), Mar. 5, 1817.

9. Constance McLaughlin Green, *Washington: Village and Capital, 1800–1878* (Princeton: Princeton University Press, 1962), pp. 67–68.

10. James Monroe, inaugural address, Mar. 4, 1817, in Stanislaus Hamilton, ed., *The Writings of James Monroe*, 7 vols. (New York, 1898–1903; reprint ed., New York: AMS Press, 1969), 6:6–14.

11. *National Intelligencer* (Washington), Mar. 5, 1817.

12. *National Register* 3 (Mar. 15, 1817): 161–63 (Joel K. Mead, editor).

13. Dearborn to Monroe, Mar. 11, 1817, James Monroe Papers, New York Public Library (hereafter, NYPL).

14. House Report 79, Feb. 21, 1825, 18 Cong., 2 Sess., serial set 123, 2:17–18; Monroe to Jefferson, Apr. 23, 1817, in Hamilton, ed., *Monroe Writings*, 6:22.

15. Biddle to Monroe, Apr. 10, 1817, Monroe Papers, NYPL.

16. Ibid.

17. Monroe to Jefferson, July 17, 1817, in Hamilton, ed., *Monroe Writings*, 6:26–27.

18. *Niles' Weekly Register* 12 (June 7, 1817): 238.

19. George Stiles, address, dated June 2, 1817, ibid.

20. Ibid., pp. 238–39.

21. Samuel Putnam Waldo, *The Tour of James Monroe, President of the United*

States, Through the Northern and Eastern States, in 1817; His Tour in the Year 1818; Together with a Sketch of His Life, 2d ed. (Hartford, Conn.: Silas Andrus, 1820), p. 61, 69–70; Joseph Gardner Swift, *The Memoirs of General Joseph Gardner Swift* (N.p., 1890), p. 153; *Niles' Weekly Register* 12 (June 14, 1817): 250.

22. *National Register* 3 (June 21, 1817): 398; *Niles' Weekly Register* 12 (June 28, 1817): 280.

23. *Niles' Weekly Register* 12 (June 21, 1817): 271.

24. *Enquirer* (Richmond), Aug. 5, 1817, quoted in Bert M. Mutersbaugh, "Jeffersonian Journalist: Thomas Ritchie and the Richmond *Enquirer,* 1804–1820" (Ph.D. diss., University of Missouri, Columbia, 1973), pp. 399–400.

25. Waldo, *Tour of James Monroe,* pp. 80–87, 98; *National Register* 3 (June 21, 1817): 398–400.

26. Reprinted in *Niles' Weekly Register* 12 (June 21, 1817): 271–72.

27. Richard Radcliffe, ed., *The President's Tour: A Collection of Addresses Made to James Monroe, Esq., President of the United States, on His Tour Through the Northern and Middle States, A.D. 1817, Accompanied with Answers from the President* (New Ipswich, N.H.: Salmon Wilder, 1822). Samuel Putnam Waldo's *Tour of James Monroe,* first published in 1819, contained extensive reprinting of Monroe's addresses.

28. Monroe to George Graham, June 15, 1817, Graham Family Papers, Virginia Historical Society.

29. Monroe to George Hay, Aug. 5, 1817, "Letters of James Monroe, 1812–1817," *Bulletin of the New York Public Library* 6 (1902): 230.

30. William Wirt, *The Letters of the British Spy,* 10th ed. (New York: Harper and Brothers, 1856), pp. 174, 176–77; Richard Beale Davis, *Intellectual Life in Jefferson's Virginia, 1790–1830* (Chapel Hill: University of North Carolina Press, 1964), pp. 176–77, 279–81.

31. Monroe to George Hay, Aug. 5, 1817, "Letters of James Monroe," 230.

32. *National Register* 3 (June 21, 1817): 400; *Niles' Weekly Register* 12 (June 21, 1817): 272; Waldo, *Tour of James Monroe,* p. 101.

33. Charles Francis Adams, ed., *The Memoirs of John Quincy Adams, Comprising Portions of His Diary from 1797 to 1848,* 12 vols. (Philadelphia: J. B. Lippincott, 1874–1877) (hereafter, Adams, *Diary*), Sept. 14, 1817, 4:4–5.

34. Waldo, *Tour of James Monroe,* pp. 133, 135, 138.

35. House Report 79, 18 Cong., 2 Sess., serial set 123, 2:15–18; Diary of Charles Jared Ingersoll, Feb. 9, 1823, in William M. Meigs, *The Life of Charles Jared Ingersoll* (Philadelphia: J. B. Lippincott, 1897), p. 117.

36. Radcliffe, ed., *President's Tour,* pp. 50–52.

37. *Niles' Weekly Register* 12 (July 12, 1817): 314.

38. Jeremiah Brainard to the president, June 25, 1817, Monroe Papers, NYPL.

39. Monroe to Jefferson, July 27, 1817, in Hamilton, ed., *Monroe Writings,* 6:27.

40. *Columbian Centinel* (Boston), July 5, 1817; *Independent Chronicle and Boston Patriot,* July 3, 4, 8, 1817; Morison, *Life and Letters of Harrison Gray Otis,* 2:207; Radcliffe, ed., *President's Tour,* pp. 24–29.

41. Gore to Jeremiah Mason, July 4, 1817, in George S. Hilliard, ed., *Memoir and Correspondence of Jeremiah Mason* (Cambridge, Mass.: Riverside Press, 1873), p. 173.

42. *Columbian Centinel* (Boston), July 5, 9, 19, 30, 1817; *Niles' Weekly Register* 12 (July 19, 1817): 327–29.

43. *Independent Chronicle and Boston Patriot*, July 8, 1817.

44. *Niles' Weekly Register* 12 (July 19, 1817): 329.

45. Monroe to Jefferson, July 27, 1817, in Hamilton, ed., *Monroe Writings*, 6:27–28.

46. *Annals of Congress*, 15 Cong., 1 Sess. (Mar. 7, 1818), p. 1169.

47. Monroe to Hay, Aug. 5, 1817, "Letters of James Monroe," 227.

48. Ibid., pp. 228–29.

49. Philemon Beecher, chairman of the committee, to the President of the United States, Aug. 26, 1817, Monroe Papers, NYPL.

50. Levin Belt to the President of the United States, Aug. 28, 1817, ibid.

51. Waldo, *Tour of James Monroe*, pp. 266–67.

52. Radcliffe, ed., *President's Tour*, pp. 72–76; Waldo, *Tour of James Monroe*, pp. 294–97.

53. Monroe to [Charles J. Ingersoll], Dec. 2, 1817, Monroe Papers, NYPL.

CHAPTER 4
THE NEW PRESIDENT AND A NEW CONGRESS

1. Adams, *Diary*, Sept. 20, 1817, 4:4–8.

2. Monroe to Adams, Oct. 11, 1817, Adams Family Papers, Massachusetts Historical Society (hereafter, MHS), microfilm edition, reel 440. See also on same reel, "Draft to Dashkoff," Oct. 13, 1817, with note by Monroe attached.

3. Monroe to George Graham, Oct. 5, 1817, Graham Family Papers, Virginia Historical Society.

4. Noble E. Cunningham, Jr., *In Pursuit of Reason: The Life of Thomas Jefferson* (Baton Rouge: Louisiana State University Press, 1987), p. 339.

5. Adams's draft, Oct. 1817, and Monroe's comments, Adams Family Papers, MHS, microfilm edition, reel 440; Adams, *Diary*, Oct. 29, 1817, 4:14.

6. Adams, *Diary*, Nov. 18, 21, 1817, 4:21–22, and Mar. 26, 1821, 5:337–38. Abbé Correa was Portuguese minister to the United States.

7. Memorandum, endorsed by Adams: "Monroe, James, P.U.S. Questions 25 Oct. 1817 proposed by P.U.S. to the Heads of Departments," Adams Family Papers, MHS, microfilm edition, reel 440; printed in Stanislaus M. Hamilton, ed., *The Writings of James Monroe*, 7 vols. (New York, 1898–1903; reprint ed., New York: AMS Press, 1969), 6:31–32.

8. Arthur Preston Whitaker, *The United States and the Independence of Latin America, 1800–1830* (New York: Russell and Russell, 1962; orig. pub., 1941), pp. 229–32.

9. Adams, *Diary*, Oct. 25–30, 1817, 4:13–16.

10. Ibid., Nov. 7, 1817, 4:16–17.

11. Monroe to Rives, Nov. 24, 1817, William C. Rives Papers, LC; Adams, *Diary,* Nov. 14, 1817, 4:21.

12. Adams, *Diary,* Nov. 28, 1817, 4:25.

13. *National Register* 4 (Dec. 6, 1817): 353–58; *Niles' Weekly Register* 13 (Dec. 6, 1817): 235–36, 240.

14. Fred Israel, ed., *The State of the Union Messages of the Presidents, 1790–1966,* 3 vols. (New York: Chelsea House, 1967), 1:148.

15. Ibid., pp. 149–150.

16. Ibid., pp. 151–52, 156.

17. Ibid., pp. 153–54.

18. Ibid., pp. 154, 155.

19. James J. Wilson to William Darlington, Senate Chamber, Dec. 1, 1817, William Darlington Papers, LC; *Annals of Congress,* 15 Cong., 1 Sess., pp. 2505–8.

20. Nelson to Charles Everett, Dec. 2, [1817], Hugh Nelson Papers, LC.

21. Mason to Rufus King, Dec. 10, 1817, in George S. Hilliard, ed., *Memoir and Correspondence of Jeremiah Mason* (Cambridge, Mass.: Riverside Press, 1873), p. 177.

22. Robert Allen Rutland, *The Presidency of James Madison* (Lawrence: University Press of Kansas, 1990), pp. 205–6.

23. Nelson to Charles Everett, Dec. 2, [1817], Hugh Nelson Papers, LC.

24. *Niles' Weekly Register* 13 (Dec. 20, 1817): 257–59. Another analysis of the message is in the *National Register* 4 (Dec. 6, 1817): 358–60.

25. Monroe to Charles J. Ingersoll, Dec. 2, 1817, James Monroe Papers, NYPL.

26. Brooks to Monroe, Dec. 8, 1817, ibid.

27. Astor to Monroe, Dec. 6, 1817, microfilm of private collection, LC.

28. Roane to Monroe, Dec. 6, 1817, Monroe Papers, College of William and Mary.

29. Madison to Monroe, Dec. 9, 1817, in Gaillard Hunt, ed., *The Writings of James Madison,* 9 vols. (New York: G. P. Putnam's Sons, 1900–1910), 8:399.

30. Monroe to Madison, Dec. 22, 1817, in Hamilton, ed., *Monroe Writings,* 6:45–46.

31. Jackson to Monroe, Mar. 4, 1817, and Monroe to Jackson, Oct. 5, 1817, in John Spencer Bassett, ed., *Correspondence of Andrew Jackson,* 6 vols. (Washington D.C.: Carnegie Institution, 1926–1933), 2:231–32.

32. Adams, *Diary,* Jan. 6, 9, 1818, 4:36–37.

33. Ibid., Dec. 6, 1817, 4:28, Mar. 18, 28, 1818, 4:62–63, 70.

34. James Sterling Young, *The Washington Community, 1800–1828* (New York: Columbia University Press, 1966), p. 90.

35. Louis McLane to Kitty McLane (wife), Dec. 2, 1817, Louis McLane Papers, LC.

36. *Annals of Congress,* 14 Cong., 1 Sess., p. 1801.

37. Tyler to his constituents, Feb. 25, 1817, in Noble E. Cunningham, Jr., ed., *Circular Letters of Congressmen to Their Constituents, 1789–1829,* 3 vols.

(Chapel Hill: University of North Carolina Press for the Institute of Early American History and Culture, Williamsburg, Va., 1978), 2:998.

38. Committee rosters are in Perry Goldman and James S. Young, eds., *The United States Congressional Directories, 1789–1840* (New York: Columbia University Press, 1973), pp. 79–82, 89–92.

39. *Niles' Weekly Register* 13 (Nov. 8, 1817): 163. Niles gave credit for the figures to the *Norfolk Herald*.

40. Williams to his constituents, Apr. 25, 1816, in Cunningham, ed., *Circular Letters*, 2:980.

41. Samuel Dickens to his constituents, Mar. 4, 1817, ibid., p. 1007.

42. Tyler to his constituents, Apr. 14, 1818, ibid., 3:1035.

43. Mason to Rufus King, Dec. 10, 1817, in Hilliard, ed., *Mason Correspondence*, p. 177.

44. Story to Ezekiel Bacon, Mar. 12, 1818, in William W. Story, ed., *Life and Letters of Joseph Story*, 2 vols. (Boston: Charles E. Little and James Brown, 1851), 1:311.

45. Act of Dec. 23, 1817, *Annals of Congress*, 15 Cong., 1 Sess., pp. 2505–8.

46. Ibid. (Mar. 14, 1818), pp. 1381–89.

47. Ibid. (Mar. 14, 28, 1818), pp. 1468, 1646; Joseph Desha to Walker Reid, Mar. 28, 1818, Joseph Desha Papers, LC; Alexander Smyth to his constituents, Apr. 13, 1818, in Cunningham, ed., *Circular Letters*, 3:1025.

48. Monroe to Fulwar Skipwith, Apr. 21, 1818, Monroe Papers, NYPL.

49. Adams to Alexander H. Everett, Apr. 6, 1818, Adams Family Collection, LC.

50. Stewart to his constituents, Apr. 13, 1818, in Cunningham, ed., *Circular Letters*, 3:1027.

51. Nathaniel Silsbee to Henry Dearborn, Mar. 22, 1818, Nathaniel Silsbee Papers, LC.

52. Monroe to Madison, Apr. 28, 1818, in Hamilton, ed., *Monroe Writings*, 6:49–50.

53. Monroe to Fulwar Skipwith, Apr. 21, 1818, Monroe Papers, NYPL.

CHAPTER 5

ANDREW JACKSON AND THE FIRST SEMINOLE WAR

1. Jackson to Monroe, Mar. 4, 1817, in Sam B. Smith, Harriet Owsley, and Harold D. Moser, eds., *The Papers of Andrew Jackson*, 4 vols. to date (Knoxville: University of Tennessee Press, 1980–), 4:93–98.

2. Monroe to Jackson, June 2, Aug. 4, 1817, in John Spencer Bassett, ed., *Correspondence of Andrew Jackson*, 6 vols. (Washington D.C.: Carnegie Institution, 1926–1933), 2:296–97, 319.

3. Monroe to George Graham, Oct. 5, 1817, Graham Family Papers, Virginia Historical Society.

4. Jackson to Monroe, Aug. 12, 1817, in Bassett, ed., *Jackson Correspondence*, 2:320–21.

5. Calhoun to Monroe, Nov. 1, 1817, in Robert L. Meriwether, W. Edwin Hemphill, and Clyde N. Wilson, eds., *The Papers of John C. Calhoun*, 21 vols. to date (Columbia: University of South Carolina Press, 1959–), 1:418–19.

6. Monroe to George Graham, Oct. 5, 1817, Graham Family Papers, Virginia Historical Society.

7. Monroe to Jackson, Oct. 5, 1817, in Bassett, ed., *Jackson Correspondence*, 2:329–31.

8. Monroe to Jackson, Dec. 2, 1817, ibid., pp. 336–37. Before sending this letter to Jackson, Monroe sent it to George Graham to review, noting that "I have not mentioned either Mr. Crawford or you for reasons that will occur." Monroe to Graham, Dec. 2, 1817, James Monroe Papers, NYPL.

9. Jackson to Monroe, Dec. 20, 1817, in Smith, Owsley, and Moser, eds., *Jackson Papers*, 4:162.

10. Calhoun to Jackson, Dec. 29, 1817, in Meriwether, Hemphill, and Wilson, eds., *Calhoun Papers*, 2:43–44. A number of historians, including Charles Wiltse, Robert Remini, John Niven, and the editors of the *Calhoun Papers*, have given Calhoun the credit for ending the confrontation between Jackson and the War Department, but the evidence indicates that Monroe settled the dispute. Charles M. Wiltse, *John C. Calhoun: Nationalist, 1782–1828* (Indianapolis: Bobbs-Merrill Company, 1944), p. 151; Robert V. Remini, *Andrew Jackson and the Course of American Empire, 1767–1821* (New York: Harper and Row, 1977), p. 343; John C. Nevin, *John C. Calhoun and the Price of Union: A Biography* (Baton Rouge: Louisiana State University Press, 1988), pp. 61–62; *Calhoun Papers*, 2:lvii–lviii.

11. Monroe to Jackson, Dec. 28, 1817, Monroe Papers, NYPL. The general order, Dec. 29, 1817, stated: "As a general rule, all orders will issue in the first instance, to the commanders of division. In cases where the nature of the duty to be performed, and the public interest may require it, orders will issue directly to officers commanding departments, posts, or detachments, and to any officer attached to the division; but in such cases, a copy of the orders will be transmitted to General of division, for his information." Meriwether, Hemphill, and Wilson, eds., *Calhoun Papers*, 2:42–43.

12. Monroe to Jackson, Dec. 28, 1817, Monroe Papers, NYPL.

13. Charles Francis Adams, ed., *The Memoirs of John Quincy Adams, Comprising Portions of His Diary from 1797 to 1848*, 12 vols. (Philadelphia: J. B. Lippincott, 1874–1877), Dec. 26, 1817, 4:31.

14. Meriwether, Hemphill, and Wilson, eds., *Calhoun Papers*, 2:20.

15. Jackson to Monroe, Jan. 6, 1818, in Smith, Owsley, and Moser, eds., *Jackson Papers*, 4:166–67.

16. Jackson to Calhoun, Jan. 12, 1818, in Bassett, ed., *Jackson Correspondence*, 2:347.

17. Calhoun to James Bankhead, Jan. 15, 1818, in Meriwether, Hemphill, and Wilson, eds., *Calhoun Papers*, 2:73–74.

18. Calhoun to Forsyth, Mar. 24, 1818, ibid., p. 207. Forsyth himself had contemplated proposing that Congress pass a bill authorizing the president to

take possession of East Florida, but he did not get the support of his committee. Adams, *Diary,* Mar. 22, 23, 24, 1819, 4:65–67.

19. Monroe to Senate and House of Representatives, Mar. 25, 1818, in James D. Richardson, ed., *A Compilation of the Messages and Papers of the Presidents, 1789–1897,* 10 vols. (Washington, D.C.: N.p., 1896–1899), 2:31–32.

20. Adams, *Diary,* May 4, 1818, 4:87; Jackson to Mrs. Jackson, Apr. 8, 1818, in Bassett, ed., *Jackson Correspondence,* 2:357–58.

21. Jackson to Calhoun, Apr. 8, 20, 26, May 5, 1818, in Bassett, ed., *Jackson Correspondence,* 2:358–59, 362–63, 365–67.

22. Jackson to Calhoun, May 5, 1818, ibid., pp. 366–68.

23. Jackson to Monroe, June 2, 1818, ibid., pp. 376, 378.

24. Jackson to Calhoun, June 2, 1818, ibid., p. 380.

25. Adams, *Diary,* June 18, 25, 26, July 8, 1818, 4:102–5.

26. Ibid., July 15, 16, 1818, pp. 107–9.

27. Ibid., July 17, 18, 20, 1818, pp. 111–13.

28. Ibid., July 18, 21, 24, 28, 1818, pp. 112, 114–17, 119.

29. Ingersoll to Monroe, Aug. 10, 1819, Monroe Papers, NYPL.

30. *National Intelligencer* (Washington), July 27, 1818.

31. Ibid.

32. Ibid.

33. Monroe to Jackson, July 19, 1818, in Smith, Owsley, and Moser, eds., *Jackson Papers,* 4:224–25.

34. Jackson to Monroe, Aug. 19, 1818, ibid., pp. 236–38.

35. Monroe to George Hay, Sept. 6, 1818, Ingrid Westesson Hoes Archives, James Monroe Museum and Memorial Library, Fredericksburg, Va.

36. Ibid.

37. Monroe to Jackson, Oct. 20, 1818, in Bassett, ed., *Jackson Correspondence,* 2:398.

38. Ibid.

39. Jackson to Monroe, Nov. 15, 1818, in Smith, Owsley, and Moser, eds., *Jackson Papers,* 4:247.

40. Adams, *Diary,* Nov. 2, 4, 5, 1818, 4:156, 162, 164.

41. Monroe to Adams, Nov. 9, 1818, Adams Family Papers, MHS, microfilm edition, reel 445. Benjamin Crowninshield resigned as secretary of the navy in September 1818. At the time of his appointment, Smith Thompson was chief justice of the Supreme Court of New York; he was also a friend of Martin Van Buren.

42. Adams, *Diary,* Nov. 7, 1818, 4:165–68.

43. Fred Israel, ed., *The State of the Union Messages of the Presidents, 1790–1966,* 3 vols. (New York: Chelsea House, 1967), 1:157–61.

44. *Annals of Congress,* 15 Cong., 2 Sess., pp. 515–18, 1132–33; *American State Papers: Documents Legislative and Executive of the United States,* 38 vols. (Washington, D.C., 1832–1861), *Military Affairs,* 1:681–769; House Document 86, 15 Cong., 2 Sess., Jan. 12, 1819; James S. Smith to his constituents, July 3, 1819, in Noble E. Cunningham, Jr., ed., *Circular Letters of Congressmen to Their Constituents, 1789–1829,* 3 vols. (Chapel Hill: University of North Carolina Press for the

Institute of Early American History and Culture, Williamsburg, Va., 1978), 3:1087.

45. Louis McLane to Kitty McLane, Jan. 20, 1819, McLane Papers, LC.

46. Margaret Bayard Smith to Jane Bayard Kirkpatrick, Jan. 1819, in Gaillard Hunt, ed., *The First Forty Years of Washington Society in the Family Letters of Margaret Bayard Smith* (New York: Frederick Ungar, 1965; orig. pub. 1906), pp. 145–46.

47. Louis McLane to Kitty McLane, Jan. 23, 1819, McLane Papers, LC.

48. John Forsyth to R. Campbell, Feb. 7, 1819, John Forsyth Papers, South Caroliniana Library, University of South Carolina.

49. James J. Wilson to William Darlington, Jan. 22, 26, 1819, William Darlington Papers, LC; Merrill D. Peterson, *The Great Triumvirate: Webster, Clay, and Calhoun* (New York: Oxford University Press, 1987), pp. 45–56; James F. Hopkins, Mary W. M. Hargreaves, Robert Seager II, Melba Porter Hay, and Carol Reardon, eds., *The Papers of Henry Clay*, 10 vols. (Lexington: University Press of Kentucky, 1959–1992), 2:636–60.

50. Louis McLane to Kitty McLane, Jan. 23, 1819, McLane Papers, LC.

51. Nelson to William C. Rives, Feb. 17, 1819, William C. Rives Papers, LC.

52. John Forsyth to R. Campbell, Feb. 7, 1819, Forsyth Papers, South Caroliniana Library. For further examination of Congress see David S. Heidler, "The Politics of National Aggression: Congress and the First Seminole War," *Journal of the Early Republic* 13 (1993): 501–30.

53. Circular letters of Jesse Slocumb, Feb. 22, 1819, and James S. Smith, July 3, 1819, in Cunningham, ed., *Circular Letters*, 3:1055, 1085.

54. James S. Smith, circular letter, July 3, 1819, ibid., p. 1089.

55. Williams, circular letter, Feb. 20, 1819, ibid., p. 1051.

56. The extensive correspondence, including that of Monroe made available to Calhoun, was published in the newspapers by Calhoun and reprinted in *Niles' Weekly Register* 40 (Mar. 5, 12, 19, 1831): 11–24, 37–40, 41–45.

57. Monroe to Calhoun, Dec. 18, 1827, in Stanislaus M. Hamilton, ed., *The Writings of James Monroe*, 7 vols. (New York, 1898–1903; reprint ed., New York: AMS Press, 1969), 7:139. See also Monroe to Calhoun, May 19, 1830, ibid., p. 209.

58. The details are presented in Richard R. Steinberg, "Jackson's 'Rhea Letter' Hoax," *Journal of Southern History* 2 (1936): 480–96.

59. Statement, signed and witnessed, June 19, 1831, in Hamilton, ed., *Monroe Writings*, 7:234–36.

60. Monroe to Madison, Feb. 7, 1819, ibid., 6:87–88.

61. Adams, *Diary*, July 16, 1818, 4:110.

62. For the treaty negotiations and maps see Samuel Flagg Bemis, *John Quincy Adams and the Foundations of American Foreign Policy* (New York: Alfred A. Knopf, 1949), pp. 317–40 and map 7; William Earl Weeks, *John Quincy Adams and American Global Empire* (Lexington: University Press of Kentucky, 1992), pp. 119–38, 161–66. For documents see *American State Papers: Foreign Relations*, 4:422–626.

63. Adams, *Diary*, Feb. 22, 1819, 4:275.

64. Monroe to Richard Rush, Mar. 7, 1819, in Hamilton, ed., *Monroe Writings*, 6:91.

65. *Journal of the Executive Proceedings of the Senate*, 41 Sess., Feb. 22, 24, 1819, 3:177–78.

CHAPTER 6
WIDENING HORIZONS AND DEEPENING PROBLEMS

1. Monroe to Fulmar Skipwith, Nov. 28, 1818, James Monroe Papers, NYPL.

2. Charles M. Wiltse, *John C. Calhoun: Nationalist, 1782–1828* (Indianapolis: Bobbs-Merrill Company, 1944), pp. 180–82.

3. *Niles' Weekly Register* 16 (May 8, 1819): 192.

4. *National Intelligencer* (Washington), May 4, 1819.

5. Ibid., May 4, 5, 8, 1819.

6. Quoted in ibid., May 11, 1819.

7. Monroe to [George Hay], May 2, 1819, Monroe Papers, NYPL.

8. Noble E. Cunningham, Jr., *Popular Images of the Presidency: From Washington to Lincoln* (Columbia: University of Missouri Press, 1991), pp. 147–48.

9. Monroe to [Hay], May 2, 1819, Monroe Papers, NYPL.

10. Ibid.

11. Ibid. For Monroe's remarks on Jefferson see *National Intelligencer* (Washington), May 5, 1819.

12. Monroe to [Hay], May 2, 1819, Monroe Papers, NYPL.

13. *National Intelligencer* (Washington), May 20, 1819.

14. Ibid., May 27, June 1, 1819.

15. Monroe to Joseph McMinn, June 5, 1819, in Robert L. Meriwether, W. Edwin Hemphill, and Clyde N. Wilson, eds., *The Papers of John C. Calhoun*, 21 vols. to date (Columbia: University of South Carolina Press, 1959–), 4:94.

16. *Niles' Weekly Register* 16 (June 26, 1819): 298. The Lancasterian plan used the more advanced students to teach the less advanced. See Bernard W. Sheehan, *Seeds of Extinction: Jeffersonian Philanthropy and the American Indian* (New York: W. W. Norton for the Institute of Early American History and Culture, Williamsburg, Va., 1974), pp. 127, 132.

17. Monroe to Adams, June 14, 1819, Adams Family Papers, MHS, microfilm edition, reel 447; *National Intelligencer* (Washington), July 2, 1819.

18. Monroe to Calhoun, June 16, 1819, in Meriwether, Hemphill, and Wilson, eds., *Calhoun Papers*, 4:110–11; Robert V. Remini, *Andrew Jackson and the Course of American Empire, 1767–1821* (New York: Harper and Row, 1977), pp. 386–87.

19. *National Intelligencer* (Washington), July 8, 9, 12, 22, 1819.

20. Ibid., July 2, 22, 1819.

21. *Niles' Weekly Register* 16 (July 24, 1819): 368.

22. Clay to Joseph Gales, Jr., July 19, 1819, in James F. Hopkins, Mary W. M. Hargreaves, Robert Seager II, Melba Porter Hay, and Carol Reardon, eds.,

The Papers of Henry Clay, 10 vols. (Lexington: University Press of Kentucky, 1959–1992), 2:700–701.

23. Monroe to Adams, July 5, 1819, Adams Family Papers, MHS, microfilm edition, reel 447.

24. Monroe to Adams, Aug. 2, 1819, ibid.; Adams, *Diary,* Aug. 8, 1819, 4:405.

25. Charles J. Ingersoll to Monroe, Aug. 10, 1819, Monroe Papers, NYPL.

26. Calhoun to Thomas A. Smith, Mar. 16, 1818, in Meriwether, Hemphill, and Wilson, eds., *Calhoun Papers,* 2:195.

27. Calhoun to Andrew Jackson, Aug. 22, 1818, Mar. 6, 1819, ibid., 3:61, 633. The Mandan villages were near the present-day Bismarck, North Dakota.

28. Monroe to Calhoun, July 5, 1819, ibid., 4:135–36.

29. Maj. Gen. Thomas A. Smith to Calhoun, June 26, 1818, ibid., 2:350.

30. Long to Monroe, Mar. 15, 1817, printed in Richard G. Wood, "Exploration by Steamboat," *Journal of Transport History* 2 (1955): 121–22; Richard G. Wood, *Stephen Harriman Long, 1784–1864: Army Engineer, Explorer, Inventor* (Glendale, Calif.: Arthur H. Clark Company, 1966), pp. 59–61; Roger L. Nichols and Patrick L. Halley, *Stephen Long and American Frontier Exploration* (Newark: University of Delaware Press, 1980), pp. 41–57, 61–65.

31. Calhoun to Long, Mar. 8, 1819, in Meriwether, Hemphill, and Wilson, eds., *Calhoun Papers,* 3:639–40.

32. Calhoun to Walsh, Mar. 11, 1819, ibid., pp. 655–56.

33. Walsh to Calhoun, Mar. 30, 1819, ibid., p. 711.

34. Calhoun to Long, Dec. 15, 1818, and Long to Calhoun, Dec. 24, 1818, ibid., pp. 396, 423.

35. Long to Calhoun, Apr. 20, 1819, ibid., 4:33; Patricia Tyson Stroud, *Thomas Say: New World Naturalist* (Philadelphia: University of Pennsylvania Press, 1992), pp. 71–73.

36. Long to Calhoun, Dec. 24, 1818, in Meriwether, Hemphill, and Wilson, eds., *Calhoun Papers,* 3:423.

37. Long to Calhoun, Apr. 20, 1819, ibid., 4:31–33.

38. *National Intelligencer* (Washington), May 10, 1819.

39. Long to Calhoun, Jan. 3, 1820, in Meriwether, Hemphill, and Wilson, eds., *Calhoun Papers,* 4:542–43; Reuben Gold Thwaites, ed., *Early Western Travels,* 32 vols. (Cleveland: Arthur Clarke Company, 1905), 14:12.

40. Calhoun to Joseph G. Swift, Sept. 19, 1819, in Meriwether, Hemphill, and Wilson, eds., *Calhoun Papers,* 4:351. For public interest in the expedition see *Niles' Weekly Register* 16 (July 31, 1819): 377–78; Norval Neil Luxon, *Niles' Weekly Register: News Magazine of the Nineteenth Century* (Baton Rouge: Louisiana State University Press, 1947), pp. 234–35.

41. Long to Calhoun, Jan. 3, 1820, in Meriwether, Hemphill, and Wilson, eds., *Calhoun Papers,* 4:542–43.

42. Wiltse, *Calhoun: Nationalist,* pp. 182–85.

43. Long to Calhoun, Oct. 28, 1819, in Meriwether, Hemphill, and Wilson, eds., *Calhoun Papers,* 4:388–89. Jessup also returned East with Long; Thwaites, ed., *Western Travels,* 14:12.

44. Long to Calhoun, Jan. 3, 1820, in Meriwether, Hemphill, and Wilson, eds., *Calhoun Papers*, 4:546–47.

45. Calhoun to Henry Atkinson, Feb. 28, 1820, and Calhoun to Long, Feb. 29, 1829, ibid., pp. 689, 695.

46. Thwaites, ed., *Early Western Travels*, 14:13–16; Long to Calhoun, Feb. 28, 1821, in Meriwether, Hemphill, and Wilson, eds., *Calhoun Papers*, 5:635. For an excellent, fuller scholarly account of Long's expedition see Stroud, *Thomas Say*, pp. 71–128.

47. Long to Calhoun, Feb. 20, 1821, in Meriwether, Hemphill, and Wilson, eds., *Calhoun Papers*, 5:637–38.

48. *Transactions of the American Philosophical Society, Held at Philadelphia, for Promoting Useful Knowledge*, vol. 2, n.s. (Philadelphia: Abraham Small, 1825).

49. Edwin James, comp., *Account of an Expedition from Pittsburgh to the Rocky Mountains, Performed in the Years 1819 and '20* (Philadelphia: H. C. Carey and F. Lea, 1822–1823), reprinted in Thwaites, ed., *Early Western Travels*, vols. 14–17.

50. Charles Coleman Sellers, *Mr. Peale's Museum: Charles Willson Peale and the First Popular Museum of Natural Science and Art* (New York: W. W. Norton, 1980), pp. 236, 240–42; Calhoun to Long, Mar. 20, 1821, in Meriwether, Hemphill, and Wilson, eds., *Calhoun Papers*, 5:692.

51. Long to Christopher Vandeventer, Feb. 18, 1821, in Meriwether, Hemphill, and Wilson, eds., *Calhoun Papers*, 5:636.

52. Sellers, *Peale's Museum*, pp. 240–42.

53. Fred Israel, ed., *The State of the Union Messages of the Presidents, 1790–1966*, 3 vols. (New York: Chelsea House, 1967), 1:156.

54. Georgia Brady Barnhill, ed., " 'Extracts from the Journals of Ethan A. Greenwood': Portrait Painter and Museum Proprietor," *Proceedings of the American Antiquarian Society* 103 (1993): 140.

55. Ingersoll to Monroe, Nov. 22, 1818, James Monroe Papers, LC.

56. Hugh Nelson to Charles Everett, Dec. 1, 1818; Hugh Nelson Papers, LC. The committee was appointed Nov. 30, 1818, *Annals of Congress*, 15 Cong., 2 Sess., p. 335.

57. William Hendricks, circular letter, Feb. 15, 1819, in Noble E. Cunningham, Jr., ed., *Circular Letters of Congressmen to Their Constituents, 1789–1829*, 3 vols. (Chapel Hill: University of North Carolina Press for the Institute of Early American History and Culture, Williamsburg, Va., 1978), 3:1046.

58. Jesse Slocumb, circular letter, Feb. 22, 1819, ibid., p. 1055.

59. Louis McLane to Kitty McLane, Jan. 16, 1818, Louis McLane Papers, LC.

60. Lewis Williams, circular letter, Feb. 20, 1819, and James Stewart, circular letter, Feb. 25, 1819, in Cunningham, ed., *Circular Letters*, 3:1052, 1064–65; *Annals of Congress*, 15 Cong., 2 Sess., pp. 552–80, 1406, 1419, 2521–22.

61. B. R. Curtis, ed., *Reports of Decisions in the Supreme Court of the United States*, 22 vols., 6th ed. (Boston: Little, Brown and Company, 1881), 4:415–39.

62. Adams, *Diary*, Jan. 8, 1820, 4:499.

63. Monroe, addresses at Georgetown, S.C., and Augusta, Ga., *National Intelligencer* (Washington), May 5, 8, 20, 27, 1819.

64. *National Intelligencer* (Washington), May 18, June 2, 1819.

65. Hay to Monroe, Apr. 11, 1819, Monroe Papers, NYPL.

66. Johnson to Calhoun, Apr. 3, 1819, in Meriwether, Hemphill, and Wilson, eds., *Calhoun Papers*, 4:10.

67. Johnson to Calhoun, Mar. 29, 1819, ibid., 3:702.

68. Pope to Monroe, Aug. 10, 1819, Monroe Papers, NYPL.

69. Worthington to Calhoun, July 30, 1819, in Meriwether, Hemphill, and Wilson, eds., *Calhoun Papers*, 4:534.

70. *Niles' Weekly Register* 16 (June 19, 1819): 273–74.

71. Ibid. (May 22, 1819): 209.

72. Hezekiah Niles to William Darlington, Oct. 9, 1819, William Darlington Papers, LC.

73. Jefferson to Adams, Nov. 7, 1819, in Lester J. Cappon, ed., *The Adams-Jefferson Letters*, 2 vols. (Chapel Hill: University of North Carolina Press for the Institute of Early American History and Culture, Williamsburg, Va.), 2:547.

74. Israel, ed., *State of the Union Messages*, 1:165, 172.

75. Ibid., pp. 165, 172, 173.

76. Adams, *Diary*, Dec. 3, 1819, 4:462.

77. Ibid., Jan. 8, 1820, pp. 500–501; Harry Ammon, *James Monroe: The Quest for National Identity* (New York: McGraw-Hill, 1971), pp. 468–69.

78. Murray N. Rothbard, *The Panic of 1819: Reactions and Policies* (New York: Columbia University Press, 1962), pp. 12–13.

79. Joseph C. Robert, *The Tobacco Kingdom: Plantation, Market, and Factory in Virginia and North Carolina, 1800–1860* (Durham, N.C.: Duke University Press, 1938), pp. 137–40.

80. Alfred G. Smith, Jr., *Economic Readjustment of an Old Cotton State: South Carolina, 1820–1860* (Columbia: University of South Carolina Press, 1958), pp. 220, 224–26; Charles S. Sydnor, *The Development of Southern Sectionalism, 1819–1848* (Baton Rouge: Louisiana State University Press, 1948), p. 104.

81. Israel, ed., *State of the Union Messages*, 1:172.

82. Bray Hammond, *Banks and Politics in America: From the Revolution to the Civil War* (Princeton: Princeton University Press, 1957), p. 282.

83. Israel, ed., *State of the Union Messages*, 1:175.

84. Adams to Jefferson, Nov. 23, 1819, in Cappon, ed., *Adams-Jefferson Letters*, 2:548 (capitalization modernized).

CHAPTER 7

THE MISSOURI COMPROMISE

1. *Annals of Congress*, 15 Cong., 1 Sess., pp. 591, 840, 1391–92, 1672, and 15 Cong., 2 Sess., p. 418.

2. Ibid., 15 Cong., 1 Sess. (Apr. 4, 1818), pp. 1675–76, and 15 Cong., 2 Sess. (Nov. 23, 1818), pp. 306–7; Glover Moore, *The Missouri Controversy, 1819–1821* (Gloucester, Mass.: Peter Smith, 1967; orig. pub. 1953), pp. 33–35.

3. *Annals of Congress*, 15 Cong., 2 Sess. (Feb. 13, 1819), p. 1166; Charles S.

Sydnor, *The Development of Southern Sectionalism, 1819–1848* (Baton Rouge: Louisiana State University Press, 1948), pp. 120–21.

4. *Annals of Congress,* 15 Cong., 2 Sess. (Feb. 15, 1819), pp. 1169–70.

5. Ibid., p. 1193.

6. Nelson to William C. Rives, Feb. 17, [1819], William C. Rives Papers, LC.

7. *Annals of Congress,* 15 Cong., 2 Sess. (Feb. 16, 1819), p. 1213; Moore, *Missouri Controversy,* p. 51.

8. *Annals of Congress,* 15 Cong., 2 Sess. (Feb. 16, 1819), pp. 1214–15; Moore, *Missouri Controversy,* p. 52.

9. Charles R. King, ed., *The Life and Correspondence of Rufus King,* 6 vols. (New York: G. P. Putnam's Sons, 1894–1900), 6:702; Robert Ernst, *Rufus King: Federalist* (Chapel Hill: University of North Carolina Press for the Institute of Early American History and Culture, Williamsburg, Va., 1968), p. 370; *Annals of Congress,* 15 Cong., 2 Sess., pp. 1433–38.

10. Scott, "To the People of the Missouri Territory," in Noble E. Cunningham, Jr., ed., *Circular Letters of Congressmen to Their Constituents, 1789–1829,* 3 vols. (Chapel Hill: University of North Carolina Press for the Institute of Early American History and Culture, Williamsburg, Va., 1978), 3:1092–93.

11. The petitions are in House Records, Record Group 233, National Archives.

12. Circular, signed by Jared Ingersoll and others, Philadelphia, Nov. 26, 1819, and minutes of meeting, Nov. 23, 1819, signed by Jared Ingersoll, chairman, and Robert Ralston, secretary; "The Memorial of the Undersigned, Inhabitants of the City and County of Philadelphia, to the Congress of the United States," referred to the Committee of the Whole on the Missouri State Bill, Dec. 16, 1819, Record Group 233, National Archives.

13. Philadephia memorial, Dec. 16, 1819, Record Group 233, National Archives.

14. "At a meeting of the citizens of Hartford . . . the 3d day of Dec. 1819," John T. Peters, chairman, and "The Memorial of the undersigned, inhabitants of the City of Hartford," endorsed "Read Jan. 21, 1820," Senate Records, Record Group 46, National Archives.

15. Resolutions, adopted at Dover, Jan. 15, 1820, signed by Caleb Rodney, endorsed "Read Feb. 2, 1820," Record Group 46, National Archives.

16. Resolutions, approved, Jan. 3, 1820, signed by Gabriel Slaughter, addressed to Benjamin Hardin, House Records, Record Group 233, National Archives.

17. Resolutions, Harrisburg, Pa., Dec. 28, 1819, signed by William Findlay; State of New York, in Assembly, Jan. 17, 1820, signed by Aaron Clark and John Bacon, Senate Records, Record Group 46, National Archives.

18. "State of New-Jersey," Jan. 15, 1820, signed David Thompson, Jr., Record Group 46, National Archives.

19. *Annals of Congress,* 16 Cong., 1 Sess. (Dec. 8, 9, 1819), pp. 704, 711.

20. Arthur Livermore to Salma Hale, Dec. 14, 1819, Arthur Livermore Papers, LC.

21. Hale to Taylor, Dec. 28, 1819, John W. Taylor Papers, New-York Histori-

cal Society; *Annals of Congress,* 16 Cong., 1 Sess., pp. 732–35, 801–2; Moore, *Missouri Controversy,* p. 86.

22. Monroe to [Hay], Dec. 20, 1819, Monroe Papers, Virginia Historical Society.

23. *National Intelligencer* (Washington), Nov. 18, 20, 23, 25, 1819.

24. Monroe to [Hay], Dec. 20, 1819, Monroe Papers, Virginia Historical Society.

25. Hay to Monroe, Dec. 24, 1819, Monroe Papers, LC.

26. Monroe to Hay, Dec. 27, 1819, Ingrid Westesson Hoes Archives, James Monroe Museum and Memorial Library, Fredericksburg, Va.

27. Monroe to Hay, Jan. 5, 1820, James Monroe Papers, NYPL.

28. Monroe to Hay, Jan. 10, 1820, ibid.

29. Adams, *Diary,* Jan. 8, 1820, 4:499.

30. Monroe to Hay, Jan. [23], 1820, Monroe Papers, Virginia Historical Society.

31. Monroe to Barbour, Feb. 3, 1820, in Lyon G. Tyler, ed., "Missouri Compromise: Letters to James Barbour," *William and Mary Quarterly,* 1st ser., 10 (1901): 9.

32. Moore, *Missouri Controversy,* 88. For Barbour's role in the Senate debates and in the Missouri Compromise, see Charles D. Lowery, *James Barbour, A Jeffersonian Republican* (University: University of Alabama Press, 1984), pp. 108–25.

33. Clay to John C. Crittenden, Jan. 29, 1820, in James F. Hopkins, Mary W. M. Hargreaves, Robert Seager II, Melba Porter Hay, and Carol Reardon, eds., *The Papers of Henry Clay,* 10 vols. (Lexington: University Press of Kentucky, 1959–1992), 2:679; see also Clay to Jonathan Russell, Jan. 29, 1820, ibid., p. 771.

34. Clay to Martin D. Hardin, Feb. 5, 1820, ibid., p. 775; see also Clay to Leslie Combs, Feb. 5, 1820, ibid., p. 774.

35. Monroe to Hay, Feb. 6, 1820, Monroe Papers, NYPL. See also Monroe to Jefferson, Feb. 7, 1820, in Stanislaus Hamilton, ed., *The Writings of James Monroe,* 7 vols. (New York, 1898–1903; reprint ed., New York: AMS Press, 1969), 6:114.

36. Yancey to Archibald Austin, Feb. 10, 1820, Austin-Twyman Papers, College of William and Mary.

37. Yancey to Barbour, Feb. 9, 1820, *William and Mary Quarterly,* 1st ser., 21 (1912): 75.

38. *Enquirer* (Richmond), Feb. 10, 1820.

39. Yancey to Archibald Austin, Feb. 10, 1820, Austin-Twyman Papers, College of William and Mary.

40. *Enquirer* (Richmond), Feb. 10, 1820.

41. Monroe to Charles Everett, Feb. 11, 1820 (copy), Monroe Papers in Virginia repositories, microfilm.

42. Monroe to Hay, Feb. 11, 1820, Monroe Papers, NYPL. The account of Monroe's role in the Missouri crisis presented here is based on a fresh, close reading of published and unpublished manuscript sources and differs from that in Glover Moore's *Missouri Controversy* (see especially pp. 235–36).

43. Monroe to Hay, Feb. 12, 1820, Hoes Archives, Monroe Museum, Fredericksburg, Va.

44. George Hay to Eliza Monroe Hay, Feb. 12, 1820, Monroe Papers, LC.

45. Printed in *Congressional Globe,* 30 Cong., 1 Sess., Appendix, p. 67.

46. James Barbour to Spencer Roane, Feb. 13, 1820, William L. Clements Library, University of Michigan. I am indebted to John C. Dann for making this letter available to me.

47. Monroe to Roane, Feb. 16, 1820, *Congressional Globe,* 30 Cong., 1 Sess., Appendix, p. 67. This letter was never sent to Roane, although that fact was not indicated when the text was published in the *Congressional Globe* in 1848.

48. Roane to Monroe, Feb. 16, 1820, "Letters of Spencer Roane," *Bulletin of the New York Public Library* 10 (1906): 174–75; Hay to Monroe, Feb. 17, 1820, Monroe Papers, LC.

49. Hay to Monroe, Feb. 17, 1820, Monroe Papers, LC.

50. Ibid.

51. Monroe to Jefferson, Feb. 19, 1820, in Hamilton, ed., *Monroe Writings,* 6:116.

52. Moore, *Missouri Controversy,* 88–90, 99–103; *Annals of Congress,* 16 Cong., 1 Sess., pp. 1572, 1586–88; Adams, *Diary,* Mar. 2, 1820, 4:3.

53. Adams, *Diary,* Mar. 3, 1820, 5:5; Monroe to Adams, Mar. 4, 1820, Adams Family Papers, MHS, microfilm edition, reel 449.

54. Adams, *Diary,* Mar. 3, 1820, 5:6–9; Adams to Monroe, Mar. 4, 1820, in Worthington C. Ford, ed., *Writings of John Quincy Adams,* 7 vols. (New York: Macmillan, 1913–1917), 7:1–2.

55. Everett Somerville Brown, ed., *The Missouri Compromises and Presidential Politics, 1820–1825: From the Letters of William Plumer, Junior* (St. Louis: Missouri Historical Society, 1926), pp. 14–15.

56. Adams, *Diary,* Mar. 3, 1820, 5:12.

57. Jefferson to John Holmes, Apr. 22, 1820, in Paul L. Ford, ed., *The Works of Thomas Jefferson,* Federal edition, 12 vols. (New York: G. P. Putnam's Sons, 1904), 12:158.

CHAPTER 8
TRANSITION TO A SECOND TERM

1. Fred Israel, ed. *The State of the Union Messages of the Presidents, 1790–1966,* 3 vols. (New York: Chelsea House, 1967), 1:169–70; Adams, *Diary,* Dec. 3, 1819, 4:459; Samuel Flagg Bemis, *John Quincy Adams and the Foundations of American Foreign Policy* (New York: Alfred A. Knopf, 1949), pp. 350–51.

2. Clay to John J. Crittenden, Jan. 29, 1820, in James F. Hopkins, Mary W. M. Hargreaves, Robert Seager II, Melba Porter Hay, and Carol Reardon, eds., *The Papers of Henry Clay,* 10 vols. (Lexington: University Press of Kentucky, 1959–1992), 2:769; Robert V. Remini, *Henry Clay: Statesman of the Union* (New York: W. W. Norton, 1991), pp. 172–73.

3. Monroe to George Hay, Feb. 10, 1820, James Monroe Papers, NYPL.

4. Stanislaus M. Hamilton, ed., *The Writings of James Monroe*, 7 vols. (New York, 1898-1903; reprint ed., New York: AMS Press, 1969), 6:124.

5. Waller Taylor to Archibald Austin, Mar. 28, 1820, Austin-Twyman Papers, College of William and Mary.

6. Adams, *Diary*, Apr. 6, 9, 1820, 5:57-58, 60-61.

7. Quoted in Lynn W. Turner, "Elections of 1816 and 1820," in Arthur M. Schlesinger, Jr., and Fred L. Israel, eds., *History of American Presidential Elections, 1789-1968*, 4 vols.(New York: McGraw-Hill, 1971), 1:316.

8. Ibid.

9. Quoted in Lynn W. Turner, *William Plumer of New Hampshire, 1759-1850* (Chapel Hill: University of North Carolina Press for the Institute of Early American History and Culture, Williamsburg, Va., 1962), p. 315.

10. Adams to Francisco Dionisio Vives, Feb. 20, 1821, Adams Family Papers, MHS, microfilm edition, reel 451; Adams, *Diary*, Feb. 22, 1821, 5:288-89; Bemis, *Adams*, pp. 351-53.

11. Monroe to Jackson, Jan. 24, 1821, and Jackson to Monroe, Feb. 11, 1821, in John Spencer Bassett, ed., *Correspondence of Andrew Jackson*, 6 vols. (Washington D.C.: Carnegie Institution, 1926-1933), 3:38-39.

12. Lewis Williams to his constituents, Feb. 26, 1821, in Noble E. Cunningham, Jr., ed., *Circular Letters of Congressmen to Their Constituents, 1789-1829* (Chapel Hill: University of North Carolina Press for the Institute of Early American History and Culture, Williamsburg, Va., 1978), 3:1134.

13. Israel, ed., *State of the Union Messages*, 1:174-81.

14. Monroe to Madison, Nov. 16, 1820, in Hamilton, ed., *Monroe Writings*, 6:160.

15. Lowndes to Elizabeth Lowndes (wife), Nov. 17, 1820, William Lowndes Papers, LC.

16. Remini, *Clay*, pp. 184-85; Glover Moore, *The Missouri Controversy, 1819-1821* (Gloucester, Mass.: Peter Smith, 1967; orig. pub. 1953), pp. 140-41.

17. *Annals of Congress*, 16 Cong., 2 Sess., pp. 10, 440.

18. William Plumer, Jr., to William Plumer, Sr., Dec. 3, 1821, in Everett Somerville Brown, ed., *The Missouri Compromises and Presidential Politics, 1820-1825: From the Letters of William Plumer, Junior* (St. Louis: Missouri Historical Society, 1926), p. 21.

19. Adams, *Diary*, Feb. 14, 1821, 5:276.

20. Remini, *Clay*, pp. 188-90.

21. Thomas H. Hall, circular letter to his constituents, Feb. 17, 1821, in Cunningham, ed., *Circular Letters*, 3:1132.

22. *Annals of Congress*, 16 Cong., 2 Sess., p. 1830.

23. Cheves to Clay, Mar. 5, 1821, in Hopkins et al., eds., *Clay Papers*, 3:58.

24. Williams to his constituents, Feb. 26, 1821, in Cunningham, ed., *Circular Letters*, 3:1136-37.

25. Jesse Slocumb to his constituents, Feb. 22, 1819, ibid., pp. 1057-58; *American State Papers: Documents Legislative and Executive of the United States*, 38 vols. (Washington, D.C., 1832-1861), *Military Affairs*, 1:779, 784.

26. Adams, *Diary*, Mar. 19, 1821, 5:331; Robert L. Meriwether, W. Edwin

Hemphill, and Clyde N. Wilson, eds., *The Papers of John C. Calhoun*, 21 vols. to date (Columbia: University of South Carolina Press, 1959–), 5:480.

27. Lewis Williams to his constituents, Feb. 20, 1819, and Jesse Slocumb to his constituents, Feb. 22, 1819, in Cunningham, ed., *Circular Letters*, 3:1049, 1057–58.

28. Calhoun to John W. Taylor, Speaker of the House of Representatives, Dec. 12, 1820, in Meriwether, Hemphill, and Wilson, eds., *Calhoun Papers*, 5:480–82, 490.

29. Trimble to Calhoun, Jan. 4, 1821, ibid., p. 529.

30. Trimble to Calhoun, Jan. 6, 1821, ibid., p. 537.

31. John C. Nevin, *John C. Calhoun and the Price of Union: A Biography* (Baton Rouge: Louisiana State University Press, 1988), p. 91; Michael S. Fitzgerald, "Europe and the United States Defense Establishment: American Military Policy and Strategy, 1815–1821" (Ph.D. diss., Purdue University, 1990), pp. 342–44.

32. Lewis Williams to his constituents, Feb 16, 1821, in Cunningham, ed., *Circular Letters*, 3:1136–37.

33. Calhoun to Jackson, Mar. 7, 1821, in Meriwether, Hemphill, and Wilson, eds., *Calhoun Papers*, 5:662.

34. William B. Skelton, *An American Profession of Arms: The Army Officer Corps, 1784–1861* (Lawrence: University Press of Kansas, 1992), pp. 109, 117, 120, 123, 126–28; *Niles' Weekly Register* 26 (Mar. 27, 1824): 50–51.

35. Calhoun to Jackson, Mar. 7, 1821, in Meriwether, Hemphill, and Wilson, eds., *Calhoun Papers*, 5:662.

36. Adams, *Diary*, Mar. 19, 1821, 5:331–33.

37. Ibid., Mar. 4, 1821, p. 317.

38. William C. Rives to Judith Rives (wife), Dec. 10, 1823, William C. Rives Papers, LC.

39. Duncan McArthur to Effie McArthur (daughter), Feb. 6, 1824, Duncan McArthur Papers, LC.

40. Adams, *Diary*, Mar. 5, 1821, 5:317–18.

41. *National Intelligencer* (Washington), Mar. 6, 1821.

42. Tompkins, who had not been in Washington during the recent session of Congress, took the oath of office twice: first on March 3, and again on March 5 after learning that the president intended to take the oath on the latter date. Adams, *Diary*, Mar. 10, 1821, 5:326; Ray W. Irwin, *Daniel D. Tompkins: Governor of New York and Vice President of the United States* (New York: New-York Historical Society, 1968), p. 264. The *National Intelligencer* (Mar. 3, 1821) reported that his absence during the session was "attributable to indisposition" and that his physicians had advised him not to make the journey to Washington for the inauguration.

43. Adams, *Diary*, Mar. 5, 1821, 5:318.

44. *National Intelligencer* (Washington), Mar. 6, 1821.

45. Adams, *Diary*, Mar. 5, 1821, 5:318.

46. Ibid., Feb. 12, Mar. 1, 1821, pp. 292, 308–9.

47. Monroe, address, Mar. 5, 1821, in Hamilton, ed., *Monroe Writings*, 6:174.

48. Ibid., p. 171.
49. See chapter 12.

CHAPTER 9
MONROE AS CHIEF EXECUTIVE

1. *Communications to a Committee of the House of Representatives, in Relation to the Duties of the Government Clerks,* House Document 194, 15 Cong., 1 Sess., Apr. 13, 1818; Noble E. Cunningham, Jr., *The Process of Government Under Jefferson* (Princeton: Princeton University Press, 1978), pp. 92–93, 325.

2. *Letter from the Secretary of War, Transmitting a Report of the Names of the Clerks Employed in that Department, and the Salaries Given to Each,* House Document 65, 15 Cong., 1 Sess., Jan. 27, 1818; Cunningham, *Process of Government Under Jefferson,* p. 326.

3. *Letter from the Secretary of the Navy, Transmitting Statements of the Names of the Clerks Employed in the Navy Department . . . and the Compensation Allowed to Each,* House Document 39, 15 Cong., 1 Sess., Jan. 7, 1818.

4. *Letter from the Secretary of State, Transmitting a List of the Names of the Clerks Employed in the Department of State, and Patent Office; and the Compensation Allowed to Each,* House Document 48, 18 Cong., 2 Sess., Jan. 14, 1825; *Letter from the Secretary of War, Transmitting a Statement of the Names of the Clerks Employed in the War Department, During the Year 1824, and the Compensation Allowed to Each,* House Document 60, 18 Cong., 2 Sess., Jan. 17, 1825; *Letter from the Secretary of the Navy Transmitting Statements of the Names of the Clerks Employed in the Navy Department . . . and the Salary Allowed to Each,* House Document 34, 18 Cong., 1 Sess., Jan. 7, 1825.

5. Leonard D. White, *The Jeffersonians: A Study in Administrative History, 1801–1829* (New York: Macmillan, 1951), pp. 173–74.

6. *Letter from the Secretary of the Treasury, Transmitting a Statement of the Names of the Clerks in the Treasury Department and the Compensation Allowed to Each, for Services Rendered During the Year 1817,* House Document 70, 15 Cong., 1 Sess., Feb. 2, 1818; *Letter of the Secretary of the Treasury, Transmitting a Statement Exhibiting the Names of the Clerks Employed in the Several Offices of the Treasury Department, During the Year 1824, and the Compensation Allowed to Each,* House Document 45, 18 Cong., 2 Sess., Jan. 12, 1825; Cunningham, *Process of Government Under Jefferson,* pp. 325–26.

7. *Letter from the Postmaster General, Transmitting a List of the Names of the Clerks Employed in His Office During the Year 1816, and the Compensation Received by Each,* House Document 134, 15 Cong., 2 Sess., Feb. 9, 1819; *Letter from the Postmaster General, Transmitting a List of the Clerks Employed in the General Post Office Department, and the Compensation Allowed Each,* House Document 15, 18 Cong., 2 Sess., Dec. 20, 1824.

8. Monroe to Lowndes, Dec. 31, 1816, *American State Papers: Documents Legislative and Executive of the United States,* 38 vols. (Washington, D.C., 1832–1861),

Miscellaneous, 2:418–19; William Wirt to Monroe, [1817], Monroe Papers, College of William and Mary.

9. White, *Jeffersonians,* p. 337.

10. Wirt to St. George Tucker, Jan. 17, 1822, Tucker-Coleman Papers, College of William and Mary.

11. Ibid.

12. *Communications to a Committee of the House of Representatives, in Relation to the Duties of the Government Clerks,* House Document 194, 15 Cong., 1 Sess., Apr. 13, 1818; Cunningham, *Process of Government Under Jefferson,* pp. 177–82, 328–32; White, *Jeffersonians,* pp. 189–90, 374–75.

13. Michael Birkner, *Samuel L. Southard: Jeffersonian Whig* (Rutherford, N.J.: Fairleigh Dickinson University Press, 1984), pp. 54–64.

14. See chapter 4.

15. Act of April 29, 1816, *Annals of Congress,* 14 Cong., 1 Sess., pp. 1374, 1886–87; Hendricks to his constituents, Apr. 10, 1820, in Noble E. Cunningham, Jr., ed., *Circular Letters of Congressmen to Their Constituents, 1789–1829,* 3 vols. (Chapel Hill: University of North Carolina Press for the Institute of Early American History and Culture, Williamsburg, Va., 1978), 3:1106.

16. Fred Israel, ed., *The State of the Union Messages of the Presidents, 1790–1966,* 3 vols. (New York: Chelsea House, 1967), 1:261; White, *Jeffersonians,* p. 269.

17. Israel, ed., *State of the Union Messages,* p. 191.

18. Adams to Monroe, Aug. 26, 1820, James Monroe Papers, LC.

19. Ibid.; Arthur Preston Whitaker, *The United States and the Independence of Latin America, 1800–1830* (New York: Russell and Russell, 1962; orig. pub. 1941), pp. 295–99.

20. Monroe to Adams, Sept. 1, 1820, Adams Family Papers, MHS, microfilm edition, reel 450.

21. See Samuel Flagg Bemis, *John Quincy Adams and the Foundations of American Foreign Policy* (New York: Alfred A. Knopf, 1949), p. 485.

22. Recommendation from legislature of Pennsylvania in favor of Alexander Brackenridge as district attorney in western district of Pennsylvania, Dec. 15, 1820, Letters of Application and Recommendation, 1817–1825, Record Group 59, M-439, National Archives.

23. Monroe to Adams, Nov. 23, 1819, Adams Family Papers, MHS, microfilm edition, reel 448.

24. Adams, *Diary,* Nov. 23. 1819, 4:445.

25. Ibid., Feb. 16, Mar. 18, 1819, pp. 263, 307.

26. Ibid., May 15, 1820, Feb. 7, 1828, 5:118, 7:424; White, *Jeffersonians,* pp. 387–89; Harry Ammon, *James Monroe: The Quest for National Identity* (New York: McGraw Hill, 1971), pp. 494–95. Chase C. Mooney, in *William H. Crawford, 1772–1834* (Lexington: University Press of Kentucky, 1974), pp. 122–26, finds the evidence inconclusive that Crawford drafted the Tenure of Office Act.

27. Jefferson to Madison, Nov. 29, 1820, in Paul L. Ford, ed., *The Works of Thomas Jefferson,* Federal edition, 12 vols. (New York: G. P. Putnam's Sons, 1904), 12:175.

28. Monroe to Andrew Jackson, Dec. 14, 1816, Stanislaus M. Hamilton, ed., *The Writings of James Monroe*, 7 vols. (New York, 1898–1903; reprint ed., New York: AMS Press, 1969), 5:342–46.

29. John Rhea to John Quincy Adams, Jan. 8, 1818; and James Trimble to Joseph Anderson (comptroller of the Treasury), July 8, 1818, Letters of Application and Recommendation, 1817–1825, Record Group 59, M-439, National Archives.

30. Monroe to Fulwar Skipworth, July 31, 1823, James Monroe Papers, NYPL.

31. Rufus King and Martin Van Buren to Return Jonathan Meigs, Jr., Jan. 3, 1822; Daniel Tompkins, King, and Van Buren to Meigs, Jan. 4, 1822; Van Buren to Monroe, Jan. 5, 1822, Martin Van Buren Papers, LC. See also Robert V. Remini, *Martin Van Buren and the Making of the Democratic Party* (New York: Columbia University Press, 1959), pp. 18–22.

32. Adams, *Diary,* Jan. 4, 5, 7, 1822, 5:479–82, 484.

33. Monroe to Jefferson, Mar. 22, 1824, in Hamilton, ed., *Monroe Writings,* 7:11–12.

34. Monroe to Rives, Nov. 24, 1817, William C. Rives Papers, LC.

35. Horace Holley to Mary Holley, Mar. 2, 1818, Horace Holley Papers, William L. Clements Library, University of Michigan.

36. Nelson to Charles Everett, Jan. 29, 1818, Hugh Nelson Papers, LC.

37. Joseph Monroe to Daniel Brent, undated memorandum, Records of the State Department, Record Group 59, E869, National Archives.

38. Joseph Monroe to Daniel Brent, dated "22d," ibid.

39. Monroe to William Clark, Apr. 21, 1820, E. G. Vocrhis Memorial Collection, Missouri Historical Society, St. Louis; Adams, *Diary,* Aug. 8, Dec. 4, 1819, 4:405, 467.

40. Morse to his mother, Nov. 28, Dec. 17, 1819, in Edward L. Morse, ed., *Samuel F. B. Morse: His Letters and Journals*, 2 vols. (Boston: Houghton Mifflin, 1914), 1:226–27. See also Noble E. Cunningham, Jr., *Popular Images of the Presidency: From Washington to Lincoln* (Columbia: University of Missouri Press, 1991), pp. 144, 146.

41. Adams, *Diary,* Feb. 22, 1821, 5:289; Monroe to unidentified correspondent, Nov. 2, 1822, "Letters of James Monroe," *Tyler's Quarterly Historical and Genealogical Magazine* 5 (July 1923): 18.

42. Monroe to Everett, Dec. 2, 1822, "Letters of Monroe," 19. See also Charles Jared Ingersoll, diary, Feb. 9, 1823, in William M. Meigs, *The Life of Charles Jared Ingersoll* (Philadelphia: J. B. Lippincott, 1897), p. 118.

43. Monroe to Everett, Nov. 13, 1823, "Letters of Monroe," 21. See also Monroe to Everett, Nov. 20, 1824, ibid., 24.

44. Adams, *Diary,* June 3, 1824, 6:374.

45. Monroe to Adams, Dec. 26, 1817, [Jan. 3, 1820], Adams Family Papers, MHS, microfilm edition, reels 441 and 449; see also Monroe to "the members of the administration," July 12, [18—], Records of the State Department, Record Group 59, E869, National Archives.

46. Adams, *Diary,* Nov. 12, 1820, 5:199–200.

47. Ibid., p. 201.

48. John Q. Adams to William Lowndes, Dec. 27, 1819, and William H. Crawford to William Lowndes, Jan. 14, 1822, William Lowndes Papers, LC.

49. William Wirt to William H. Crawford, Apr. 9, 1818, sending a draft of a bill to Crawford who forwarded it to William Lowndes, chairman of the House Ways and Means Committee, William Lowndes Papers, LC; John C. Calhoun to Joseph Hemphill, chairman of a House select committee on roads and canals, Dec. 29, 1821, enclosing the draft that Hemphill had requested, House Records, Committee on Roads and Canals, Record Group 233, National Archives.

50. Adams, *Diary,* Jan. 8, 1820, 4:497.

51. Ibid., Mar. 9, 1821, 5:323–24.

52. Rufus King to John A. King, Jan. 19, 1821, in Charles R. King, ed., *The Life and Correspondence of Rufus King,* 6 vols. (New York: G. P. Putnam's Sons, 1894–1900), 6:378.

53. King to Christopher Gore, Feb. 3, 1822, quoted in George R. Nielson, "The Indispensable Institution: The Congressional Party During the Era of Good Feelings" (Ph.D. diss., University of Iowa, 1968), p. 130.

54. Louis McLane to Kitty McLane, Apr. 18, 1822, Louis McLane Papers, LC.

55. Monroe to Madison, May 10, 1822, in Hamilton, ed., *Monroe Writings,* 6:286.

56. Madison to Monroe, May 18, 1822, in Gaillard Hunt, ed., *The Writings of James Madison,* 9 vols. (New York: G. P. Putnam's Sons, 1900–1910), 9:97.

57. Adams, *Diary,* Apr. 8, 12, 1822, 5:486–88.

58. Crawford to Gallatin, May 13, 1822, in Henry Adams, ed., *The Writings of Albert Gallatin,* 3 vols. (New York: Antiquarian Press, 1960; orig. pub. 1879), 2:242–43.

59. Monroe to Madison, May 10, 1822, in Hamilton, ed., *Monroe Writings,* 6:288–89.

60. Crawford to Monroe, July 4, 1822, Monroe Papers, LC; see also Mooney, *William H. Crawford,* pp. 196–205.

61. Monroe to Crawford, Aug. 22, 1822, Monroe Papers, NYPL.

62. Crawford to Monroe, Sept. 3, 1822, ibid.

63. Monroe to Crawford, Sept. 17, 1822, ibid.

64. Monroe to Rush, Jan. 16, 1823, The FORBES Magazine Collection, New York, N.Y.

65. Taylor to Archibald Austin, Feb. 13, 1822, Austin-Twyman Papers, College of William and Mary.

66. Louis McLane to Kitty McLane, Dec. 29, 1821, McLane Papers, LC; John A. Munroe, *Louis McLane: Federalist and Jacksonian* (New Brunswick, N.J.: Rutgers University Press, 1973), pp. 126–27.

67. Lacock to Monroe, July 7, 1822, Monroe Papers, LC.

CHAPTER 10
LIFE IN MONROE'S WASHINGTON

1. Noble E. Cunningham, Jr., *In Pursuit of Reason: The Life of Thomas Jefferson* (Baton Rouge: Louisiana State University Press, 1987), pp. 257–58.

2. Adams, *Diary,* March 29, 1819, 4:314.

3. Circular, Dept. of State, Nov. 21, 1818, inviting foreign ministers to a drawing room at the president's on the evening of Nov. 25, 1818, Adams Family Papers, MHS, microfilm edition, reel 445.

4. Adams, *Diary,* Feb. 17, 1819, 4:263–64.

5. Ibid., Dec. 31, 1819, pp. 493–94.

6. Lacock to Monroe, June 4, 1821, Monroe Papers, LC.

7. Adams, *Diary,* Mar. 13, 1819, 4:295–97, Nov. 21, 1820, 5:204.

8. Jefferson to Monroe, Feb. 12, 1823, in Paul L. Ford, ed., *The Works of Thomas Jefferson,* Federal edition, 12 vols. (New York: G. P. Putnam's Sons, 1904), 12:276.

9. Charles Jared Ingersoll, diary, Feb. 9, 1823, in William M. Meigs, *The Life of Charles Jared Ingersoll* (Philadelphia: J. B. Lippincott, 1897), p. 118.

10. Gouverneur to Monroe, Dec. 11, 1823, Ingrid Westesson Hoes Archives, James Monroe Museum and Memorial Library, Fredericksburg, Va.

11. Louis McLane to Kitty McLane, Jan. 1, 9, 1822, Louis McLane Papers, LC; Samuel Flagg Bemis, *John Quincy Adams and the Foundations of American Foreign Policy* (New York: Alfred A. Knopf, 1949), p. 274.

12. Adams, *Diary,* Dec. 19, 1817, 4:29.

13. Louis McLane to Kitty McLane, Jan. 19, 1818, McLane Papers, LC.

14. Adams, *Diary,* Dec. 9, 10, 11, 12, 1818, 4:187–90.

15. William C. Rives to Judith Rives (wife), April 22, 1824, William C. Rives Papers, LC.

16. Adams, *Diary,* June 1, Dec. 20, 1819, 4:383–84, 480–81.

17. Adams, *Diary,* Jan. 22, 1818, 4:45–46, June 1, Dec. 20, 1819, 4:383–84, 480–81.

18. William Wirt to Elizabeth Wirt, Nov. 17, 1817, William Wirt Papers, Maryland Historical Society, microfilm edition.

19. James Sterling Young, *The Washington Community, 1800–1828* (New York: Columbia University Press, 1966), pp. 65–83; Noble E. Cunningham, Jr., *The Process of Government Under Jefferson* (Princeton: Princeton University Press, 1978), pp. 282–87.

20. Louis McLane to Kitty McLane, Dec. 5, 1817, McLane Papers, LC.

21. Louis McLane to Kitty McLane, Dec. 19, 1817, ibid.

22. Louis McLane to Kitty McLane, Jan. 1, 1818, ibid.

23. Job Durfee to Judith Durfee, Dec. 4, 1821, Job Durfee Papers, LC.

24. Job Durfee to Judith Durfee, Feb. 6, 1823, ibid.

25. William C. Rives to Judith Rives, Dec. 24, 1823, Rives Papers, LC.

26. Ibid.

27. Daggett to Jeremiah Mason, Feb. 10, 1819, in George S. Hilliard, ed., *Memoir and Correspondence of Jeremiah Mason* (Cambridge, Mass.: Riverside Press, 1873), p. 191.

28. William C. Rives to Judith Rives, Dec. 31, 1823–Jan. 1, 1824, Rives Papers, LC.

29. William C. Rives to Judith Rives, Jan. 3, 1824, ibid.

30. Robert P. Henry to John F. Henry, Jan. 3, 1824, Papers of the Short-Harrison-Symmes Families, LC.

31. Axel Leonhard Klinkowström, *Baron Klinkowström's America, 1818–1820*, trans. and ed. Franklin D. Scott (Evanston, Ill.: Northwestern University Press, 1952), pp. 28–29.

32. Horace Holley to Mary Holley, Mar. 21, 1818, Horace Holley Papers, William L. Clements Library, University of Michigan.

33. Horace Holley to Mary Holley, Apr. 3, 1818, ibid.

34. Horace Holley to Mary Holley, Apr. 8, 1818, ibid.

35. Ibid.

36. Ibid.

37. *Quarterly Review* (London) 17 (Apr. and July 1817): 260–286.

38. Act of Mar. 3, 1817, *Annals of Congress*, 14 Cong., 2 Sess., pp. 1045, 1299–1300.

39. House Report 79, 18 Cong., 2 Sess., serial set 123, 2:15–16. For the complicated story of the "furniture fund," see Lucius Wilmerding, Jr., *James Monroe: Public Claimant* (New Brunswick, N.J.: Rutgers University Press, 1960), pp. 11–25.

40. Mary Lee Mann, ed., *A Yankee Jeffersonian: Selections from the Diary and Letters of William Lee of Massachusetts Written from Washington from 1796 to 1840* (Cambridge: Harvard University Press, 1958), pp. 20, 299–300.

41. Monroe to Samuel Lane, May 30, 1818, James Monroe Papers, NYPL.

42. House Records, 15th Cong., Document 13.1, Record Group 233, National Archives.

43. *National Register* (Washington) 4 (Nov. 29, 1817): 351.

44. Monroe, *Message from the President of the United States, upon the Subject of the Furniture Necessary for the President's House*, Feb. 10, 1818 (Washington D.C.: E. De Kraft, 1818), House Document 91, 15 Cong., 1 Sess., serial set 7, 3:1–2; House Report 79, 18 Cong., 2 Sess., serial set 123, 2:14.

45. *Statement of William Lee, Esquire, Agent for the Procuring Furniture for President's House*, Mar. 9, 1818, House Document 143, 15 Cong., 1 Sess., serial set 10, 6:1–5.

46. *Annals of Congress*, 15 Cong., 1 Sess., p. 2580.

CHAPTER 11

THE MONROE DOCTRINE

1. Monroe to Joel Barlow, Nov. 27, 1811, in Stanislaus M. Hamilton, ed., *The Writings of James Monroe*, 7 vols. (New York, 1898–1903; reprint ed., New York: AMS Press, 1969), 5:364.

2. John Quincy Adams to Manuel H. de Aquirre, Aug. 27, 1818. Adams's draft is in the Adams Family Papers, MHS, microfilm edition, reel 444; the letter is printed in William R. Manning, ed., *Diplomatic Correspondence of the United States Concerning the Independence of the Latin-American Nations*, 3 vols. (New York: Oxford University Press, 1925), 1:76–78.

3. Monroe's changes and additions to Adams's draft of his letter to Manuel

H. de Aquirre, Aug. 27, 1818, Adams Family Papers, MHS, microfilm edition, reel 444.

4. Adams, *Diary*, Nov. 12, 1820, 5:200.

5. Fred Israel, ed., *The State of the Union Messages of the Presidents, 1790–1966*, 3 vols. (New York: Chelsea House, 1967), 1:177–78, 188–89.

6. Monroe to the Senate and House of Representatives, Mar. 8, 1822, in Hamilton, ed., *Monroe Writings*, 6:207–11.

7. *Annals of Congress*, 17 Cong., 1 Sess. (Mar. 20, 1822), pp. 1314–1320.

8. Williams to his constituents, Apr. 15, 1822, in Noble E. Cunningham, Jr., ed., *Circular Letters of Congressmen to Their Constituents, 1789–1829*, 3 vols. (Chapel Hill: University of North Carolina Press for the Institute of Early American History and Culture, Williamsburg, Va., 1978), 3:1151–52.

9. Adams, *Diary*, Nov. 16, 1819, 4:438.

10. Ibid., Jan. 27, 1821, 5:252–53, July 17, 1823, 6:163; Dexter Perkins, *The Monroe Doctrine, 1823–1826* (Gloucester, Mass.: Peter Smith, 1965; orig. pub. 1927), p. 11.

11. Observations accompanying Adams to Henry Middleton, July 22, 1823, *American State Papers: Documents Legislative and Executive of the United States*, 38 vols. (Washington, D.C., 1832–1861), *Foreign Relations*, 5:445; Perkins, *Monroe Doctrine*, pp. 6–7, 13.

12. Adams, *Diary*, Nov. 25, 1822, 6:104; Perkins, *Monroe Doctrine*, pp. 10–11.

13. Adams, memorandum to Monroe, Nov. [13], 1823, Monroe Papers, NYPL.

14. Rush to Adams, Aug. 19, 1823, in Hamilton, ed., *Monroe Writings*, 6:361–65.

15. Canning to Rush, Aug. 20, 1823, ibid., p. 365.

16. Samuel Flagg Bemis, *John Quincy Adams and the Foundations of American Foreign Policy* (New York: Alfred A. Knopf, 1949), pp. 380–81.

17. Monroe to Madison, Oct. 17, 1823, James Madison Papers, LC.

18. Monroe to Jefferson, Oct. 17, 1823, in Hamilton, ed., *Monroe Writings*, 6:323–25.

19. Jefferson to Monroe, Oct. 24, 1823, in Paul L. Ford, ed., *The Works of Thomas Jefferson*, Federal edition, 12 vols. (New York: G. P. Putnam's Sons, 1904), 12:318–21.

20. Madison to Monroe, Oct. 30, 1823, in Gaillard Hunt, ed., *The Writings of James Madison*, 9 vols. (New York: G. P. Putnam's Sons, 1900–1910), 9:157–59.

21. Adams, *Diary*, Nov. 7, 1823, 6:178–80; Monroe to Madison, Dec. 29, 1823, Madison Papers, LC; Bemis, *Adams*, pp. 384–85; Perkins, *Monroe Doctrine*, pp. 70–72.

22. Chase C. Mooney, *William H. Crawford, 1772–1834* (Lexington: University Press of Kentucky, 1974), pp. 187, 241.

23. Adams, *Diary*, Nov. 7, 1823, 6:177–79.

24. Ibid., Nov. 13, 1823, p. 185.

25. Ibid., Nov. 15, 1823, p. 186; Mooney, *Crawford*, p. 241.

26. The political aspects are fully explored in Ernest R. May, *The Making of*

the Monroe Doctrine (Cambridge: Harvard University Press, 1975), especially pp. 190–253.

27. Adams, *Diary,* Nov. 15, 1823, 6:186.

28. Ibid., Nov. 17, 1823, p. 188.

29. Ibid., Nov. 21, 1823, pp. 193–94. Adams's draft, Monroe's amendments, and Adams's substitute are printed in Worthington C. Ford, ed., "Some Original Documents on the Genesis of the Monroe Doctrine," *Proceedings of the Massachusetts Historical Society,* 2d ser., 15 (1902): 405–9.

30. Adams, *Diary,* Nov. 21, 1823, 6:194.

31. Bradford Perkins, *Castlereagh and Adams: England and the United States, 1812–1823* (Berkeley and Los Angeles: University of California Press, 1964), p. 328.

32. Adams, *Diary,* Nov. 21, 1823, 6:195–96.

33. Ibid., Nov. 22, 1823, pp. 196–98.

34. Ibid., Nov. 24, 1823, p. 199.

35. Ibid., Nov. 25, 1823, pp. 199–200.

36. Ibid., pp. 200–204.

37. Ibid., Nov. 26, 1823, pp. 204–10.

38. Ibid., Nov. 25, 27, 1823, pp. 203, 210.

39. The document is printed, showing omitted passages, in Ford, ed., "Documents on the Genesis of the Monroe Doctrine," pp. 405–9.

40. Adams, *Diary,* Nov. 27, 1823, 6:213.

41. Monroe to Adams, Nov. 27, [1823], published in Worthington C. Ford, "John Quincy Adams and the Monroe Doctrine," *American Historical Review* 8 (1902): 45.

42. Adams, *Diary,* Nov. 27, 1823, 6:213.

43. Ford, ed., "Documents on the Genesis of the Monroe Doctrine," pp. 408–9.

44. Ibid., p. 408.

45. On the subject of West and East Florida see Irving Brant, *James Madison: The President, 1809–1812* (Indianapolis: Bobbs-Merrill Company, 1956), pp. 173–89, 239–49.

46. "Resolution relative to the occupation of the Floridas by the United States of America," approved Jan. 15, 1811, in Richard Peters, ed., *The Public Statutes at Large of the United States of America, 1789–1845,* 8 vols. (Boston: Charles C. Little and James Brown, 1850), 2:666. For the journal of secret proceedings see *Annals of Congress,* 11 Cong., 3 Sess., pp. 1117–48.

47. Israel, ed., *State of the Union Messages,* 1:204; Perkins, *Monroe Doctrine,* pp. 13–14.

48. Adams, memorandum to Monroe, Nov. [13], 1823, Monroe Papers, NYPL.

49. Monroe, message to Congress, Dec. 2, 1823, in Israel, ed., *State of the Union Messages,* 1:212–13.

50. Crowninshield to Henry A. Dearborn, Dec. 19, 1823, Benjamin W. Crowninshield Papers, LC.

51. Webster to Edward Everett, Dec. 6, 1823, in Charles M. Wiltse and

Harold Moser, eds., *The Papers of Daniel Webster: Correspondence,* 7 vols. (Hanover, N.H.: University Press of New England, 1974–1986), 1:339.

52. Addington to Canning, Jan. 5, 1824, quoted in Perkins, *Monroe Doctrine,* p. 144. Arthur Preston Whitaker, in *The United States and the Independence of Latin America, 1800–1830* (New York: Russell and Russell, 1962; orig. pub. 1941), concluded that there was "surprisingly little articulate opposition in the press" to the policy Monroe presented in his message (pp. 524–25).

53. Crittenden to Monroe, Dec. 30, 1823, Monroe Papers, NYPL.

54. George M. Bibb to Monroe, Dec. 30, 1823, ibid.

55. Adair to Monroe, Jan. 10, 1824, enclosing "Resolutions approbatory of the course of the President of the United States in relation to the struggles of the Greeks and South Americans for freedom, and in relation to the administration of the General Government," approved Jan. 7, 1824, ibid. The Kentucky resolutions gave more emphasis to the Greek struggle for independence than the president would have welcomed.

56. Copies of the resolutions, adopted Feb. 23, 1824, were sent to the President of the United States, the President of the Senate, and the Speaker of the House of Representatives. Senate Records, 18 Cong., 1 Sess., Apr. 5, 1824, Record Group 46, National Archives.

57. Mangum to Thomas D. Bennehan, Dec. 15, 1823, in Henry T. Shanks, ed., *The Papers of Willie Person Mangum,* 5 vols. (Raleigh, N.C.: State Department of Archives, 1950–1956), 1:89.

58. Perkins, *Monroe Doctrine,* pp. 161–62, 167–68, 183.

59. Monroe to Madison, Mar. 27, 1824, in Hamilton, ed., *Monroe Writings,* 7:14, 14n; Perkins, *Monroe Doctrine,* pp. 149–64.

60. Monroe to Jefferson, Dec. [8], 1823, in Hamilton, ed., *Monroe Writings,* 6:344–45.

61. Monroe to Madison, Dec. 4, 1823, Madison Papers, LC.

62. Monroe to Madison, Dec. 20, 1823, ibid.

CHAPTER 12
DOMESTIC CONCERNS

1. Adams, *Diary,* Dec. 3, 4, 1819, 4:462–64, 468–70.

2. The bill passed the House of Representatives on Apr. 29, 1822, and the Senate on May 3, 1822. *Annals of Congress,* 17 Cong., 1 Sess., pp. 439, 443–44, 1734.

3. Veto message, May 4, 1822, in James D. Richardson, ed., *A Compilation of the Messages and Papers of the Presidents, 1789–1897,* 10 vols. (Washington, D.C.: N.p., 1896–1899), 2:142–43.

4. "Views of the President of the United States on the Subject of Internal Improvements," ibid., p. 144; Stanislaus M. Hamilton, ed., *The Writings of James Monroe,* 7 vols. (New York, 1898–1903; reprint ed., New York: AMS Press, 1969), 6:216–84. See also William Hendricks to his constituents, Apr. 16, 1822, in Noble E. Cunningham, Jr., ed., *Circular Letters of Congressmen to Their Constituents,*

1789–1829, 3 vols. (Chapel Hill: University of North Carolina Press for the Institute of Early American History and Culture, Williamsburg, Va., 1978), 3:1156–57.

5. Monroe, sixth annual message, Dec. 3, 1822, in Fred Israel, ed., *The State of the Union Messages of the Presidents, 1790–1966*, 3 vols. (New York: Chelsea House, 1967), 1:198.

6. Story to Monroe, June 24, 1822, Monroe Papers, LC.

7. Marshall to Monroe, June 13, 1822, ibid.

8. Monroe, annual message, Dec. 2, 1823, in Israel, ed., *State of the Union Messages*, 1:211.

9. *Annals of Congress*, 18 Cong., 1 Sess. (May 7, 1824), p. 2556.

10. Monroe, annual message, Dec. 2, 1823, in Israel, ed., *State of the Union Messages*, 1:211.

11. *Register of Debates in Congress*, 18 Cong., 2 Sess., Appendix, p. 99; George Dangerfield, *The Awakening of American Nationalism, 1815–1828* (New York: Harper and Row, 1965), p. 200.

12. The bill passed the House of Representatives on Feb. 11, 1824, and was signed by the president on Apr. 30, 1824. *Annals of Congress*, 18 Cong., 1 Sess., p. 1471, 3217.

13. David Trimble to his constituents, May 20, 1824, in Cunningham, ed., *Circular Letters*, 3:1212, 1227–28.

14. *Register of Debates in Congress*, 18 Cong., 2 Sess., p. 334, and Appendix, p. 110; Duncan McArthur to Thomas J. McArthur, Jan. 21, Feb. 2, 1825, Duncan McArthur Papers, LC.

15. Tucker to his constituents, Apr. 18, 1825, in Cunningham, ed., *Circular Letters*, 3:1307. On internal improvements see also Joseph H. Harrison, Jr., "The Internal Improvement Issue in the Politics of the Union, 1783–1825" (Ph.D. diss., University of Virginia, 1954).

16. Monroe, annual message, Dec. 2, 1823, in Israel, ed., *State of the Union Messages*, 1:210.

17. Daniel Webster to Jeremiah Mason, Apr. 19, 1824, in Charles M. Wiltse and Harold Moser, eds., *The Papers of Daniel Webster: Correspondence*, 7 vols. (Hanover, N.H.: University Press of New England, 1974–1986), 1:337; Duncan McArthur to Effie McArthur, Feb. 25, 1824, Duncan McArthur Papers, LC; Benjamin W. Crowninshield to Henry A. Dearborn, Apr. 10, 1824, Benjamin W. Crowninshield Papers, LC; *Annals of Congress*, 18 Cong., 1 Sess., pp. 2429, 3221–26.

18. Robert Allen to his constituents, Feb. 22, 1825, in Cunningham, ed., *Circular Letters*, 3:1285.

19. Calhoun to Micah Sterling, Jan. 5, 1824, and Calhoun to Virgil Maxcy, Feb. 27, 1824, in Robert L. Meriwether, W. Edwin Hemphill, and Clyde N. Wilson, eds., *The Papers of John C. Calhoun*, 21 vols. to date (Columbia: University of South Carolina Press, 1959–), 7:447, 554.

20. Mangum to Duncan Cameron, Dec. 10, 1823, and Mangum to Thomas D. Bennehan, Dec. 15, 1823, in Henry T. Shanks, ed., *The Papers of Willie Person*

Mangum, 5 vols. (Raleigh, N.C.: State Department of Archives, 1950–1956), 1:83, 89.

21. Mangum to Seth Jones, Feb. 11, 1824, ibid., 115. See also Benjamin W. Crowninshield to Henry A. Dearborn, Dec. 19, 1823, Crowninshield Papers, LC.

22. Houston to Abram Maury, Dec. 13, 1823, Samuel Houston Papers, LC.

23. Duncan McArthur to Nancy McArthur, Jan. 14, 1824, Duncan McArthur Papers, LC; Adams, *Diary*, Jan. 8, 1824, 6:229.

24. Louisa Kalisky, journal, Jan. 6, 1824, Lee-Palfrey Family Papers, LC.

25. Ibid., Jan. 20, 1824. Louisa Kalisky was a houseguest of William Lee of Massachusetts, second auditor of the Treasury. Her journal was written in German and translated by a member of her family. Mary Lee Mann, ed., *A Yankee Jeffersonian: Selections from the Diary and Letters of William Lee of Massachusetts Written from Washington from 1796 to 1840* (Cambridge: Harvard University Press, 1958), pp. 211, 293.

26. Daniel Webster to Ezekiel Webster, Dec. 4, 1823, in Wiltse and Moser, eds., *Webster Papers*, 1:337.

27. James S. Chase, *Emergence of the Presidential Nominating Convention, 1789–1832* (Urbana: University of Illinois Press, 1973), pp. 52–59.

28. *Anti-Caucus* [1824], broadside, New-York Historical Society.

29. William Plumer, Jr., to William Plumer, Feb. 16, 1824, in Everett Somerville Brown, ed., *The Missouri Compromises and Presidential Politics, 1820–1825: From the Letters of William Plumer, Junior* (St. Louis: Missouri Historical Society, 1926), p. 99; Chase, *Nominating Convention*, p. 60.

30. Williams to Newton Cannon, Mar. 13, 1824, Newton Cannon Papers, LC.

31. Adams, *Diary*, Jan. 8, 1824, 6:229–30.

32. Harry Ammon, "Executive Leadership in the Monroe Administration," in John B. Boles, ed., *America, the Middle Period: Essays in Honor of Bernard Mayo* (Charlottesville: University Press of Virginia, 1973), pp. 124–26; Samuel Flagg Bemis, *John Quincy Adams and the Foundations of American Foreign Policy* (New York: Alfred A. Knopf, 1949), pp. 432–35.

33. Stanley J. Idzerda, Anne C. Loveland, and Marc H. Miller, *Lafayette, Hero of Two Worlds: The Art and Pageantry of His Farewell Tour of America, 1824–1825* (Hanover, N.H.: University Press of New England, 1989), pp. 106–7, 195–96.

34. Adams, *Diary*, June 10, 1824, 6:378; for voluminous excerpts from newspaper reports on Lafayette's tour see Edgar E. Brandon, ed., *Lafayette, Guest of the Nation*, 3 vols. (Oxford, Ohio: Oxford Historical Press, 1950–1957).

35. William Lee to Susan Lee, Oct. 13, 1824, in Mann, ed., *A Yankee Jeffersonian*, pp. 226–27.

36. On Monroe's welcoming of Lafayette at the White House see Brandon, ed., *Lafayette*, 3:27–29, 46–47.

37. Idzerda, Loveland, and Miller, *Lafayette*, p. 12.

38. Monroe to Jefferson, Oct. 18, 1824, in Hamilton, ed., *Monroe Writings*, 7:41.

39. Monroe to Madison, Oct. 18, 1824, in Hamilton, ed., *Monroe Writings*, 7:40.

40. Monroe to Jefferson, Oct. 18, 1824, ibid., pp. 41–42. On Lafayette's visit see also Sylvia Neely, "The Politics of Liberty in the Old World and the New: Lafayette's Return to America in 1824," *Journal of the Early Republic* 6 (1986): 151–71.

41. Monroe to Jefferson, Oct. 31, 1824, in Hamilton, ed., *Monroe Writings*, 7:42–43; Noble E. Cunningham, Jr., *In Pursuit of Reason: The Life of Thomas Jefferson* (Baton Rouge: Louisiana State University Press, 1987), pp. 344–45.

42. Israel, ed., *State of the Union Messages*, 1:214–15, 220–21, 228–29.

43. Ibid., p. 229.

44. Ibid., p. 228.

45. Monroe to the Senate and House of Representatives of the United States, Mar. 30, 1824, in Hamilton, ed., *Monroe Writings*, 7:14–15.

46. Ibid., pp. 16–17; *American State Papers: Documents Legislative and Executive of the United States*, 38 vols. (Washington, D.C., 1832–1861), *Indian Affairs*, 2:460.

47. Monroe to Madison, Apr. 1824, in Hamilton, ed., *Monroe Writings*, 7:18. See also Monroe to Jefferson, Apr. 1824, ibid., pp. 20–21.

48. The letter is published in *American State Papers: Indian Affairs*, 2:476–77.

49. Israel, ed., *State of the Union Messages*, 1:223.

50. Monroe, message to Senate, Jan. 27, 1825, *American State Papers: Indian Affairs*, 2:541–42.

51. Gist to his constituents, Feb. 21, 1825, in Cunningham, ed., *Circular Letters*, 3:1281.

CHAPTER 13
CLOSING A PRESIDENCY

1. William C. Rives to Judith Rives, Dec. 11, 1824, William C. Rives Papers, LC.

2. Ibid.

3. Fred Israel, ed., *The State of the Union Messages of the Presidents, 1790–1966*, 3 vols. (New York: Chelsea House, 1967), 1:227–28; Stanley J. Idzerda, Anne C. Loveland, and Marc H. Miller, *Lafayette, Hero of Two Worlds: The Art and Pageantry of His Farewell Tour of America, 1824–1825* (Hanover, N.H.: University Press of New England, 1989), pp. 12–13.

4. Adams, *Diary*, Dec. 12, 1824, 6:440; Harry Ammon, *James Monroe: The Quest for National Identity* (New York: McGraw-Hill, 1971), pp. 541–42; Edgar E. Brandon, ed., *Lafayette, Guest of the Nation*, 3 vols. (Oxford, Ohio: Oxford Historical Press, 1950–1957), 3:170–72.

5. The act was approved on Dec. 28, 1824, *Annals of Congress*, 18 Cong., 2 Sess., Appendix, p. 83; Joseph Gist to his constituents, Feb. 21, 1825, and Robert Allen to his constituents, Feb. 22, 1825, in Noble E. Cunningham, Jr., ed., *Circular Letters of Congressmen to Their Constituents*, 3 vols. (Chapel Hill: Univer-

sity of North Carolina Press for the Institute of Early American History and Culture, Williamsburg, Va., 1978), 3:1280–81, 1284.

6. Adams, *Diary*, Jan. 1, 1825, 6:457; Brandon, ed., *Lafayette*, 3:180.

7. Louis McLane to Kitty McLane, Jan. 2, 1825, Louis McLane Papers, LC.

8. Louis McLane to Kitty McLane, Dec. 5, 1817, ibid.

9. Mangum to Seth Jones, Feb. 11, 1824, in Henry T. Shanks, ed., *The Papers of Willie Person Mangum*, 5 vols. (Raleigh, N.C.: State Department of Archives, 1950–1956), 1:116.

10. Webster to Jeremiah Mason, Feb. 15, 1824, in Charles M. Wiltse and Harold Moser, eds., *The Papers of Daniel Webster: Correspondence*, 7 vols. (Hanover, N.H.: University Press of New England, 1974–1986), 1:353–54.

11. "Presidential Election," printed circular, Washington D.C., May 25, 1824, addressed to W. P. Mangum, Willie Person Mangum Papers, LC; reprinted in Shanks, ed., *Mangum Papers*, 1:147–49.

12. Johnson to Charles S. Morgan, Dec. 8, 1824, Joseph Johnson Papers, LC.

13. Johnson to Morgan, Dec. 16, 1824, ibid.; William Plumer, Jr., to William Plumer, Dec. 16, 1824, in Everett Somerville Brown, ed., *The Missouri Compromises and Presidential Politics, 1820–1825: From the Letters of William Plumer, Junior* (St. Louis: Missouri Historical Society, 1926), p. 123.

14. Robert P. Henry to John F. Henry, Jan. 3, 1825, Papers of the Short-Harrison-Symmes Families, LC.

15. Ibid.

16. Clay to Francis P. Blair, Jan. 8, 1825, in James F. Hopkins, Mary W. M. Hargreaves, Robert Seager II, Melba Porter Hay, and Carol Reardon, eds., *The Papers of Henry Clay*, 10 vols. (Lexington: University Press of Kentucky, 1959–1992), 4:9; James F. Hopkins, "Election of 1824," in Arthur M. Schlesinger, Jr., and Fred L. Israel, eds., *History of American Presidential Elections, 1789–1968*, 4 vols. (New York: McGraw-Hill, 1971), 1:377.

17. Clay to Adams, Jan. 9, 1825, in Hopkins et al., eds., *Clay Papers*, 4:9; Adams, *Diary*, Jan. 9, 1825, 6:464–65.

18. Louis McLane to Kitty McLane, Jan. 13, 1825, McLane Papers, LC.

19. Taylor to Archibald Austin, Jan. 23, 1825, Austin-Twyman Papers, College of William and Mary.

20. Adams, *Diary*, Jan. 25, 1825, 6:478; see also William Plumer, Jr., to William Plumer, Jan. 24, 1825, in Brown, ed., *Missouri Compromises and Presidential Politics*, pp. 135–36.

21. Hopkins, "Election of 1824," in Schlesinger and Israel, eds., *History of American Presidential Elections*, 1:380.

22. Monroe to Samuel L. Gouverneur, June 10, 1823, Monroe Papers, NYPL.

23. William Lee to Susan and Mary Lee, Aug. 29, 1824, in Mary Lee Mann, ed., *A Yankee Jeffersonian: Selections from the Diary and Letters of William Lee of Massachusetts Written from Washington from 1796 to 1840* (Cambridge: Harvard University Press, 1958), p. 222.

24. *Message from the President of the United States, in Relation to His Accounts with the Public,* House Document 33, 18 Cong., 2 Sess., Jan. 6, 1825, p. 3.

25. House Report 79, Feb. 21, 1825, 18 Cong., 2 Sess., serial set 123, 2:1–286.

26. Ammon, *Monroe,* pp. 116, 124, 208, 210.

27. Monroe to Skipwith, Mar. 11, 1823, Monroe Papers, LC.

28. Ibid.

29. Ibid. (Skipwith's reply not located.)

30. Monroe to Samuel L. Gouverneur, June 5, 1823, Monroe Papers, NYPL. Advertisements for the sale of the Albemarle property appeared in the *Enquirer* (Richmond), June 17, 20, 27, and July 1, 1823.

31. Monroe to [George Graham], June 4, 1823, Graham Family Papers, Virginia Historical Society.

32. Monroe to George Graham, Sept. 29, 1823, ibid.

33. The advertisement, dated Oak Hill, Loudoun County, Va., Apr. 12, [1825], was the same as that published in 1823, except for a note adding: "With a view to a sale of the lands above described, to the highest bidder, in small tracts, and with liberal credit, I will attend on the premises, on the first Monday in June next." *Enquirer* (Richmond), May 17, 1825.

34. Monroe to Gouverneur, Oct. 19, 1823, Monroe Papers, NYPL.

35. Gouverneur to Monroe, Nov. 1, 1823, Ingrid Westesson Hoes Archives, James Monroe Museum and Memorial Library, Fredericksburg, Va.

36. Ibid.

37. Ibid.

38. Gouverneur to Monroe, Dec. 11, 1823, ibid.

39. House Report 79, 18 Cong., 2 Sess., pp. 3–5; Lucius Wilmerding, Jr., *James Monroe: Public Claimant* (New Brunswick, N.J.: Rutgers University Press, 1960), pp. 53–56, 83, 138.

40. House Report 79, 18 Cong., 2 Sess., pp. 5–11; Wilmerding, *Monroe: Public Claimant,* pp. 66–70, 83.

41. A summary of the claims and the allowances granted is in Wilmerding, *Monroe: Public Claimant,* p. 83; Ammon, *Monroe,* p. 556.

CHAPTER 14
THE END OF AN ERA

1. *Niles' Weekly Register* 26 (May 8, 1824): 151; Norval Neil Luxon, *Niles' Weekly Register: News Magazine of the Nineteenth Century* (Baton Rouge: Louisiana State University Press, 1947), p. 128.

2. Marshall to Monroe, Dec. 13, 1824, James Monroe Papers, LC. See also Marshall to Monroe, Mar. 7, 1825, Stanislaus M. Hamilton, ed., *The Writings of James Monroe,* 7 vols. (New York, 1898–1903; reprint ed., New York: AMS Press, 1969), 7:56n.

3. *Journal, Acts and Proceedings, of the Convention, Assembled at Philadelphia,*

Monday, May 14, and Dissolved Monday, September 17, 1787, Which Formed the Constitution of the United States (Boston: Thomas B. Wait, 1819).

4. Noble E. Cunningham, Jr., *Popular Images of the Presidency: From Washington to Lincoln* (Columbia: University of Missouri Press, 1991), pp. 93–96.

5. Monroe to Jefferson, Feb. 23, 1817, in Hamilton, ed., *Monroe Writings*, 6:2; Irma B. Jaffe, *John Trumbull: Patriot-Artist of the American Revolution* (Boston: New York Graphic Society, 1975), pp. 234–37.

6. Trumbull was to be paid $32,000—$8,000 with the signing of the agreement and $6,000 with the completion and delivery of each painting. Articles of Agreement, March 15, 1817, House Records, Record Group 233, National Archives.

7. Theodore Sizer, ed., *The Autobiography of Colonel John Trumbull: Patriot-Artist, 1756–1843* (New Haven, Conn.: Yale University Press, 1958), pp. 271–77.

8. Monroe to John Q. Adams, Aug. 3, 1820, in Hamilton, ed., *Monroe Writings*, 6:146; report of Senate committee relative to the appropriation of a room for the third painting of Col. Trumbull, Mar. 13, 1822, Senate Records, Record Group 46, National Archives.

9. Adams, *Diary*, Sept. 1, 1818, 4:128; Louis McLane to Kitty McLane, Feb. 21, 1819, Louis McLane Papers, LC.

10. Adams, *Diary*, Nov. 28, 1826, 7:188–89.

11. Horace Holley to Mary Holley, Apr. 2, 1818, Horace Holley Papers, William L. Clements Library, University of Michigan.

12. Job Durfee to Judith Durfee, Dec. 4, 1821, Job Durfee Papers, LC; Louis McLane to Kitty McLane, Jan. 1, 1818, McLane Papers, LC.

13. Monroe to Madison, May 10, 1822, in Hamilton, ed., *Monroe Writings*, 6:289 91. See also Ralph Ketcham, *Presidents Above Party: The American Presidency, 1789–1829* (Chapel Hill: University of North Carolina Press for the Institute of Early American History and Culture, Williamsburg, Va., 1984), pp. 124–27.

14. *Niles' Weekly Register* 27 (Feb. 26, 1825): 401; and 28 (Mar. 19, 1825): 36, 42–43.

15. Monroe to Susan M. Hubbard, Mar. 8, 1825, Ingrid Westesson Hoes Archives, James Monroe Museum and Memorial Library, Fredericksburg, Va.

16. Reynolds to his constituents, Feb. 26, 1825, in Noble E. Cunningham, Jr., ed., *Circular Letters of Congressmen to Their Constituents, 1789–1829*, 3 vols. (Chapel Hill: University of North Carolina Press for the Institute of Early American History and Culture, Williamsburg, Va., 1978), 3:1288.

17. Inaugural address, Mar. 4, 1817, in Hamilton, ed., *Monroe Writings*, 6:12.

18. Monroe, annual message, Dec. 3, 1821, in Fred Israel, ed., *The State of the Union Messages of the Presidents, 1790–1966*, 3 vols. (New York: Chelsea House, 1967), 1:190.

19. Monroe, annual message, Dec. 2, 1823, ibid., p. 210.

20. Monroe to Calhoun, Aug. 4, 1828, in Hamilton, ed., *Monroe Writings*, 7:176.

21. Resolutions of Maryland General Assembly, Feb. 10, 1825, Hoes Archives, Monroe Museum and Memorial Library.

22. Resolutions of the General Assembly of Louisiana, Feb. 18, 1825, ibid.

23. Resolutions of the legislature of Maine, Feb. 26, 1825, ibid.

24. Resolutions, State of New York, in Assembly, March 1, 1825, ibid.

BIBLIOGRAPHICAL ESSAY

The correspondence and other papers of James Monroe—though not so vo-luminous as those of Thomas Jefferson or James Madison—are extensive, but only a small portion of Monroe's papers for his presidential years has been pub-lished. The largest collections of Monroe manuscripts are in the Library of Con-gress (LC) and the New York Public Library (NYPL); both collections are avail-able on microfilm. Numerous Monroe papers are scattered among the files in the National Archives. Smaller collections are at the College of William and Mary, Williamsburg; the University of Virginia, Charlottesville; the Virginia His-torical Society, Richmond; and in the Ingrid Westesson Hoes Archives at the James Monroe Museum and Memorial Library, Fredericksburg, Virginia. Some papers from the Hoes Archives are included in the microfilm of the Monroe pa-pers in the Library of Congress; other papers in Virginia collections are available on the microfilm of the James Monroe Papers in Virginia repositories. The major published collection of Monroe's papers is Stanislaus M. Hamilton, ed., *The Writings of James Monroe*, 7 vols. (New York, 1898–1903; reprint ed., New York: AMS Press, 1969). Volume 6 and a section of volume 7 cover the presidential years.

The papers of key members of Monroe's cabinet are invaluable in studying his presidency. The most important single record is the diary kept by Secretary of State John Quincy Adams. Large portions of the diary were published in Charles Francis Adams, ed., *The Memoirs of John Quincy Adams, Comprising Por-tions of His Diary from 1797 to 1848*, 12 vols. (Philadelphia: J. B. Lippincott, 1874–1877); volumes 4, 5, and 6 (cited in notes as Adams, *Diary*) are devoted to the period of Monroe's presidency. The manuscript diary, letters, and other papers of John Quincy Adams are available in the Adams Family Papers, Massachusetts Historical Society (MHS), Boston (microfilm edition). Some of Adams's letters are published in Worthington C. Ford, ed., *Writings of John Quincy Adams*, 7 vols. (New York: Macmillan, 1913–1917).

John Quincy Adams's record of Monroe's administration, which has long dominated accounts of Monroe's presidency, must be supplemented by the papers of other members of the administration and of congressional leaders. The most important of these are the papers of the influential Secretary of War John C. Calhoun, whose letters and other papers are being comprehensively published in Robert L. Meriwether, W. Edwin Hemphill, and Clyde N. Wilson, eds., *The Papers of John C. Calhoun*, 21 vols. to date (Columbia: University of South Carolina Press, 1959–). Also essential is James F. Hopkins, Mary W. M. Hargreaves, Robert Seager II, Melba Porter Hay, and Carol Reardon, eds., *The Papers of Henry Clay*, 10 vols. (Lexington: University Press of Kentucky, 1959–1992).

Reports on congressional proceedings sent by members to their constituents are published in Noble E. Cunningham, Jr., ed., *Circular Letters of Congressmen to Their Constituents, 1789–1829*, 3 vols. (Chapel Hill: University of North Carolina Press for the Institute of Early American History and Culture, Williamsburg, Va., 1978).

A number of collections of manuscripts in the Library of Congress provide valuable material for the study of the presidency of James Monroe. Among them are papers of the following: Adams Family Collection, Newton Cannon, William H. Crawford, Benjamin W. Crowninshield, William Darlington, Joseph Desha, Job Durfee, Samuel Houston, Joseph Johnson, Lee-Palfrey Family, Arthur Livermore, William Lowndes, Duncan McArthur, Louis McLane, Hugh Nelson, William C. Rives, Short-Harrison-Symmes Families, Nathaniel Silsbee, Margaret Bayard Smith, Samuel Smith, and Martin Van Buren.

Other useful manuscript sources include the John W. Taylor Papers at the New-York Historical Society; William Wirt Papers at the Maryland Historical Society, Baltimore (microfilm edition); Graham Family Papers at the Virginia Historical Society; Tucker-Coleman Papers and Austin-Twyman Papers at the College of William and Mary; and Horace Holley Papers at the William L. Clements Library, University of Michigan.

At the National Archives, extensive documentary evidence relating to Monroe's presidency can be found in the House and Senate Records of the Fifteenth through the Eighteenth Congresses and in the records of the executive departments. Many documents from these records have been published separately or in *American State Papers: Documents Legislative and Executive of the United States*, 38 vols. (Washington, D.C., 1832–1861). Others are on microfilm, including Letters of Application and Recommendation, 1817–1825 (Record Group 59, M-439). Among unpublished papers in the State Department Records is a small file of Drafts of Letters and Memoranda of Monroe, 1818–1824 (Record Group 59, E869), which contains miscellaneous notes from Monroe's private secretary to the chief clerk of the State Department and other papers that reveal Monroe's administrative style.

Because Monroe was a close friend and political ally of Jefferson and Madison, their papers are useful sources for studying Monroe. The extensive collections of the manuscripts of both Jefferson and Madison in the Library of Congress are available on microfilm. The editorial projects currently publishing the definitive editions of the papers of Jefferson and of Madison have not reached the years of Monroe's presidency. The most important earlier editions of published papers are Paul L. Ford, ed., *The Works of Thomas Jefferson*, Federal edition, 12 vols. (New York: G. P. Putnam's Sons, 1904); Andrew A. Lipscomb and Albert E. Bergh, eds., *The Writings of Thomas Jefferson*, 20 vols. (Washington, D.C.: Thomas Jefferson Memorial Association, 1903-1904); and Gaillard Hunt, ed., *The Writings of James Madison*, 9 vols. (New York: G. P. Putnam's Sons, 1900-1910).

Additional published papers include John Spencer Bassett, ed., *Correspondence of Andrew Jackson*, 6 vols. (Washington, D.C.: Carnegie Institution, 1926-1933); Sam B. Smith, Harriet Owsley, and Harold D. Moser, eds., *The Papers of Andrew Jackson*, 4 vols. to date (Knoxville: University of Tennessee Press, 1980-); Charles R. King, ed., *The Life and Correspondence of Rufus King*, 6 vols. (New York: G. P. Putnam's Sons, 1894-1900); Samuel Eliot Morison, *The Life and Letters of Harrison Gray Otis*, 2 vols. (Boston: Houghton Mifflin, 1913); Everett Somerville Brown, ed., *The Missouri Compromises and Presidential Politics, 1820-1825: From the Letters of William Plumer, Junior* (St. Louis: Missouri Historical Society, 1926); Charles M. Wiltse and Harold Moser, eds., *The Papers of Daniel Webster: Correspondence*, 7 vols. (Hanover, N.H.: University Press of New England, 1974-1986); George S. Hilliard, ed., *Memoir and Correspondence of Jeremiah Mason* (Cambridge, Mass.: Riverside Press, 1873); Henry Adams, ed., *The Writings of Albert Gallatin*, 3 vols. (New York: Antiquarian Press, 1960; orig. pub. 1879); Henry T. Shanks, ed., *The Papers of Willie Person Mangum*, 5 vols. (Raleigh, N.C.: State Department of Archives, 1950-1956); Gaillard Hunt, ed., *The First Forty Years of Washington Society in the Family Letters of Margaret Bayard Smith* (New York: Frederick Ungar, 1965; orig. pub. 1906); and Mary Lee Mann, ed., *A Yankee Jeffersonian: Selections from the Diary and Letters of William Lee of Massachusetts Written from Washington from 1796 to 1840* (Cambridge: Harvard University Press, 1958).

The major biography of James Monroe is Harry Ammon, *James Monroe: The Quest for National Identity* (New York: McGraw-Hill, 1971); also still useful is W. P. Cresson, *James Monroe* (Chapel Hill: University of North Carolina Press, 1946). Harry Ammon focused on Monroe's presidency in an important essay, "Executive Leadership in the Monroe Administration," in John B. Boles, ed., *America, the Middle Period: Essays in Honor of Bernard Mayo* (Charlottesville: University Press of Virginia, 1973). The early American presidency and political parties have been studied in Ralph Ketcham, *Presidents Above Party: The American Presidency, 1789-1829* (Chapel Hill: University of North Carolina Press for the Institute of Early American History and Culture, Williamsburg, Va., 1984). George Dangerfield, *The Awakening of American Nationalism, 1815-1828* (New York: Harper and Row, 1965), offers a general survey of the period. The years of Monroe's presidency are incisively covered in Charles Sellers, *The Market Revolution: Jacksonian America, 1815-1846* (New York: Oxford University Press, 1991).

John Quincy Adams as secretary of state is treated in Samuel Flagg Bemis,

John Quincy Adams and the Foundations of American Foreign Policy (New York: Alfred A. Knopf, 1949), and in William Earl Weeks, *John Quincy Adams and American Global Empire* (Lexington: University Press of Kentucky, 1992). Chase C. Mooney, *William H. Crawford, 1772–1834* (Lexington: University Press of Kentucky, 1974), provides a biography of Monroe's secretary of the Treasury. Secretary of War John C. Calhoun has attracted numerous biographers, the most useful being Charles M. Wiltse, *John C. Calhoun: Nationalist, 1782–1828* (Indianapolis: Bobbs-Merrill Company, 1944), the first volume of a three-volume biography; John C. Nevin, *John C. Calhoun and the Price of Union: A Biography* (Baton Rouge: Louisiana State University Press, 1988); and Irving H. Bartlett, *John C. Calhoun: A Biography* (New York: W. W. Norton, 1993). Navy Secretary Samuel L. Southard has been studied in Michael Birkner, *Samuel L. Southard: Jeffersonian Whig* (Rutherford, N.J.: Fairleigh Dickinson University Press, 1984).

Henry Clay, Speaker of the House during most of Monroe's presidency, has been thoroughly studied by historians. The best recent works are Robert V. Remini, *Henry Clay: Statesman of the Union* (New York: W. W. Norton, 1991), and Merrill D. Peterson, *The Great Triumvirate: Webster, Clay, and Calhoun* (New York: Oxford University Press, 1987). The life of Vice-president Daniel D. Tompkins is covered in Ray W. Irwin, *Daniel D. Tompkins: Governor of New York and Vice President of the United States* (New York: New-York Historical Society, 1968).

Other relevant biographies include Robert Ernst, *Rufus King: American Federalist* (Chapel Hill: University of North Carolina Press for the Institute of Early American History and Culture, Williamsburg, Va., 1968); Charles D. Lowery, *James Barbour, A Jeffersonian Republican* (University: University of Alabama Press, 1984); John A. Munroe, *Louis McLane: Federalist and Jacksonian* (New Brunswick, N.J.: Rutgers University Press, 1973); Robert V. Remini, *Andrew Jackson*, 3 vols. (New York: Harper and Row, 1977–1984); Lynn W. Turner, *William Plumer of New Hampshire, 1759–1850* (Chapel Hill: University of North Carolina Press for the Institute of Early American History and Culture, Williamsburg, Va., 1962); and Patricia Tyson Stroud, *Thomas Say: New World Naturalist* (Philadelphia: University of Pennsylvania Press, 1992).

Thomas Jefferson during the time of Monroe's presidency is covered in Dumas Malone, *Jefferson and His Time*, vol. 6, *The Sage of Monticello* (Boston: Little, Brown and Company, 1981); Merrill D. Peterson, *Thomas Jefferson and the New Nation* (New York: Oxford University Press, 1970); and Noble E. Cunningham, Jr., *In Pursuit of Reason: The Life of Thomas Jefferson* (Baton Rouge: Louisiana State University Press, 1987). James Madison during his successor's presidency is discussed in Irving Brant, *James Madison: Commander in Chief, 1812–1836* (Indianapolis: Bobbs-Merrill Company, 1961); Ralph Ketcham, *James Madison: A Biography* (New York: Macmillan, 1971); and Drew R. McCoy, *The Last of the Fathers: James Madison and the Republican Legacy* (Cambridge: Cambridge University Press, 1989).

Specialized studies relevant to Monroe's presidency include Leonard D. White, *The Jeffersonians: A Study in Administrative History, 1801–1829* (New York: Macmillan, 1951); James Sterling Young, *The Washington Community, 1800–1828* (New York: Columbia University Press, 1966); Shaw Livermore, Jr., *The Twilight of Federalism: The Disintegration of the Federalist Party, 1815–1830* (Princeton: Princeton University Press, 1962); Norman K. Risjord, *The Old Republicans: Southern Conservatism in the Age of Jefferson* (New York: Columbia University Press, 1965); William B. Skelton, *An American Profession of Arms: The Army Officer Corps, 1784–1861* (Lawrence: University Press of Kansas, 1992); Murray N. Rothbard, *The Panic of 1819: Reactions and Policies* (New York: Columbia University Press, 1962); Bray Hammond, *Banks and Politics in America: From the Revolution to the Civil War* (Princeton: Princeton University Press, 1957); Douglass C. North, *The Economic Growth of the United States, 1790–1860* (New York: W. W. Norton, 1966; orig. pub. 1961); Glover Moore, *The Missouri Controversy, 1819–1821* (Gloucester, Mass.: Peter Smith, 1967; orig. pub. 1953); and Lucius Wilmerding, Jr., *James Monroe: Public Claimant* (New Brunswick, N.J.: Rutgers University Press, 1960).

For the background and formation of the Monroe Doctrine, important works include William R. Manning, ed., *Diplomatic Correspondence of the United States Concerning the Independence of the Latin-American Nations*, 3 vols. (New York: Oxford University Press, 1925); Arthur Preston Whitaker, *The United States and the Independence of Latin America, 1800–1830* (New York: Russell and Russell, 1962; orig. pub. 1941); Dexter Perkins, *The Monroe Doctrine, 1823–1826* (Gloucester, Mass: Peter Smith, 1965; orig. pub. 1927); Bradford Perkins, *Castlereagh and Adams: England and the United States, 1812–1823* (Berkeley and Los Angeles: University of California Press, 1964); and Ernest R. May, *The Making of the Monroe Doctrine* (Cambridge: Harvard University Press, 1975).

Extensive extracts from newspaper reports on Lafayette's visit to America in 1824–1825 have been published in Edgar E. Brandon, ed., *Lafayette, Guest of the Nation*, 3 vols. (Oxford, Ohio: Oxford Historical Press, 1950–1957). Lafayette's tour is studied from a special angle in Stanley J. Idzerda, Anne C. Loveland, and Marc H. Miller, *Lafayette, Hero of Two Worlds: The Art and Pageantry of His Farewell Tour of America, 1824–1825* (Hanover, N.H.: University Press of New England, 1989).

Portraits, engravings, and other images of Monroe are included in Noble E. Cunningham, Jr., *Popular Images of the Presidency: From Washington to Lincoln* (Columbia: University of Missouri Press, 1991). Additional annotated bibliographical references can be found in Harry Ammon, *James Monroe: A Bibliography* (Westport, Conn.: Meckler, 1991).

INDEX